Organizational Systems

Raul Espejo · Alfonso Reyes

Organizational Systems

Managing Complexity with the Viable System Model

 Springer

Raul Espejo
Syncho Ltd.
Nettleham Road 3, North P
LN2 1RE Lincoln
United Kingdom
r.espejo@syncho.org

Alfonso Reyes
Universidad de Ibague
Carrera 22 Calle 67
Ibague
Colombia
areyes12345@yahoo.com

ISBN 978-3-642-43834-9   ISBN 978-3-642-19109-1 (eBook)
DOI 10.1007/978-3-642-19109-1
Springer Heidelberg Dordrecht London New York

Cover design: SPi Publisher Services

Printed on acid-free paper

Springer is part of Springer Science+Business Media (www.springer.com)

Preface

During 1971–1973 the first author of this book was involved in Project Cybersyn in Chile. This was conceived by the cybernetician Stafford Beer for the recently elected government of Salvador Allende (Beer gives a vivid account of this work in the second edition of his book *Brain of the Firm*, 1981). This project was a holistic attempt to address issues of governance in Chile, with particular emphasis on the management of complexity. Far from the centralist approach characteristic of planned economies and the laissez-faire approach characteristic of the capitalist economies, Beer was offering a 'third way' that required the contribution of all stakeholders in the creation, regulation and production of the country's industrial economy. He made it clear that, since this economy was exceedingly complex, any attempt to 'represent' it in a plan was doomed to failure, and any attempt to rely exclusively on market forces naively assumed a fair distribution of information and decision capacity in society. This 'third way' was performative in the sense that all stakeholders required learning platforms to develop their capabilities for adaptation and change. The embodiment of this platform was his Viable System Model (Beer 1972), which is the main focus of this book. The emphasis of the work in Chile was creating communication and information networks to support distributed decision-making and to give stakeholders resources to coordinate their actions throughout the economy. Independent of the historical events that aborted Allende's government, the experience of being involved in the project made apparent that Beer's approach was bold but too optimistic; producing *effective relationships* between stakeholders and policy-makers was far more complex than building up communication networks and information systems.

Relationships became the main concern of the next large cybernetic project, this time with the contribution of both authors. In the mid 1990s both authors were involved in a large project aimed at improving the auditing practices of the National Audit Office of Colombia (Espejo 2001; Espejo et al. 2001; Espejo and Reyes 2001; Reyes 2001). The aim of this project was to support organizational learning and create effective structures at all levels of government with the support of the Viable System Model. We expected that an ongoing auditing of communication mechanisms in government and other public institutions could help diagnose necessary improvements to reduce the misuse of resources and to improve their deployment. The thrust of this work was building up trust between stakeholders and reducing corruption. For 4 years we supported auditors of government institutions in this endeavour. Afterwards a post-graduate programme in systemic auditing was set up at the Universidad de Los Andes to continue the training of new generations of auditors. The emphasis of all this work was more appreciative of relationships than making information available. Its impact may take several years to get a fair assessment. However, its evolution has clearly confirmed that changing organizational structures, in particular the relationships that produce them, is a tall order that requires more research. This book is a contribution to this research. Hundreds of organizations were diagnosed and more organizations of all kinds continue to be diagnosed using the same method in varied contexts. No one should be surprised that many of our examples in this book come from this experience. However, our purpose here is not a report of this work; it is sharing our understanding of the Viable System Model and more specifically of the main tools underpinning the work in Colombia: the Viplan Method and the Viplan Methodology.

The book's aim is to clarify the application of cybernetic ideas to organizational design and problem solving in organizational systems. In Part I the reader goes through a journey that starts with making a simple distinction in a background and ends up with a model of the organization structure of any viable system. This journey continues in Part II, with a method to model these structures and to braid business, organizational and information processes, which opens the space for a detailed management of complexity in organizations. Finally in Part III we acknowledge that often people in organizations experience problematic situations that can be ameliorated or dissolved by improving the structures in which they emerge. This part offers methodological support and highlights how to think systemically when experiencing these problematic situations. The three parts offer a comprehensive journey through which readers hopefully will learn to appreciate the complexity of organizational problem situations and the relevance of seeing the systemic coherence of the world. The book argues that many of the problems we experience in enterprises of all kinds are rooted in our practice of fragmenting what needs to be connected as a whole.

The scope of this book is the management of complexity in an uncertain world. It builds on Ashby's Law of Requisite Variety (Ashby 1964) and Stafford Beer's Viable System Model (Beer 1979, 1981, 1985). Its contributions are methodologies to deal with problem situations and a method to study, manage and engineer an organization's complexity.

Organizational cybernetics is capturing the imagination of many; unfortunately so far there has been limited *methodological* support to make effective use of this body of knowledge. Beer's work, in particular his book *Diagnosing the System for Organizations* (Beer 1985), offers a guide to apply the Viable System Model but not an epistemology to understand organizations. Several books have been published recently on organizational cybernetics (for instance Achterbergh and Vriers 2009; Schwaninger 2009; Christopher 2007) however, these publications have offered limited methodological support. Our book attempts to fill this gap. It is the outcome of many years of working in projects such as Cybersyn and the project with the National Audit Office of Colombia, as well as work with all kinds of public and private enterprises throughout the world. At a more detailed level we offer an in depth discussion of *variety engineering* that is not available either in the primary or secondary literature. Variety engineering helps directly in the *design of organizational, business and information processes*.

Here we offer the Viable System Model (VSM) as a problem solving heuristic. This model is of increasing relevance in today's digital world. It is built using the concept of variety, a measurement of complexity, which helps to map the proliferating states of our day-to-day situations. Radical tools for this type of mapping were unavailable before the digital revolution. Today communications and computers make possible not only globalization but also dealing with business tasks beyond anything that was possible in the pre-digital world. Organizations are already achieving higher performance with fewer resources, but the scope for further improvements is indeed large; this is the scope for variety engineering in this book.

The VSM is used as a tool to study the systemic context of processes in organizations and to reconfigure the use of their resources with the support of new technologies. They offer the possibility to respond with ingenuity to challenging situations. The *Viplan Methodology* explained in Part III is used for this reconfiguration, which is supported by the Viplan Method developed in Part II. This method (Espejo 1989) helps to work out the boundaries of organizational systems, modelling organizational and environmental complexity, working out strategies to manage this complexity and distributing accountability and resources in the organization. It offers a framework to braid the organization's value chain with regulatory and informational processes. This framework, a detailed application of variety engineering, helps to work out strategic, structural and informational aspects of an organization.

This book should be particularly relevant to students of management, organizational/industrial engineering and information/knowledge management. Indeed not only students but managers, civil servants, policy-makers and community operators can benefit from a novel way of understanding relationships and organizational processes. Naturally, this book should also be of interest to academics carrying out research and teaching in the above topics. Last but not least, these topics should be of interest to consultants involved in managing change in organizations. The book offers many 'real world' examples and its emphasis is on diagrams rather than on mathematics, but requires the reader's maturity to relate abstract ideas to personal experience and practice.

November 2010   Raul Espejo
                                                                                   Alfonso Reyes

References

Achterbergh J, Vriers D (2009) Organizations: social systems conducting experiments. Springer Verlag, Berlin, Heidelberg

Ashby R (1964) An introduction to cybernetics. Methuen & Co, Ltd., London

Beer S (1972) Brain of the firm. Allen Lane The Penguin Press, London

Beer S (1979) The heart of enterprise. Wiley, Chichester

Beer S (1981) Brain of the firm, second edition. Wiley, Chichester

Beer S (1985) Diagnosing the system for organizations. Wiley, Chichester

Christopher WF (2007) Holistic management; managing what matters for company success. Wiley, Hoboken, NJ

Espejo R (1989) A method to study organizations. In: Espejo R, Harnden R (eds) The viable system model: interpretations and applications of Stafford Beer's VSM. Wiley, Chichester, UK, pp 361–382

Espejo R (2001) Auditing as a trust creation process. Syst Pract Action Res 14(2):215–236

Espejo R, Bula G, Zarama R (2001) Auditing as the dissolution of corruption. Syst Pract Action Res 14(2):139–156

Espejo R, Reyes A (2001) The state of the state: introduction. Syst Pract Action Res 14(2): 135–137

Reyes A (2001) Second-order auditing practices. Syst Pract Action Res 14(2):157–180

Schwaninger M (2009) Intelligent organizations: powerful models for systemic management. Springer Verlag, Berlin, Heidelberg

Acknowledgments

This book has been written over a number of years. Many people have contributed to its content and form. Its content principally owes to Stafford Beer, who had a deep influence on Espejo's work; also to John Watt, from the University of Aston, who enabled Espejo's work on Viplan, method and methodology, which is at the core of this book. Syncho's people contributed with their practice to the grounding of this book's model, method and methodology. Early briefings about the Viable System Model benefited from Antonia Gill's skills clarifying what were indeed difficult ideas. Diane Bowling and Tony Gill helped not only applying these ideas with varied customers but also supported their further elaboration. In particular Diane Bowling had a major contribution in the implementation of the electronic book Viplan Learning System, which can be considered precursor of this book. Tony Gill's contributions were significant in several projects, in particular the SYCOMT Project, for collaborative work with the support of ICTs in the National Westminster Bank and the RISCOM project for policy transparency in nuclear waste management in Sweden. Aspects of these projects are reported in this book. Also, in the context of Syncho´s work, Robert Gilmore contributed developing the COMLIS case study that we use in Chapter 10. The contributions of multiple students of Aston University in Birmingham, UK, the University of Los Andes in Bogotá, and the University of Ibague, Colombia, were fundamental in the clarification of the Viplan method and methodology. Equally our work together with German Bula and Roberto Zarama at the National Audit Office of Colombia enabled the work in structural and identity archetypes reported in the final chapter of this book.

Our particular gratitude goes to Silvia Bonilla who prepared many of the figures used in this book and also to David Whittaker for reading and editing the manuscript.

The book is dedicated to our wives Zoraida and Silvia ...

Raul Espejo
Alfonso Reyes

Contents

Part I
Concepts and the Viable System Model

The first part of this book develops a theoretical framework to understand the Viable System Model. It is in this part that we clarify the distinction between a black box and an operational description of a system. The former is focused on the transformation of inputs into outputs; the latter is focused on the relationships that produce a whole from a set of components. This distinction has important implications for the management of complexity. A black box description is often related to the idea of someone trying to control a situation from the outside; a form of unilateral control. An operational description is more connected to on-going interactions between components that are striving for stability in their relationships. Control in this case has a very different connotation to the unilateral control of a management viewpoint; it is all about communications, accommodation and mutual influence. Our argument here is that these two forms of description are not incompatible. Quite on the contrary, they are complementary and both are necessary to manage and measure the complexity of organizational activities.

Chapter 2 goes to the roots of cybernetics and offers a discussion of control and communications. A key distinction introduced in this chapter is between intrinsic and extrinsic control. The former is the control that is in-built in the interactions of the components and therefore suggests a form of operational control. If these interactions are well designed then the situation will maintain an inherent control. The latter is control from the outside; it does not have an inherent control capacity but depends on an outside intervention. If the agent responsible for this intervention does not have capacity, or simply forgets to respond to changes, then we may expect that the situation will go out of control. This is an important distinction that has design implications; organisational systems need capacity to maintain stability in their interactions with environmental agents and this stability cannot depend on extrinsic control. This proposition has two implications for organizational systems; first, the design of regulatory mechanisms with capacity to maintain their stable operation over time and second, the viability of these systems depends on their capacity to respond to unanticipated situations. These two aspects are at the core of the last four chapters of Part I.

Ashby's Law of Requisite Variety (Ashby 1964) is paramount for the design of regulatory -control- mechanisms with *capacity* to maintain stable interactions. Chapters 3 and 4 develop the ideas of complexity and the management of complexity. In these chapters we highlight the idea of *residual variety*; an effective management of complexity requires regulators that enable self-regulation and self-organization in the situation being regulated and therefore do not need capacity to match all its states; they only need to match their residual variety. This idea drives our discussion of variety engineering, a key concern throughout the book.

The last two chapters of this part of the book are focused on the identity and structure of organizational systems. We distinguish a black-box and an operational definition of an organization's identity. This distinction, emerging from the definition of a system in Chap. 1, will help us in Part II to work out the boundaries of an organization and to model its complexity. As for the structure, we explain complexity management strategies that are necessary for an organizational system to achieve cohesion and adaptability in a dynamic and changeable environment. In Chap. 6 Beer's Viable System Model (Beer 1972, 1979, 1981, 1985) is explained following Espejo's interpretation of this model (Espejo 1989, 2003). In this presentation of the model we use several examples of the work done in Colombia for the National Audit Office and others. Espejo's interpretation of the VSM highlights five *systemic functions* -policy, intelligence, cohesion, coordination and implementation- rather than Beer's systems 1, 2, 3, 4 and 5. Cohesion, intelligence and policy constitute the adaptation mechanism whereas implementation, coordination and cohesion constitute the cohesion mechanism. This interpretation is mostly consistent with Beer's original work except for the coordination function, which is understood as more than an anti-oscillatory system. Additionally, this systemic function is produced by all shared cultural aspects that support the components' operational coordination of their actions.

References

Ashby R (1964) An introduction to cybernetics. Methuen & Co., Ltd., London
Beer S (1972) Brain of the firm. Allen Lane The Penguin Press, London
Beer S (1979) The heart of enterprise. Wiley, Chichester
Beer S (1981) Brain of the firm, second edition. Wiley, Chichester
Beer S (1985) Diagnosing the system for organizations. Wiley, Chichester
Espejo R (1989) The VSM revisited. In: Espejo R, Harnden R (eds) The viable system model: interpretations and applications of Stafford Beer's VSM. Wiley, Chichester, pp 77–100
Espejo R (2003) The viable system model: a briefing about organizational structure. Syncho, Ltd, Lincoln, UK (www.syncho.com)

Chapter 1
On Systems

Abstract A system is a set of interrelated parts that we experience as a whole. While we may be able to observe and bump into these parts, their systemicity emerges from their relationships, which are abstract. As such, a system is different to a thing 'out there'. In this chapter we discuss different types of systems. We take the view that though all of them are observer dependent, some are well grounded in shared realities that allow us to describe something; others are intellectual (epistemological) devices that allow us to explore existing situations and possibly create something new. We experience and talk about systems, but we do not bump into systems 'out there'. We name them and by doing this we bring them into existence. Systems link events in time, helping to see the big picture in spatial and temporal terms and helping to see patterns of relationships and processes. In short, systems help to avoid unnecessary fragmentation. From an ethical perspective systems thinking helps us to connect distant events and work out the hidden consequences of our actions.

Etymologically SYSTEM is a word that has a Greek root that means 'organized whole' (Greek: σύστημα; Latin: *systēma*). This root implies that, originally, the word was used to signal a process of integration or adding together things to produce a sort of a synthesis. Its current use, however, is much broader. It has become a very fashionable word used as a short cut to refer to a set of related things with a purpose. In fact, the OED[1] defines system as 'complex whole; set of connected things or parts; organized body of material or immaterial things'. That is how we commonly speak about the 'immune *system*', a 'document management *system*', the 'braking *system* of a car', the 'prison *system*' or the 'National Health *system*' of a country and so on.

All these examples refer to things or parts that are working together as a whole. But it is worth noticing that in the way we normally talk about a system we imply some sort of 'objectivity' to it. We are used to talk of a prison system in the same way as we talk of a car; that is, as an 'object' that everybody can observe, touch or 'kick'. We think, however, that this common way to refer to a system deserves further revision.

---

[1]Oxford English Dictionary.

R. Espejo and A. Reyes, *Organizational Systems*,
DOI 10.1007/978-3-642-19109-1_1, © Springer-Verlag Berlin Heidelberg 2011

We shall start this revision by stating that a system is a set of interrelated parts that we experience as a whole. While we may be able to observe and bump into these parts their systemicity emerges from their relationships, which are abstract. As such, a system is different to a thing 'out there'. Later in this chapter we discuss different types of systems, however, we take the view that all of them are mental constructs; some are well grounded in shared realities that allow us to describe something, others are intellectual (epistemological) devices that allow us to explore existing situations and possibly create something new. We experience and talk about systems, but we do not bump into systems 'out there'. We name them and by doing this we are bringing them into existence.

This applies to all the examples mentioned above. To begin with, when we name a system we arbitrarily choose its parts and relations, according to a purpose we ascribe to it. A car, for instance, has many parts necessary for it to be driven. By talking about a 'braking system' we are selecting some parts that we consider the most closely related to perform the act of stopping the car. Of course, we are leaving outside of this system many other parts of the car. A similar reasoning can be applied to the other examples listed above. Therefore, selecting the parts and their relations according to a purpose is inherent to naming a system. These parts can be imaginary, physical, biological, or whatever. In a sense, by going back to the etymological root, this is a process of synthesis.

But naming a system implies distinguishing it from its background or, in other words, separating its parts and relations from its environment by means of specifying a border (Spencer-Brown 1969). Therefore, before going any further in our discussion about systems, it seems important to explore with more detail the process of making distinctions.

Drawing a distinction is, in a general sense, a basic cognitive operation by which we come to know or distinguish the world around us. Any distinction is composed by three different elements that come into being all at the same time: the 'inside', the 'outside' and the 'border'. If we draw a circle on a piece of paper, for instance, we are making a distinction; if we point to a car we are also making a distinction. In any case, a distinction is drawn as soon as we completely specify its border: the circle is distinguished as soon as we close its circumference, not before; a car is distinguished as soon as we recognize and make apparent the heap of metals and other materials defining its border; and an enterprise is distinguished by its people and their relationships, which define a more abstract border but equally one that separates the inside, indicating those included by the relationships, from the outside, those excluded.

Once a distinction is made, we are free to refer to any of its aspects. We usually do this by assigning a name to each aspect of the distinction. For instance, we may call the 'outside' of a distinction its 'environment'. However, it is quite important to differentiate between a distinction and the *name* we ascribe to it. This difference is similar to that between the label we put to a variable and its content, while the former corresponds to the name, the latter correspond to the distinction itself. The name is ascribing purpose to the distinction.

Making distinctions is a basic cognitive operation; it makes sense to ask what sort of distinctions we can actually make. To approach this question it is important to notice that the space of possible distinctions we can make is bounded by the biological structure that we all share as human beings. This structure determines the kind of interactions we can maintain in any specific domain of action. For instance, in the domain of our hearing, the structure of our inner and middle ear determines what kind of stimuli may trigger a reaction of the related parts of our nervous system. Our hammer and eardrum only react to sound waves ranging between 20 and 20,000 Hz. Outside these limits our auditory nerve will not be effective to this kind of stimuli. On the other hand, a dog can listen to the sound produced by the owner's training whistle (that is outside these limits) while the owner cannot hear (i.e., distinguish) this sound. This point holds for all the distinctions we can make through our other senses. Therefore, it is clear that our biological make-up as living beings is directly connected to our capability to make distinctions.

Interestingly enough, the above discussion suggests that we may enhance the number of distinctions we can make in a particular domain of action by using different observational tools to increase the range of our possible interactions in that domain. By using a radio telescope, for instance, we can distinguish some astronomical bodies we will be unable to distinguish with our naked eyes. Similarly, by using a scanner doctors can distinguish some parts of a body that they otherwise would be unable to observe. We will go back to this point later on in the book.

In general terms, we claim that external stimuli may *trigger* but not determine a distinction at a particular moment in time. Instead, the distinctions we actually make are determined by our biological structure at that particular moment. This is a consequence of the *structural determination* that characterizes our nervous system (Maturana and Varela 1992). But because our nervous system has plasticity, its structure may go through changes as a result of each interaction with its environment. In other words, an external stimulus not only may trigger a distinction but it may also trigger a change in the structure of our nervous system in such a way that our capacity for further distinctions may change as well. Consider, for instance, the extreme case in which we hear (i.e., distinguish) a very high-frequency sound that produces some damage in our eardrum. This particular stimulus not only triggered a distinction but also produced a change in our biological structure in such a way that our capacity to distinguish further sounds may be affected. Research in biology has proven that changes that are less extreme in our nervous system happen all the time as a result of our interaction with our surroundings (Maturana and Varela 1992). The history of all these structural changes is what is known as *ontogeny*.

This fact has an extremely important consequence for the process of making distinctions because as we all go through different ontogenies, we never make exactly the same distinctions that others do. Indeed, even if we assume that two persons receive the same sort of stimuli at a given moment in time, because they certainly have gone through different ontogenies, the structure of their nervous systems may differ and therefore they may react to each stimulus in a slightly different way. One may ask then how is it possible that although biologically we cannot make exactly the *same* distinctions we are still able to communicate with each other in a coordinated way? In addition, how is it that we seem to observe a world full of regularities that we all agree upon?

The answers to these questions are at the core of the epistemological grounding of the ideas and concepts developed in this book. We should first notice that however different it may be from person to person, the process of making distinctions is rooted in our biology and we all share a similar biological structure, as we all pertain to the same kind of mammals. Secondly, and mainly in relation to the persons we encounter (and the environment) in our daily lives, we have been raised in traditions (i.e., cultures) that have set predominant (i.e., common) criteria for making distinctions that we usually follow. Therefore, we do live in a world of *shared regularities* that we cannot alter at whim. But, it is important to recognise here that this 'shared world' is the outcome of an ongoing process of cultural agreements and not an ontological reality 'out there'. We will go back to this point later on but now let us continue exploring the consequences of having different ontogenies in the process of making distinctions.

It is in this sense that we say that the distinctions we make are deeply rooted in what we are in a particular moment in time (i.e., the present state of our ontogeny). They are grounded in our particular biology and in our personal history. Any distinction therefore, is intrinsically related to a particular observer who experiences the distinction. In fact, notice that when we make a distinction, we are not only bringing it forth but also we are making apparent our own cognitive capacities, our emotions and our intentions. It seems a bit paradoxical that we, as human beings, distinguish ourselves by precisely distinguishing what we are not, that is, the 'world' around us (Varela 1975, p. 22). When we claim, for instance, that a prison is a place in which inmates are kept locked in order to protect us (people in a community) from their wrong doings, we are not only distinguishing a prison system but we are simultaneously exposing our viewpoints about criminal punishment.

Experiments have shown the close relation between our emotions and the distinctions we make (Clore and Storbeck 2006). In one such experiment, different persons who were walking by a park were asked to say, by using their hands, how steep was a hill they were about to climb. Before asking the question, some of them were invited to listen to a piece of Mozart whereas others listened to part of a Mahler symphony. The outcome of the experiment was that the people listening to Mahler 'saw' the hill much steeper than those listening to Mozart. Here, the music was used as a means to set the emotional state of the subjects. In another experiment, people were asked to describe with their hands how steep was a downhill road in front of them. Some of them, however, were invited to approach the edge of the road by wearing a pair of roller-skates. These subjects 'saw' a much steeper road than those wearing regular tennis shoes. In this case, fear was the emotional state that influenced the distinctions they made. Similar experiments with children, much more sensitive than adults, have also shown how emotions play an important role in the distinctions they make at school (Maturana and Verden-Zoeller 1993).

'Everything that is said is said by an observer that could be him or herself' (Maturana 1988, p. 27). This is a claim that synthesises our discussion about making distinctions. It stresses the role of the observer in the process but avoids going into solipsism. Namely, it should be clear by now, that in performing a distinction the 'object' *and* the 'observer' constitute each other simultaneously.

There is no prevalence either of the object distinguished or of the observer making a distinction. The old objectivists claim that 'the properties of the observer shall not enter into the description of his observations', is replaced by a rather different one. Indeed, 'the description of observations shall reveal the properties of the observer' (von Foerster 1984). In this way, we are moving away from both the common objectivist and subjectivist epistemologies toward a more *constructivist* approach; an objectivity within parenthesis (Maturana 1988).

Let's go back now to the process of cultural agreements. When a community of observers share a set of distinctions in a particular domain of action and ground them in their recurrent practices as a way of coordinating their actions in that domain, these distinctions appear to them as objective, as if they had an ontological reality. However, this is so only in that particular action domain of that particular community of observers; those are the limits implied by the objectivity within parenthesis.

By moving outside these limits this apparent ontological reality may start to vanish. This could be nicely exemplified by recalling the popular Hollywood movie *The Gods Must be Crazy* in which a bottle of coke is accidentally dropped from an aeroplane and falls into the hands of an isolated tribe in Botswana[2]: For most of us it is obvious what a bottle of coke is and (consequently) what it is used for, even if we haven't tasted it yet. This certainty points to its ontological status as an 'objective' object in our culture. However, for this particular African community that object (i.e., a distinction without a name) went from *being* a useful hammer to *being* a deadly weapon. Therefore, the ontological status of the 'bottle of coke' (notice the use of the quotation marks here) is not *intrinsic* to this object; instead this community is constructing it. At the end of the day what this object will *be* for that community depends on the shared practices they develop (if any) to coordinate their actions with it.

Those distinctions grounded by recurrent conversations and coordination of actions produce shared meanings for a community. They are deeply rooted in the particular history and culture of that community and, therefore, support their tacit views about their world. Notice that these distinctions have a different *ontological status* from those that are drawn by observers as insightful new ideas about the world but lack this grounding. The former are useful for supporting people's coordination of actions in a particular action domain; the latter are useful for opening new possibilities and therefore for creating new domains of actions. We will come back to this point later on.

By now, let us go back to revisit the definition of a system by using all the elements we have discussed so far. We take the view that a system is a *distinction* that brings forth a set of parts non-linearly related exhibiting *closure*. In this way, systems are a particular class of distinctions and, therefore, all we have said before about making distinctions also applies to the process of naming systems. Let us be

---

[2]http://www.youtube.com/watch?v=GorHLQ-jLRQ

clear about this, we say that a system is a distinction but not every distinction is a system.

We are ascribing two conditions to this particular class of distinctions or, in other words, two conditions that will allow us to recognise a distinction as belonging to this particular class: a systems-class. These conditions are: observing non-linear interactions among its parts and observing closure. Let us briefly expand more about these conditions.

Regarding the first condition, what makes the world unpredictable is that interactions among parts do not add up in a simple manner. Their interactions are non-linear, and are not determined by cause-effect relations. The non-linearity of interactions among the system's parts is responsible for its *emergent properties*. That is, we observe properties that are not observable in any of the system's parts taken in isolation. This is precisely what makes of a system a 'whole' that is different from a collection of parts. A popular way to describe this is by saying that *the whole is greater*[3] *than the sum of its parts* or that we observe synergy in a system. This corresponds with the OED's definition of a system as a set of parts 'working together as a whole'. So, emergent properties are intrinsic to the systems we observe.

Recent developments of complexity and chaos theories recognise this non-linearity of interactions in the constitution of an observable system:

> The conjunction of a few small events can produce a big effect if their impacts multiply rather than add. The overall effect of events can be unforeseeable if their consequences diffuse unevenly via the interaction patterns within the system. In such worlds, current events can dramatically change the probabilities of many future events. (Axelrod and Cohen 1999, p. 14)

These theories are mainly concerned with studying the behaviour of dynamic systems far from equilibrium. It is nowadays agreed that most of observable physical and social systems share this non-linearity characteristic (Beinhocker 2006; Sawyer 2005). It is claimed that this is exactly what makes apparent their complexity. We will go back to this in chapter 3 when we develop the concept of complexity.

Regarding the other condition, we say that exhibiting closure is necessary to distinguish a system. Of course, we have said that when observers make a distinction they are already drawing a border but when this distinction is a system, its parts will show operational closure. The observer will observe that the parts' relations are enough to sustain the system's border; there are no open ended relations requiring external actions for closure. The network of relations specifies in full the distinction that is being made and is self-referential. This is the condition of closure for a system. The border will relate to a meaning that is grounded by the parts and their

---

[3]Or more precisely: *the whole is different to the sum of the parts*, since unfortunately it may be the case that an emergent property is negative, or in other words, that synergy is negative (e.g., members of a family cancelling each other's capabilities or a football team where individual abilities are not coordinated).

relations in the consensual domain of a group of observers. For instance, this is the distinction that observers tacitly make when they agree that a National Health Service is a system to improve the health of a community. However, some observers may challenge this grounded distinction by offering other meanings for the emergent system; they are recognising different purpose to the system. This is in consonance with our claim that the system specified by a named distinction has no truth-value; it is more or less grounded in a community of observers.

In fact, this border specification, as will be discussed later in the book with reference to social systems, (cf. Chap. 7 about naming systems) relates to the purposes and values of the parts producing the system through their relations. Indeed, drawing borders requires considering in detail who are the stakeholders of the system. On the other hand, considering who ought to be the stakeholders and their relations is drawing a border for social systems beyond its current grounding; it is making boundary judgments (Ulrich 2000). We will consider social systems throughout this book with this critical perspective.

But here our point is to avoid a rather vague use of the term system and to differentiate it from its use as a wild card. In fact, our definition claims that a system, in a particular action domain, emerges from those distinctions that, as we mentioned before, are deeply grounded in the recurrent coordination of actions of the people acting in that domain. Therefore, social systems are closed networks of recurrent interactions producing, and produced by, people's coordination of actions.

Systems as defined above are different from holons (Checkland and Scholes 1990). Holons are mental constructs, ideas, hypotheses of wholes triggered by observations in the world, regardless of whether they have as referent closed networks of interacting people. In this sense holons are offered only as intellectual (epistemological) devices to think about the world. They are important to support people's conversations for possibilities (Espejo 1994).

We have explained so far what we meant when we said at the beginning of this chapter that a system is a collective's culturally shared construct of a whole produced in the world by a set of interrelated parts. Let us expand now how a system can be used to account for particular issues of concern. In order to do this, we will show that considering a system as a particular kind of distinction enables the emergence of two complementary paths of system's descriptions. We will see that, in fact, each one of these paths generates different epistemologies (i.e., different ways to know and to deal with named systems). Then, we will move on to explore possible typologies of systems in order to point to the kind of systems we are referring to in this book.

Remember, we said that a distinction splits the world into two parts, 'this' and 'that'. In this way, the 'thing' being distinguished is separated from its 'background'. But, after distinguishing a system, we are free to choose to focus our attention on either of the two sides split by the act of distinction. If we choose to see the system from *its environment* (i.e., we, as observers, are situated in the 'outside'), we treat the system as a simple entity, ascribe to it some *attributes* and study its interactions with its environment. The system is viewed as having inputs and outputs and as being constrained by the environment. On the other hand, if we choose to see the system from within (i.e., we, as observers, are situated on the 'inside') the *properties* of the system emerge from the interactions of its components and the environment is viewed as a source of perturbations. The system has no inputs or outputs (Varela 1979, p. 85).

The first type of description constitutes a system as a *black-box*. Here, the observers are in a privileged position because they can observe both the system and its environment simultaneously and establish correlations between the two through time. In other words, they may describe the system's behaviour in terms of the history of these correlations. It would be apparent to them that the environment is affecting the system through certain inputs that produce certain outputs. Although the inside of the system is not accessible (i.e., it is a black-box) they may establish a correlation between inputs and outputs and observe that the environment is, in a sense, constraining the system's behaviour.

Notice that this has been the standard mode of describing systems in general. We shall call this a *black-box* type of *description*. It has associated with it a mode of inference in which information affecting the inputs of the system determines its future behaviour. We may think of this mode of inference in terms of an arrow going from the outside to the inside of the system. It is a mode of inference that has associated with it a discourse about controlling a system's behaviour by choosing the appropriate controllable inputs. In this type of description control is understood as restricting the system's behaviour to reach desirable outcomes or goals (Rosenblueth et al. 1943).

As we will see in Chap. 3, this type of description is sometimes necessary to cope with the complexity of the world. It recognises that often 'it is not necessary to enter the black box to understand the nature of the function it performs'. This is Beer's First Regulatory Aphorism (Beer 1979, p. 59). This aphorism implies that the transformation of inputs into outputs is governed by regularities and that these regularities can be established through observation. This observation permits us to work out the inputs (controllable and non-controllable variables) and outputs (monitored variables) relevant to the observer's purpose in the situation. The border of the system is thus defined by the variables the observer chooses to study. This type of description is referred to as functionalist and often is dismissed as mechanistic. We take it as one valuable though restricted form of a system's description.

In the second type of descriptions, the observer is accounting for the system's behaviour standing on its 'inside'. The focus is on the nature of the internal coherence of the system that arises out of the interconnectedness of its constituting components (or parts). We concentrate on this inner coherence and from this standpoint what used to be specific environmental inputs in the previous type of descriptions are now seen as unspecified perturbations or simply noise (Varela 1984). In other words, because the observer is not in a privileged position anymore (i.e., 'outside the system') there is neither an environment nor a set of inputs, outputs or a transformation process (i.e., a function relating the outputs with the inputs) to account for the system's behaviour. All we have at hand are the relations of the parts constituting the system as a whole.

We shall call these types of descriptions *operational descriptions*. Again, they have associated with them a mode of inference, but one in which the internal coherence of the system determines its possible behaviours. Here the arrow representing this mode of inference points to the opposite direction: from the inside to the outside. External perturbations may trigger changes in the internal structure of the system but they do not determine its future behaviour. A lion, for instance, looking at a young gazelle may behave in different ways depending on its internal biological states (is it hungry? is it tired? does it feel in danger? etc.). This is why this mode of description is more appropriate with a discourse about autonomy and, therefore, for describing the behaviour of autonomous systems. In this type of description control is understood in terms of self-regulation.

By now, it should be clear the difference between these two types of system descriptions. But remember that these two types of descriptions are complementary; they arise from an indication chosen by an observer after he or she distinguishes a system. In a sense, these two types of system descriptions relate to each other and to an observer in the same way as the inside and the outside of a circle relate to each other and to the hand drawing the circumference that separates them. They correspond to different uses of a system as a cognitive device. What has to be stressed, however, is that the consequences of choosing one or the other type of description are very different. Let us explore this claim with more detail by approaching different issues using both types of descriptions.

For instance, when the named system is the phenomenon of cognition, it has usually been studied by describing human beings as black boxes. Here the brain is normally depicted as a computer machine that picks up information from its environment ('out there') throughout the sensory system, processes it and stores the output somewhere inside. Under this type of description it is commonly said that the brain operates with a representation of the information content from the environment (Pickering 2010).

If we now switch to an operational description, cognition is understood as an emergent property of the internal coherence of the nervous system that arises as a result of its relative interconnectivity. Under these circumstances, it is the structure of the nervous system that selects which patterns of disturbances in its environment are going to be 'seen', 'heard', or in general 'perceived'. It is the internal structure of the nervous system that makes sense of the world 'out there'. It is in this sense that we say that the nervous system is *structure-determined*. We are moving from psychology of cognition to biology of cognition (Maturana 1988, 2002).

In the above example the concept of *information* changes dramatically under these two types of system's descriptions. Information as referential, instructional and representational is a concept that pertains to the black-box type of descriptions (Simon 1996). On the other hand, in the operational type of descriptions, we use the word *information* in the original etymological sense of *informare* (Latin 'to shape or form') to characterize a quality of an autonomous system to endow its environment with meaning (Varela 1986, p. 119). With this distinction, we are moving from questions about semantic correspondence to questions about structural patterns. Colour, for instance, passes from being considered as a property of objects (i.e., external to us) to be the outcome of an internal (structural) mechanism of our nervous system to which we have no direct experiential access (Maturana 1983).

Similarly, other phenomena like evolution, language, and learning may be explained using one or the other type of description. Our Western tradition, based on a Newtonian-Cartesian paradigm, has supported and generalised the use of the black-box type of system descriptions and the functionalist way of inference (i.e., the behaviour of the system can be established by unveiling the transformation function relating its outputs to its inputs). For a long time this form of description has been the best we have had at hand to characterize and deal with complex phenomena. But the consequences of this input/output type of intervention can be indeed undesirable if applied to aspects of a system's autonomy; for example when using electro-shock to deal with mental illnesses or chemotherapy to deal with cancer (Pert 1997). However, as we develop more complex and sophisticated tools, like the Viable System Model to study organizations, the operational type of descriptions and related forms of intervention are becoming increasingly more relevant and are super-seding the black-box type of descriptions. Yet, in spite of recent developments in complexity theory, the study of economic and social phenomena still depend to a large degree on the latter form of descriptions.

The study of autonomous systems needs using operational descriptions where linear forecasting is replaced by the system's structural dynamic capabilities to deal with the unexpected (i.e., the system's behaviour is determined by the internal capabilities and coherences of the system as a whole).

In effect, these two types of descriptions are not contradictory but complementary. However, as we have tried to show with the examples presented, they lead to radically different consequences. We may choose to use one or the other in studying a particular phenomenon but we have to be fully aware when and why we are using each type of description, and when we are switching from one to the other. This is not a claim for exclusivity but for a 'clean epistemological accounting' (Varela 1984). There are many instances in which these two types of system descriptions are conflated in a single explanation of a particular phenomenon. We know, for instance, that a frog's eye reacts only to shadows in motion, which means that a frog will not react at all if it is standing in front of a steady fly, even if it is starving (Lettvin et al. 1968). If we claim, from this observation, that an explanation of this 'strange' behaviour is because the frog does not *see* the fly; we are conflating two different domains of explanation; the domain of the observations carried out by scientists in which they can simultaneously observe the frog and the fly and establish a correlation between the two; and the frog's domain of interactions (i. e., the frog's 'world'). In this latter domain, the fly does not exist at all. The first explanatory domain comes from the use of a black-box type of descriptions; the other comes from the use of an operational type of description. For the rest of the book we will make explicit which path of description we are following in approaching each one of the issues we discuss.

The topic we need to address now is that of the typology of systems. In the literature about systems there are many of these typologies (see for example Beer 1959, p. 18; Mingers 1995, p. 83). The first point we must notice, according to what we have said so far, is that any typology of systems is arbitrary, reflecting no objective claim at all. We cannot say, therefore, that any particular typology of systems is correct or not, what we can do is refer to its coherence and usefulness as a token for the coordination of actions in a particular domain or as an insight to explore new possibilities in that domain.

We can use different criteria to classify systems. We may, for instance, classify them according to the kinds of parts and relations that constitute them. These typologies may include a differentiation between physical systems, like the car's braking system, biological systems, the digestive system, social systems, the family and so on.

Here we will focus our attention on distinguishing between the two constructs that were implied by the above discussion: *black box systems* and *organizational systems*. These two constructs are relevant for our purpose in this book. Black box systems help us to discuss an organization's strategy to manage complexity while organizational systems help us to discuss their relationships and structure.

Black box systems help us to focus attention on achieving desirable outcomes. First of all managers need to work out what they want to achieve, these are the variables they want to monitor, and secondly the inputs they want to control, these are the controllable variables. The human activities that transform these inputs into the desirable outputs constitute the system in focus. Although quite naturally, managers are part of this system their managerial role requires that they see it as a black box; they cannot possibly get involved in its detailed operations. They have to find responses to deal with any contingency that may take the monitored variables outside the space of desirable outcomes; if they fail the performance of the system suffers. These are responses not only to discrepancies now, but more fundamentally to unanticipated challenges. Managers are managing the complexity of current and unanticipated discrepancies through the system. For this purpose they define strategies to transform inputs into outputs taking into account environmental uncertainty (Beer 1979). These are strategies that break down or decompose the total transformation into more manageable tasks (i.e., more detailed transformations) taking into account aspects such as technology, market segmentation, geography and time (Espejo and Bowling 1996).[4] A production process is a strategy to manage the complexity of a system's transformation. Black box systems are focused on these production processes. In this book, these types of systems provide the platform to distinguish organizational systems.

The second construct (coming from operational descriptions of systems) we would like to examine briefly arises from imposing three conditions to the process by which organizational systems are constituted. The first condition establishes that we are able to observe that the parts or components of the system constitute a *network* of relations or *organizational processes*. The second condition states that the outcomes of this network of processes are the components of the system themselves. The third condition is that some of these components engage in

---

[4]Electronic book available from www.syncho.com

preferential neighbourhood interactions producing the system's boundary. These systems are called autopoietic systems (Maturana and Varela 1992, pp. 47–52).

Autopoietic systems have many interesting characteristics. Let us see a few of them. First of all, they are dynamic systems continually producing themselves (this is literally the meaning of the word *autopoiesis* (Greek 'self-producing'); secondly, because an autopoietic system continually produces its own boundary, it distinguishes itself from its background in the domain of its interactions. That implies that observers will distinguish an autopoietic system only if their observational mechanism interacts with it in the same domain defined by the system's interactions. A cell is an example of an autopoietic system in the domain of physicochemical interactions; therefore, only by interacting with a cell in that domain (for example by using a microscope) an observer will be able to distinguish it. Finally, though we do not take the view that organizational systems are autopoietic (in the biological sense), in epistemological terms autopoietic systems point at self-referential systems that refer to themselves, like the artist M. C. Escher's drawing of two hands drawing each other. These characteristics, we argue later in the book, allow bootstrapping of organizational processes and permit observers to distinguish organizational systems beyond formal institutional definitions.

A theory of autopoietic systems has been developed extensively during the last 30 years with many implications and applications in different fields in the understanding of cognition (Maturana and Varela 1980; Varela et al. 1991); family therapy (Watzlawick 1984; Efran and Lukens 1985; Simon 1985a, b); the legal system (Teubner 1987, 1993; Luhmann 1987); Information Systems (Winograd and Flores 1986; Kensing and Winograd 1991); and Social Systems (Luhmann 1995).

In this book we are interested in applying systems thinking to address issues that pertain to the social domain and more specifically to organizational systems. One of these issues is that of autonomous social organizations, however, as implied above, we do not want to get into the debate of whether social systems are autopoietic systems or not. Instead, we will hypothesise that social systems are 'organizationally closed' but are open to energy and disturbances (what we usually call information, see Chap. 5). These are systems that also exhibit autonomy, and are constituted by *organizational processes* (similar to an autopoietic system) producing their own components and *business processes* producing outcomes of a different kind, like products or services (see Chap. 10). Therefore we see them both from the perspectives of transformational (black-box) and network (operational) descriptions. The boundaries of organizationally closed systems are continually generated by the braiding of these two types of processes, making apparent the relevance of purpose and identity in the generation of these boundaries. Together they clarify what the organizational system does (its purpose) and is (its identity). We will expand on this theme in more detail later on in our chapters about organization and identity (i.e., Chaps. 5 and 7).

It is important to notice that according to our discussion about different system constructs, autopoietic systems are clearly more useful to generate operational descriptions of phenomena like autonomy and cognition. We, of course, can also elaborate black-box type of descriptions of phenomena beyond organizations, modelling inputs, transformations and outputs of social and economic processes. One instance of this kind of description is system dynamics (Forrester 1961, 1969, 1971; Senge 1990), that is, systems constituted by a closed network of activities connected by regulated flows of information and materials. The type of systems we refer to in such a way are distinguished from autopoietic systems as allopoietic systems, that is, systems whose processes of production constitute a transformation function that produces some outputs from its inputs. They are called allopoietic because the system produces something different from itself, something that is defined by an external observer. In this sense, autopoietic systems and allopoietic systems are two complementary ways to approach dynamic phenomena from the standpoint of systems thinking.

There is another distinction about systems we would like to highlight; this is the distinction between human communication systems (HCSs) and human activity systems (HASs). HCSs are the ones we have explained throughout this chapter. They emerge when people's communications achieve closure. We have also called them organizational systems. Let us say a few more words about these systems and contrast them with HASs.

There is a fundamental discontinuity between a HCS and other systems we have been referring to so far. In physical and biological systems (i.e., in the physical and biological domains) for instance, there are observers who bring forth systems but they do not actively constitute the system itself. In other words, observers may not participate in the relations among the system's components. The observer is neither one of the system's components nor participates in the production of such components. On the other hand, a HCS is a name used to indicate a system that is brought forward by a group of observer-participants engaged in a set of recurrent interactions that defines a particular consensual domain of action.

Let us clarify the point. We have discussed the process by which an observer *brings forth* a system (i.e., distinguishes it). We are concerned now with understanding the way by which a group of observer-participants *constitute* a Human Communication System. It is in their recurrent interactions that people negotiate and renegotiate (not necessarily with the same negotiating power) their own distinctions in the particular domain in which they are interacting. As long as they use these shared distinctions to coordinate their actions, they constitute a consensual domain for action, a particular Human Communication System (e.g., a health system, a prison system, a business school). The emergent properties of such a HCS will remain the same as long as the consensual domain of action is dynamically maintained. One such emergent property is its identity, a set of stable relationships that observers may call, for instance, a prison system. This emergent identity has a far deeper meaning than the name generated as an outcome of conversations about the system (Espejo 1994, p. 204) even if the people constituting the system are the ones carrying out these conversations. We will explore this point with more detail in our chapters about organizations and identity later on (Chaps. 5 and 7).

Recalling what we have said about different types of system descriptions, we say that we shall use HCS to elaborate operational descriptions of organizational issues like, for instance, the study of the identity and structure of an organization and the study of autonomous organizations.

On the other hand, holons, or *ideal* types, about purposeful human activities are called Human Activity Systems (HASs), in concordance with Soft Systems Methodology (Checkland 1981). We shall use HASs to hypothesise HCSs; these are mental constructs of systems that may not have emerged yet. Therefore, while a HCS is the name we give to the *distinction* emerging from people's 'interactions' in the world, a HAS is an intellectual device that helps us exploring and thinking about a particular domain of action.

As a HAS is purposeful, we usually name it by explicitly describing the intended transformation of some inputs into some outputs. We may name a prison, for instance, as a HAS in the following way: 'An institution that provides a service to a community by receiving and maintaining as inmates people convicted by a criminal court, for as long as established by their sentence, in order to protect the community from their wrong doings.' The holon in this example is a mental construct of the human activity that takes as input convicted people and transforms them into people with completed sentences (see Chap. 7).

We may, of course, produce many other possible HASs for a prison, for instance: 'An institution that provides psychological treatment, medical care and training to people that have been convicted by a criminal court, in order to help them to join a productive life in society after they accomplish their punishment.'

We can use HAS and HCS to approach the study of phenomena that we distinguished as constituted by recurrent interactions of observer-participants. Their use generates two different ways of understanding such phenomena. HASs are not concerned with organizational closure but with purposeful activities. It is important to stress, however, that they belong to different logical domains; while Human Activity Systems pertain to the domain of people's ideas, Human Communication Systems belong to the domain of people's interactions. We will discuss these two domains in more detail in the chapter about complexity (Chap. 3).

Summarising: our epistemological stance about organizational systems is that they are closed networks of interactive people. They emerge as individuals coordinate successfully their actions with others. We, as observers, name a system when we make a distinction expressing the meaning that we experience from observing a particular closed network of people's interactions. In this book we are concerned with both the process by which an observer names a system and, by naming it, brings it forth into existence (see Chap. 7) and the process by which a group of observer-participants, in their day-to-day recurrent interactions, constitute a consensual domain of action as a Human Communication System (Chap. 5).

The purpose of this chapter was to develop an account of the concept of a system, an account that stresses the relevance of the observer in bringing forth systems. Its grounding is in second-order – cybernetics (von Foerster 1984) and the biology of cognition (Maturana 1988).

But after developing this framework to systems a question still remains to be answered: what is systemic thinking? This question is at the core of this book and will be discussed in depth in Chap. 11. We hope that readers will come out with their own answer as triggered by the reading of this book. However, we may offer as a provoking starter the following comments (Espejo 1994).

We claim that systemic thinking is a particular way of approaching issues of concern that includes seeing wholes.

System thinking is a way of thinking that sees phenomena in context. It is a way of thinking that alerts us about networks of interactions producing wholes. It also helps us to think about required wholes in order to produce desirable outcomes. One of the characteristics of systemic phenomena is that it is complex and therefore difficult to appreciate. This complexity emerges from the relations among the components producing a whole, as well as from the co-development of a system with the many others in its surroundings. The former complexity is responsible for the emergence of autonomous systems, the latter for the unexpected outcomes of a system's behaviour, particularly as counter-intuitive co-developmental behaviours make apparent the interconnected nature of phenomena. Systemic thinking also underlies an ethics, which makes visible the requirements for ethical behaviour in a complex world. It makes apparent that ethical behaviour is one that increases possibilities for others and in particular does not restrict their viability (von Foerster 1984).

In terms of our earlier discussion of systems, when the indication is made from within the system, systems thinking implies developing an understanding of how the parts constituting a perceived system relate to each other. It also implies understanding the processes by which these parts produce a system, that is, it implies understanding self-organizing processes. It also implies developing an understanding of the processes by which social meanings are grounded as systems in a consensual domain of action by a community. It is about understanding the likely effects in the whole of local behaviours, and vice versa; and it is about understanding the language and emotions (i.e., conversations) needed to produce stable, viable systems.

When the indication is made from outside the system, systems thinking implies understanding loops of mutual causality, it implies understanding the consequences of a system's behaviour. It implies working out the effects on others and the way these others respond to these behaviours. It implies understanding the webs of interlocked behaviours affecting each other's actions. System thinking helps to connect distant events, it helps to work out the hidden consequences of our actions, it links events in time, it helps seeing the big picture in spatial and temporal terms and it helps seeing patterns of relationships and processes. In short, it helps to avoid unnecessary fragmentation (Beer 2009).

Offering tools to enable this kind of thinking is the aim of this book.

References

Axelrod R, Cohen MD (1999) Harnessing complexity. Free Press, New York
Beer S (1959) Cybernetics and management. English Universities Press, London
Beer S (1979) The heart of enterprise. Wiley, Chichester

Beer S (2009) The culpabliss error: a calculus of ethics for a systemic world. In: Whittaker D (ed) Think before you think: social complexity and knowledge of knowing. Wavestone Press, Charlbury, Oxfordshire, pp 233–247

Beinhocker ED (2006) The origin of wealth. Harvard Business School Press, Cambridge, MA

Checkland P (1981) Systems thinking, systems practice. Wiley, Chichester

Checkland P, Scholes J (1990) Soft systems methodology in action. Wiley, Chichester

Clore GL, Storbeck Jl (2006) Affect as information about liking, efficacy, and importance. In: Forgas J (ed) Affect in social thinking and behavior. Psychology Press, New York, pp 123–142

Efran J, Lukens M (1985) The world according to Humberto Maturana. Fam Ther Networker 9(3):72–75

Espejo R (1994) What's systemic thinking? Syst Dyn Rev 10(2–3 Summer–Fall):199–212

Espejo R, Bowling D (1996) Viplan learning system: a method to learn the viable system model. Syncho Ltd., Birmingham, UK

Forrester J (1961) Industrial dynamics. MIT Press, Cambridge, MA

Forrester J (1969) Urban dynamics. Pegasus Communications, Waltham, MA

Forrester J (1971) World dynamics. Wright-Allen, Cambridge, MA

Kensing F, Winograd T (1991) The language/action approach to design of computer-support for cooperative work: a preliminary study in work mapping. In: Stamper RK, Kerola RP, Lee R, Lyytinen K (eds) Collaborative work, social communications and information systems. Elsevier-North Holland, Amsterdam, pp 311–332

Lettvin JY, Maturana HR, McCulloch WS, Pitts WH (1968) What the frog's eye tells the frog's brain. In: Corning WC, Balaban M (eds) The mind: biological approaches to its functions. Wiley, Hoboken, NJ, pp 233–258

Luhmann N (1987) The unity of the legal system. In: Teubner G (ed) Autopoiesis and the law. de Gruyter, Berlin, pp 12–35

Luhmann N (1995) Social systems. Stanford University Press, Stanford, CA

Maturana H (1983) What is to see. Arch Biol Med Experimentation 16:255–269

Maturana H (1988) Reality: the search for objectivity or the quest for a compelling argument. Ir J Psychol 9(1):25–82

Maturana H (2002) Autopoiesis, structural coupling and cognition: a history of these and other notions in the biology of cognition. Cybern Hum Knowing 9(3–4):5–34

Maturana H, Varela F (1980) Autopoiesis and cognition: the realization of the living. Reidel, Dordrecht

Maturana H, Varela F (1992) The tree of knowledge. Shambhala, Boston & London

Maturana H, Verden-Zoeller G (1993) Amor y Juego: Fundamentos Olvidados de lo Humano. Editorial Instituto de Terapia Cognitiva, Santiago, Chile

Mingers J (1995) Self-producing systems: implications and applications of autopoiesis. Plenum Press, New York

Pert C (1997) Molecules of emotion: why you feel the way you feel. Scribner, New York

Pickering A (2010) The cybernetic brain. The University of Chicago Press, London

Rosenblueth A, Wiener N, Bigelow J (1943) Behavior, purpose and teleology. Philos Sci 10:18–24

Sawyer K (2005) Social emergence: societies as complex systems. Cambridge University Press, Cambridge

Senge P (1990) The fifth discipline: the art and the practice of the learning organization. Doubleday/Currency, New York

Simon R (1985a) An interview with Humberto Maturana. Fam Ther Networker 9(3):41–43

Simon R (1985b) A frog's eye view of the world. Fam Ther Networker 9(3):34–35

Simon H (1996) The sciences of the artificial. MIT Press, Cambridge, MA

Spencer-Brown G (1969) The laws of form. Allen & Unwin, London

Teubner G (ed) (1987) Autopoiesis and the law. Walter de Gruyter, Berlin

Teubner G (1993) Law as an autopoietic system. Blackwell, Oxford

Ulrich W (2000) Reflective practice in the civil society: the construction of critically systemic thinking. Reflective Pract 1(2):247–268

Varela F (1975) A calculus for self-reference. Int J Gen Sys 2:5–24

Varela F (1979) Principles of biological autonomy. Elsevier-North Holland, New York

Varela F (1984) Two principles for self-organization. In: Ulrich H, Probst G (eds) Self-organization and management of social systems. Verlag, Berlin

Varela F (1986) Steps to a cybernetics of autonomy. In: Trappl R (ed) Power, autonomy, utopia. Plenum, New York

Varela F, Thompson E, Rosch E (1991) The embodied mind. MIT Press, Cambridge, MA

von Foerster H (1984) Observing systems. Intersystems, Salinas, CA

Watzlawick P (ed) (1984) The invented reality. Norton, New York

Winograd T, Flores F (1986) Understanding computers and cognition. Ablex Publishing, Norwood, NJ

Chapter 2
On Control and Communication: Self-regulation and Coordination of Actions

Abstract The term control is a loaded one and the term communication needs much clarification. In 1948 Wiener encapsulated the outcome of discussions about feedback loops and circular causality in self-regulating systems in his book *Cybernetics: or Control and Communication in the Animal and the Machine* and this was formally the beginning of cybernetics as a discipline. The name comes from the Greek for steersman (the equivalent in Latin is gubernatur), a term that Plato used to describe the art of steering ships; much later, in the nineteenth century, the French scientist Ampère, used it in reference to the science of government. In the second edition of his book, Wiener added a few chapters showing the relevance of cybernetics to learning, artificial intelligence, adaptation and language. Today feedback mechanisms are ubiquitous; they happen whenever part of the output of a system returns as its input, which is thereby changed. This is the case of a normal heating system and any servo-mechanism ranging from missiles to robots. It is also the case of complex systems, which depend on memory to learn; feedback is happening when input information is affected by the output of the previous observation. As for communication we understand it as coordination of actions, going beyond making sure that the message has been received; only when we manage to produce coordinated actions we can claim that communication has been achieved.

During the last years of the Second World War, the Office of Scientific Research and Development of the USA focused most of its efforts and resources on finding solutions to two strategic problems: the first one was the development of the atomic bomb, the second was the construction of an antiaircraft cannon to attack German bombers. While the research for the first problem was carried out at Los Alamos as the Manhattan Project under the direction of Robert Oppenheimer, the antiaircraft project was assigned to Norbert Wiener, a brilliant mathematician who was working at the Massachusetts Institute of Technology (MIT) (Heims 1987).

Wiener was a mathematician prodigy and at the age of ten wrote his first paper entitled 'The Theory of Ignorance', when he was sixteen he got a degree in mathematics and philosophy from Harvard University and at nineteen received a PhD in philosophy from the same university. With this impressive background, it was no surprise that he was appointed to lead the project at MIT.

R. Espejo and A. Reyes, *Organizational Systems*,
DOI 10.1007/978-3-642-19109-1_2, © Springer-Verlag Berlin Heidelberg 2011

The main problem was to predict the position of an aircraft. This was so because given the limited speed of the cannon's projectiles, the operator of the cannon should not point it directly towards the plane. If he did so, when the projectile reached its intended target, of course, the aircraft would not be there anymore. In addition, pilots surely will move randomly to avoid being destroyed. Wiener's approach was to develop a mathematical theory to predict future events by extrapolating incomplete information from the past which, in passim, was the basis of modern statistical communication theory (Heims 1987, p. 184). Working with a young engineer, Julian Bigelow, they built an antiaircraft machine by connecting a cannon to the recently developed radar. Figure 2.1 shows the operation of the machine.

When the radar first detected the plane, it followed it for a few seconds gathering information about its course. Then, by using the mathematical theory developed by Wiener, a possible position of the plane was estimated. This information was fed on to the cannon mechanism which used it to set the target position and fire. If the plane was not destroyed, the radar gathered additional information and adjusted the prediction mechanism to calculate the new probable position of the plane. Again the information was passed on to the cannon that adjusted the firing mechanism and so on. As soon as the plane would follow a pattern, almost certainly it would be destroyed.

But notice that this was an entirely automatic process, nobody was controlling the cannon! Imagine the generals' astonishment when Wiener was showing this

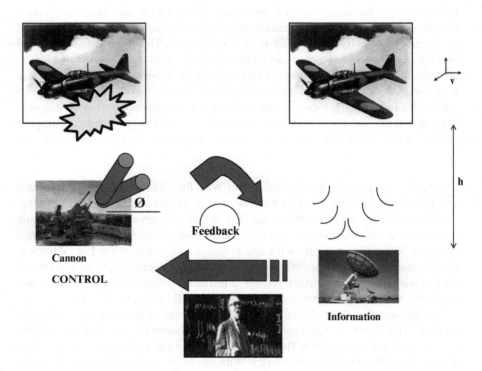

Fig. 2.1 Antiaircraft cannon built by Norbert Wiener and Julian Bigelow

invention to them. What they saw was an antiaircraft device that was activated as soon as a plane came into the range of the radar, they then saw that the cannon started to shoot automatically following and anticipating the movements of the target. It seemed as if the mechanism had an in-built purpose: to shoot down enemy aircraft. We will come to this point later on.

The mechanism was very successful though, of course, many people died, regardless of being enemies or not, Wiener publicly proclaimed that he would not participate in military projects again (Heims 1987). He moved towards the philosophy of science and organized several congresses about the subject. Here he met Arturo Rosenblueth who had been working for several years in understanding the nature of ataxia, a neurological disorder that, among other manifestations, led patients to an erratic and oscillatory movement of their arms when they wanted to pick up an object. During the course of their conversations, Wiener soon realised that it was possible to explain this biological disorder by applying the same ideas used for the construction of the antiaircraft machine.

What made it possible for the antiaircraft cannon to reach its goal (i.e., to shoot down the plane) was the feedback mechanism built into the operation of the system. Information gathered from the radar was fed onto the control mechanism of the cannon, the outcome of its operation led to gather additional information from the radar that was fed back again to the cannon and so on. This feedback loop that allowed the interlocking of communication and control in real time was the common explanatory device that Weiner recognised.

With this insight, Wiener and Rosenblueth suggested that the reason why persons suffering from ataxia started to move their arms in an oscillatory manner was because there was a delay in this feedback mechanism. Indeed, when a person tried to pick up an object (i.e., fixed a goal) and started moving his arm towards it, he initiated this feedback loop. If he observes that his arm is moving in the wrong direction, his brain will signal his muscles to correct the movement. But if they do not respond, a reinforcement signal will occur. When the muscles finally respond, the arm will pass on and move wrongly in the other direction. When the person notices this, he will promptly react to correct in the opposite direction. But if the delay continues, the outcome is that the arm will swing back again to the previous incorrect movement. In other words, an oscillatory movement will occur.

It turned out that further research found that persons suffering from ataxia had this delay in their sensory-motor system. Wiener and Rosenblueth wrote together with Bigelow a joint paper inspired by these ideas (Rosenblueth et al. 1943). The paper proposed that feedback mechanisms could be used as explanatory devices to understand phenomena either pertaining to the mechanical realm (as the operations of an anti aircraft cannon) or to a biological realm (as in ataxia). The paper was a hit because it showed an alternative way to the old debate between mechanistic principles and vitalism. The former claiming that all phenomena could be explained in terms of the operation of physico-chemical laws and the latter claiming that biological phenomena needed an additional category, that of the intrinsic purpose of the being, its soul, that regulates its behaviour.

From 1946 to 1953 there was a series of meetings in New York sponsored by the Josiah Macy Jr. Foundation to discuss the application of these ideas in different domains (Heims 1991). The meetings were led by Warren McCulloch, an American neurophysiologist, whose work in modelling the operation of the nervous system gave rise, among other things, to the modern theory of neural networks (McCulloch 1989; Bishop 1995); nowadays a field with many practical applications that goes from the design of robots to the understanding of customers' shopping behaviour in supermarkets via the use of data mining techniques (Berry and Linoff 1997)

In 1948 Wiener encapsulated the outcome of many of these discussions about feedback loops and circular causality in self-regulating systems in a book that he entitled *Cybernetics: Or Control and Communication in the Animal and the Machine* (Wiener 1948); this was formally the beginning of cybernetics as a discipline. This name comes from the Greek κυβερνήτηζ or steersman (the equivalent in Latin is *gubernatur*) a term that Plato used to describe the art of steering ships. In the nineteenth century the French scientist Ampère, used it for the science of government. In the second edition of the book, Wiener added a few chapters showing the relevance of cybernetics to learning, artificial intelligence, adaptation and language (Wiener 1961).

To understand control and communication mechanisms of these kinds of systems the Macy Meeting of the cybernetic group, as it was called (Heims 1991), developed a deep understanding of concepts like feedback, homeostasis and the black-box. Today feedback mechanisms are present in many applications; they are used to regulate certain variables (outputs) by a continuous observation of others (inputs) in such a way that the input is affected by the output of the previous observation. This is the case of a normal heating system and any servo-mechanism ranging from missiles to robots.

A special case of a feedback system is called a homeostat. Here a set of variables are maintained among expected values regardless of the nature of perturbations that may affect them. An interesting mechanical example, known as the centrifugal governor, is shown in Fig. 2.2. It was designed by the Scottish inventor James Watt to regulate the speed of a steam engine in 1765. Given the maximum expected speed (w), Watt arranged a couple of solid balls weighing m, as shown in Fig. 2.2. If the amount of steam increases, the balls will move up because of the centrifugal force over them. This, in turn, will move up the valve (v) reducing, in this way, the amount of steam going into the engine. But this reduction in steam will force the balls to fall down (as the centrifugal force will decline) making the valve move down as well. This will allow the entrance of more steam and so on. Notice that as long as the regulating mechanism does not break down, the governor will regulate the speed of the steam engine regardless of the nature of perturbations that may affect it. This special characteristic of certain control systems is commonly known as ultrastability (Ashby 1964). This is a nice example of a self-regulating system, that is, of a system that has intrinsic control. In the biological realm the internal mechanism of the body to maintain the inner temperature within a steady range (around 36–37°C for an adult) regardless of being in Alaska or near a furnace is

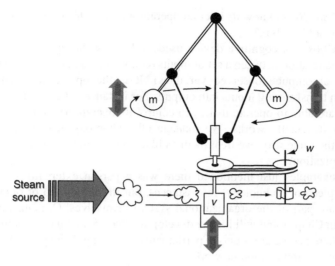

Fig. 2.2 The centrifugal governor of James Watt

another example of a homeostat. In the domain of organizations, we used the same concept at the end of Chap. 4.

Other members of the cybernetics group were John von Neumann, a Hungarian born (but later American nationalized) mathematician who, after participating in the Manhattan Project, developed the conceptual framework that allowed the construction of the first electronic computer (called ENIAC) in 1947 (von Neumann 1946); Gregory Bateson an English anthropologist who later developed (from notions of feedback) the theory of the double bind as a major contribution to understanding schizophrenia (Bateson 1972); Margaret Mead, then wife and fellow anthropologist of Bateson, who studied the behaviour and culture of tribes in Samoa (Mead 1961); and Heinz von Foerster, an Austrian physicist who was the secretary of the Macy Conferences and founder, many years later of the Biological Computer Laboratory at Illinois for studying the dynamics of observing systems or what he called second-order cybernetics (von Foerster 1984).

In 1959 Stafford Beer wrote his first book making a connection between cybernetics and management. This novel discipline, called management cybernetics, studies the design of communication and control mechanisms in organizations (Beer 1959). These are two crucial concepts for the purpose of this book. Let us explore in more detail the meaning we ascribe to them here.

Controlling a system is usually associated with the idea of reducing the uncertainty about its operation. It is believed that by increasing the knowledge we have about the specific operation of a system, we increase the chances of its effective regulation. However, this can be misleading because uncertainty is part of the natural dynamic of any complex system (see Chap. 1). From one of the control aphorisms proposed by Beer in *Diagnosing the System for Organizations* we can conclude that *given particular constraints* it is always possible to regulate a black box even if we do not know its internal operation (Beer 1985). But what exactly do we mean by a black box?

A black box is a cognitive device used to describe the operation of a system based on the relation between a set of inputs (controlled and uncontrolled variables) and a set of outputs (observed variables). It is the operation of an invisible mechanism transforming inputs into outputs. For instance, when we use our mobile phone we are able to operate it (i.e., to control its operation) without any need to know how it actually works. We manage all technology at our disposal today exactly in the same way; we treat them as black boxes. But what about the control of an organization?

In the examples just mentioned there was a person externally controlling a system (a piece of technology, for instance), but in the domain of organizations, managers are part of the organizational system themselves. Organizations, as we advanced in Chap. 1 and will further develop in Chap. 5 are human communication systems where people are observer participants producing their system by engaging in recurrent communication networks.

Therefore, control in organizations does not refer to its naïve interpretation as a crude process of coercion, but instead it mostly refers to self-regulation, a homeostatic process similar to the ones explained before. A general model for a self-regulating mechanism in an organizational context is shown in Fig. 2.3.

This is a feedback mechanism whose operation demarcates the purpose of the organizational system. Once this purpose is defined, it is possible to identify a set of aspects (sometimes called critical success factors – CSF) relevant to observe the behaviour of the system vis-à-vis this purpose. These are called indices in the diagram. Because the organizational system is not static, external and internal events will occur that affect the value of indices. When these risks materialize we

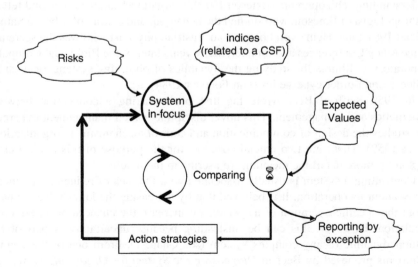

Fig. 2.3 A general model for self-regulation in an organizational system

need to work out a set of strategies to define a new course for action. The effects of its implementation will be observed in the on-going reading of the indices. The loop goes on and on and can be seen as the basis for learning mechanisms. We will go back to this point in Chap. 10.

From the perspective of an effective management of complexity (see Chap. 4) control in organizational systems should mean, to a significant degree, self-regulation. However self-regulation is not the only form of control. In organizations we distinguish between intrinsic control or self-regulation, and extrinsic control or control from outside. Examples of intrinsic control, like the thermostat or the Watt's governor, have the constraints built into the control process. However, it is always possible to change externally the desired temperature or speed thus changing the nature of the control process from intrinsic to extrinsic control. Unfortunately, with extrinsic control it is always possible that a necessary change in expected values does not take place simply because those responsible can be out of the loop when a necessary resetting of parameters is necessary. We will discuss the complementarity of intrinsic and extrinsic control while discussing the Viable System Model in Chap. 6.

But in operational terms, as we saw from its origin in cybernetics, it is not possible to separate control from communication. How then do we understand communication in this context?

We normally understand communication as a process of information transmission. Even more, we usually have in mind a model to describe this process as the one shown in Fig. 2.4. This model, broadly extended today, comes from the early work by Claude Shannon during the late 1940s (Shannon and Weaver 1949). In his Mathematical Theory of Communication, Shannon developed a basic model that has been regarded as a paradigm ever since.

According to the model, after choosing a message, a sender uses a codifier to translate it to a form that could be sent without losing its integrity through a noisy channel. The receiver, at the other end of the channel, will use a de-codifier to translate the message back into its original form. Shannon formulated and demonstrated a beautiful theorem in which he proved that given that we know the nature of the noise in the communication channel, we can always find a codifier such that the

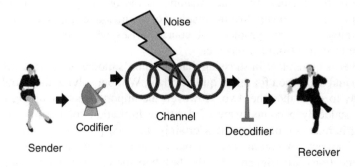

Fig. 2.4 Shannon's model of communication

codified message will go through the channel successfully. This is known as Shannon's 10th Theorem of Communication and has been used to develop many of our current devices and communication mechanisms from the telephone to radar and from satellite systems to mobile technology. This same theorem is also underpinning Ashby's Law of Requisite Variety (Ashby 1964) that we will use in Chap. 4 when we develop the concept of complexity management.

But the model has been used also in other areas. It is behind the design and implementation of modern computer networks, including the Internet, and psychologists have used it to study communication problems among individuals. Even biologists used this model to solve one of their hardest problems, the question about inheritance: how is it that certain characteristics of living beings go from one generation to the next? In fact, the well-known double-helix model of the DNA was developed because a famous physicist pointed in this direction when many scientists were looking for explanations somewhere else. In his book *What is Life*, Erwin Shrödinger suggested that this problem could be better understood if approached from the point of view of a communication mechanism at the molecular level from one 'individual' to the other (Shrödinger 1944). This is precisely the reason why nowadays scientists talk about the genetic 'code' and of being able to break this code to reveal the 'language' of the human genome (Marshall 1997).

This short historical detour should make evident the importance of Shannon's model to the current and broad understanding of the phenomenon of communication. The model's dictum is: *communication is information transmission*. However, as Weaver himself pointed out when presenting the implications of the model (Shannon and Weaver 1949), the problem of communication can be approached from three different questions emerging from the model itself. The first question is: How can we manage to send successfully a message from a sender to a receiver through a noisy communication channel? As we mentioned above, this is precisely the problem generally solved by Shannon's mathematical theory. But, there are two other problems to be solved.

The second one could be established as follows: given that a receiver successfully received a message, how can we assure that the meaning she or he ascribes to it is the same as the one ascribed by the sender? The third problem could be stated in the following way: given that a message successfully reached a receiver and given that she or he ascribes the same meaning as the one originally ascribed by the sender, how can we ensure that the receiver of the message responds to the sender's expectations? This last problem, of course, arises when the sender expects an effective response from the receiver.

Weaver is quite clear in stressing that Shannon's model only deals with the first problem and the reason for this is quite evident. Without solving this problem, there is no way to solve the other two. However, the importance of realizing this fact is that we suddenly become aware of the huge limitations of the model in understanding human communications. Certainly, the first problem covers most of the technical aspects of communication but the most pervasive problems in human communications are triggered by the last two, precisely the ones Shannon left consciously aside. However, as we explained before, the model has permeated all realms of communication from computer science to biology, from engineering to psychology and organizational theory and, most importantly, it is now part of our common sense in this matter.

With this in mind, we can go back to explore the implications of communication in organizational systems. It is often believed, as we said before, that communication is information transmission, which implies that whenever a message is successfully transmitted and received by the receiver the communication has been successful. We claim that this way of understanding communication is not enough in an organizational context for the reasons mentioned above. The problems of interpretation and coordinated action are left aside. In this book, we are using a rather different understanding of communication, one whose dictum could be expressed in the following way: *communication is coordination of actions*. It refers to the structural coupling (Maturana and Varela 1992, p. 75) of organizational actors, that is to their structural adjustments in a history of recurrent interactions. Communication, in this way, is a concept that belongs to the operational domain of the organization rather than the informational domain of sending messages (see Chap. 5).

Notice that communication, in Shannon's terms, implies a 'one way' process in the sense that it is effective when the message arrives successfully. On the other hand, communication as coordination of actions implies a *circular process*, a continuum of 'negotiation' between the sender and the receiver until their actions are coordinated. Once this coordination is achieved, we can say that the communication has been successful. A common metaphor to characterize the former model of communication is one of a conduit through which messages are delivered. A useful metaphor to characterize the latter model is one of an on-going dance between sender-receiver-sender.

It should be apparent that embodying one or the other when we engage in relations with others has important consequences. In terms of accountability, for instance, communication as information transmission implies that my responsibility in communicating effectively with others ends whenever I am sure that they got the message. This is perhaps one of the reasons why it was so common in many organizations (especially in public ones) to hold a signed copy of a message as evidence that the receiver had 'got it'. Today there are electronic equivalents of this practice. If there is a breakdown in the communication the one to be blamed is the receiver not the sender and the evidence is used to 'prove' that the message had been successfully communicated.

On the other hand, if we truly understand communication as coordination of actions, then in an analogous situation as before, my responsibility for effective communication goes beyond making sure that the message has been received. Only when I manage to produce a coordinated action can I claim that the communication has been effective. It is too easy to blame the others for our lack of competence in getting commitments from others. This understanding of communication has implications for our understanding of control; control emerges from the mutual adjustments, negotiations, dynamic stability of persons, groups, units in interaction and not from the unilateral impositions of one over the other. Of course control may also be achieved by unilateral impositions but, in general, this is an ineffective control.

Most of the main themes of this book revolve around the concept of communication. Therefore, from now on, whenever we talk about communication we will be referring to communication as coordination of actions and not simply as information transmission. Notice that this approach to communication clearly takes into account the two problems left aside by Shannon's model. In fact, we recover the full complexity of human communication by going beyond the technical aspects; emotions, for instance, play a fundamental role in human communication. To develop this line of thought even further, we would say that communication requires more than conversations; it also requires sharing cultural contexts. Here, we understand a conversation as the braiding of language and emotions in recurrent interactions with others (Maturana 1988). In other words, the language we use (verbal, written, signs, body language, etc.) and our emotions constitute our conversations. When these recurrent interactions produce meanings that go beyond the particular people in interaction then the affected community is sharing a cultural context. This is further elaborated below.

It is useful to distinguish, when communicating with others, among different types of conversations (Flores 1982). We may distinguish, for instance, between a conversation for possibilities and a conversation for action. The former is intended to open up new alternatives, perhaps bringing forth fresh insights into the topic being discussed; the latter is intended to generate commitments and produce actions. We will mention conversations for possibilities in Chap. 4 when talking about creating new distinctions as the outcome of our interactions (i.e., conversations) with others. In an organizational context, making new distinctions is a necessary condition for people to invent and re-invent their organizations; it usually implies questioning the assumptions, values and norms we normally take for granted. On the other hand, in the same context, conversations for actions are the building blocks of individual's relations. A simple model of such a conversation is shown in Fig. 2.5 (Winograd and Flores 1986, p. 65).

In this model we can appreciate the circular structure of a communication process that we mentioned before. A conversation for action is effective if, and only if, the loop is closed by a declaration of satisfaction from the person who made the request. Of course, before reaching this point, the loop can iterate many times. In a broader organizational context many people can participate in closing a single conversational loop and many different conversational loops are going on all the time. It is precisely in this sense that an organization can be visualized as a closed network of recurrent individual relations. Notice that although the conversation model here is based on a *request* made by A to B, the same structure holds in a conversation where A makes an *offer* to B.

It should be clear by now how recurrent conversations among individuals may produce stable relations, which, in turn, may produce relationships as we will explain in Chap. 5. But, notice that at the same time, the values, norms and beliefs emerging from these relationships, and shared by individuals, define their cultural context and provide a powerful influence on the way individual conversations take place in the organization. This is, again, an illustration of the circular causality between human relations and organizational relationships. A consequence of this

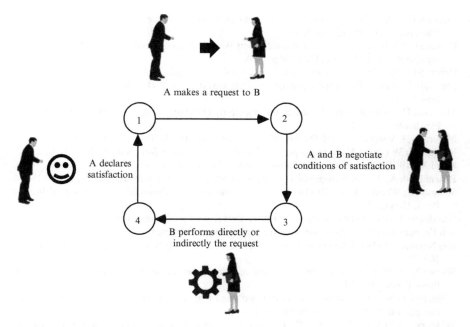

Fig. 2.5 A model of a conversation for action

circularity, as is mentioned in Chap. 5, is that the stronger the cultural links between organizational members (i.e., the stronger their relationships) the larger the capacity of the communication channels supporting their conversations (Espejo et al. 1996), which, in turn, may reinforce the organizational relationships.

Control, understood as self-regulation and communication as coordination of actions along with the meanings of complexity, systems, institutions and organizations that are given in the following chapters are necessary conditions to develop a methodological approach to study and design communication and control processes in viable complex organizations. The final chapters of this book unfold this methodological approach.

References

Ashby R (1964) An introduction to cybernetics. Methuen, London

Bateson G (1972) Steps to an ecology of mind. Ballantine, New York

Beer S (1959) Cybernetics and management. English Universities Press, London

Beer S (1985) Diagnosing the system for organizations. Wiley, Chichester

Berry M, Linoff G (1997) Data mining techniques: for marketing, sales and customer support, vol 2. Wiley, Chichester

Bishop C (1995) Neural networks for pattern recognition. Oxford University Press, Oxford

Espejo R, Schuhmann W, Schwaninger M, Bilello U (1996) Organizational transformation and learning. Wiley, Chichester

Flores CF (1982) Management and communication in the office of the future. PhD Thesis. University of California, Berkeley

Heims SJ (1987) John von Neumann and Norbert Wiener: from mathematics to the technologies of life and death. MIT Press, Cambridge, MA

Heims SJ (1991) The cybernetics group. MIT Press, Cambrigde, MA

Marshall E (1997) The human genome project: cracking the code within us. Franklin Watts, New York

Maturana H (1988) Reality: the search for objectivity or the quest for a compelling argument. Ir J Psychol 9(1):25–82

Maturana H, Varela F (1992) The tree of knowledge. Shambhala, Boston and London

McCulloch W (1989) Collected papers of Warren S. McCulloch. Intersystems, Salinas, CA

Mead M (1961) Coming of age in Samoa. Harper Collins Books, New York

Rosenblueth A, Wiener N, Bigelow J (1943) Behavior, purpose and teleology. Philos Sci 10:18–24

Shannon C, Weaver W (1949) The mathematical theory of communication. University of Illinois Press, Urbana, IL

Shrödinger E (1944) What is life? Cambridge University Press, Cambridge

von Foerster H (1984) Observing systems. Intersystems, California

von Neumann J (1946) The principles of large-scale computing machines. Ann Hist Comp 3(3): 263–273

Wiener N (1948) Cybernetics: or control and communication in the animal and the machine. MIT Press, Cambridge, MA

Wiener N (1961) Cybernetics: or control and communication in the animal and the machine, 2nd edition. MIT Press, Cambridge, MA

Winograd T, Flores F (1986) Understanding computers and cognition. Ablex Publishing, Norwood, NJ

Chapter 3
On Complexity: How to Measure It?

Abstract During the past couple of decades the study of complexity has grown as one of the most fashionable themes of research. A cursory review shows that thousands of books have been published on the topic during this period and several journals are continuously addressing different aspects related to it. The work by the Santa Fe Research Institute is perhaps one of the most famous recent efforts to approach the topic in an interdisciplinary way. Yet, despite the different particular applications of these works or perhaps because of this, there is no single generally agreed definition of complexity, let alone one practical measurement of complexity. However, in this chapter inspired by Ross Ashby's concept of variety we attempt a precise definition of the concept of complexity. This definition is necessary to approach the kind of issues that interest us throughout this book, such as self-regulation, self-organization and variety engineering.

During the past decades the study of complexity has grown as one of the most fashionable themes of research. A cursory review shows that thousands of books have been published on the topic during this period[1] and several journals are continuously addressing different aspects related with it. The work by the Santa Fe Research Institute (Arthur et al. 1997; Blume and Durlauf 2006)[2] is perhaps one of the most continuous recent efforts to approach the topic in an interdisciplinary way. Yet, despite the different particular applications of these works or perhaps because of this, naturally there is no single generally agreed definition of complexity, let alone one practical measurement of complexity (Waldrop 1993; Lewin 1993).

In fact, the following quote reflects some of the despair that the explosion of publications about this topic is causing:

> And what is "complexity" anyway? I looked forward to the two 1992 science books identically titled Complexity, one by Mitch Waldrop and one by Roger Lewin, because I was hoping one or the other would provide me with a practical measurement of complexity.

---

[1] This large number of publications can be confirmed through a search on Amazon.

[2] For more information you may visit the Santa Fe Research Institute at: http://www.santafe.edu/

R. Espejo and A. Reyes, *Organizational Systems*,
DOI 10.1007/978-3-642-19109-1_3, © Springer-Verlag Berlin Heidelberg 2011

But both authors wrote books on the subject without hazarding a guess at a usable definition. How do we know one thing or process is more complex than another? Is a cucumber more complex than a Cadillac? Is a meadow more complex than a mammal brain? Is a zebra more complex than a national economy? I am aware of three or four mathematical definitions for complexity, none of them broadly useful in answering the type of questions I just asked. We are so ignorant of complexity that we haven't yet asked the right question about what it is (Kelly 1994).

It is our intention in this chapter to define the concept of complexity in order to approach not only the kind of questions posed by Kelly but also the kind of issues that we are interested to explore in this book. Issues about self-regulation, self-organization, autonomy, communication and control from the perspective of systemic thinking could be explored by using conceptual and methodological tools based on the management of complexity.

Complexity management, in fact, is not a new topic. It has been at the core of cybernetics (Ashby 1964) and of management cybernetics since the 1950s (Beer 1959) and this book revolves around this theme exploiting its use both as an explanatory device and as a methodological tool for design.

While the next chapter will be dedicated to developing the basic principles of managing complexity, this chapter builds up a set of conceptual definitions of complexity starting from our discussion on systems as presented in our previous chapter.

In this chapter we shall distinguish among situational, individual and collective complexity and variety. Along with the definitions themselves, we will illustrate their use as explanatory devices with simple examples. To begin with, it is important to note that in our day-to-day language we usually associate complexity with difficulty. We say that something is complex if we find it difficult to understand or to explain. If we go to the OED, however, a more precise definition of complexity may be found. According to this definition, something is complex when it is 'made of (usually several) closely connected parts'.[3] Thus, following this line, it seems that the complexity we see in something relates to our ability *to distinguish* the parts and relations constituting this something. In fact, we will argue that the *complexity* we see in a situation is the *number* of *behavioural distinctions* we make in it. Indeed, we are likely to see very little complexity in situations we are not familiar with; while we may define standards in those situations we are experts in.

By seeing complexity in this way, we are taking into account again the fundamental ability of human beings to make distinctions and, therefore, what we said about distinctions in the first chapter also applies to complexity here. In particular, we are stressing once more the role of the observer. But before going any further and for the sake of simplicity in our presentation, we will address first the complexity of a *situation* (whether material, biological or social) in general terms and then we will look at it in more precise terms with the support of the idea of a *system*.

---

[3]See the Oxford Advanced Learner's Dictionary, Oxford University Press.

A consequence of our general definition of complexity given above is that we don't see complexity as an intrinsic *property* of a situation.[4] Instead, it is an *attribute* ascribed by observers according to the number of distinctions that they are able to make in the domain in which they interact with that particular situation (that is what we mean by *behavioural distinctions*). For instance, drivers who know nothing about mechanics see relatively little complexity in the car they are driving. But the same car seen by engineers is far more complex in terms of the number of parts they are able to distinguish while repairing it.

The above example suggests that the complexity we appreciate in a situation depends also on the means we use to interact with it. The number of distinctions that physicians are able to make, for instance, in examining a patient's body may vary dramatically whether they are using their hands to sense the organs, a scalpel to operate with inside, or a scanner.

Summarizing so far, the more distinctions an observer is able to make in a situation, the more complex it will appear to him or her. These distinctions, in turn, are made in the domain in which the observer interacts with the object and, therefore, depend on the 'observational instrument' used by the observer.

So, what is more complex: a cucumber or a Cadillac? According to our discussion, in order to answer this question we need to explicitly mention both the domain on which we are going to interact with these objects in order to address their complexity and the level of resolution of our observations. Both of these are related to the observational mechanism that we are going to use. For instance, let's say that the domain in which we are going to interact with a cucumber and a Cadillac is the one defined by simply looking at them. If we simply use our naked eyes to observe them, then the answer to the question is that a Cadillac will appear more complex because we will distinguish many more parts than in a cucumber.

On the other hand, if we choose to use a microscope to observe a cucumber then we may come up with exactly the opposite answer. This is because now we may distinguish many more parts or elements in the cucumber than the number of elements or parts we can distinguish by simply looking at a Cadillac. However, in this case we are making a logical mistake. The mistake here is that we are observing the objects at different levels of resolution and using these observations to compare results. It is like comparing the length of two objects by counting the number of marks along a measurement stick but in one case we put the marks an inch apart and in the other a millimetre apart. Therefore, we have to be careful of using the same metrics (i.e., interacting in the same domain and at the same level of resolution) whenever we want to measure and compare the complexity of different objects.

But if we are free to choose an observational domain (i.e., a domain of interactions) and the level of resolution when measuring the complexity of a situation, which one do we need to use in each case? We claim that the answer to this relates to the purpose of making the measurement in the first case. In other words, what are

---

[4]Though efforts have been made by authors like Gell-Mann (1995) to offer a more 'objective' definition.

we going to do with the measurement of the complexity of something? Suppose, for instance, that we want to establish the complexity of animals in order to study the different basic functions that their bodies can perform. One metric for this purpose could be counting the number of different cell types in the animal. This, in fact, according to John Tyler Bonner, of Princeton University, gives a sense of the number of specialized functions that an organism can perform (Lewin 1993, p.135). In this way (i.e., with this metric), we could say that a bacterium is less complex than a frog, which, in turn, is less complex than a human being.

Our claim here is that complexity is not an objective measurement of something. Instead, we should indicate the criteria we are using when measuring the complexity of that something; in other words, we should make explicit the domain in which we are interacting with that particular situation and the level of resolution of our observations. This implies, of course, the need to use the same criteria in order to compare the complexity of different situations, especially if they pertain to different classes like a meadow and a mammal brain.

Looking for a unique and objective measurement of complexity, while attempting to leave aside the relevance of the observer, is an attempt to impose a particular criterion to the way observers interact with something. What we can do, however, is to define and agree on different criteria for the study of complexity of situations pertaining to different domains; like counting the different types of cells in animals or establishing the different kinds of agents and their relationships in a national economy. All these metrics for measuring the complexity of something, however, are a particular instance of our general definition of complexity as the number of distinctions made in a situation.

Let us move on from this general appreciation of situational complexity to its more rigorous definition with the support of the idea of a system. If the complexity of a situation is the number of distinctions we can make in it, how can we actually measure it?

A very simple form to measure the complexity of a situation is by establishing the number of its possible states. This measure is called *variety* and was first proposed by the British cybernetician Ross Ashby in the 1950s (Ashby 1964).

Ashby's definition, of course, assumes that we have bounded the situation (i.e., named a system) as far as defining a particular state of that system. For example, if we are observing a traffic light being used to regulate the flow of cars at a crossroad and we define a state as a triplet (a, b, c) where each letter corresponds to the colour of a light we may say that the variety of this system is eight because they are all the *possible* combinations of the three colours. Of course, assuming that we are in a British city, if the traffic light is functioning well, we do not observe more than four states, (i.e., red, yellow, green, red and yellow). The point we want to make here is that the distinctions we *actually* make are the *complexity* of the system; its *variety*, on the other hand, is defined by all the *possible* states that we can compute.

This distinction between variety and complexity is particularly significant. While variety measures the situation's potentiality, complexity measures its actuality. The fact that the number of possible states of any situation is huge (as we will illustrate below) is a measurement of the almost limitless number of behavioural possibilities we have in producing a situation, something which opens the space for creative design. On the other hand, it also shows the large complexity we have to manage, something which opens the space for unilateral restriction and domination. When the emphasis is creativity we will emphasise autonomy in the description of the situation, on the other hand, when the emphasis is management response we will emphasise a black-box as presented in Chap. 1. Now, we will stress management in what follows. Notice that, in this case, a system is represented by a transformation function producing some outputs from certain inputs.

The concept of variety is very useful to understand some basic cybernetic principles that we are going to use later on, so we will briefly explore its implications in what follows and then we will go back to the concept of complexity.

To begin with, to compute all the possible states of a system (i.e., its variety) we represent a state as the $n + m$-tuple $(x_1, x_2, \ldots, x_n, y_1, y_2, \ldots, y_m)$ where each x_i represents a value of an input and each y_j represents a value of an output (here we have n inputs and m outputs). Then, we can compute easily the variety of the system by using standard combinatory methods.

Suppose, for instance, that we have a simple case of a black box with one input and one output, as shown in Fig. 3.1, and both the input and the output can take only two values (say 1 and 0), then it is easy to see that the variety generated by this black box is four. Certainly, the possible states of this black-box are (0,0); (0,1); (1,0) and (1,1) where the first component denotes its input and the second its output. It is interesting to note that while the black box has only two output values it has four outcomes. In other words, the four states above are four patterns of behaviour in time. If the input is a light {which can be *on* (0) or *off* (1)} and the output is a sound {which can be *on* (0) or *off* (1)} the first outcome is one where the light is *on* and there is sound all the time, the second is one where the light is *on* but there is no sound all the time, the third is one where there is no light but there is sound and the fourth is one where there is neither light nor sound all the time.

This procedure seems quite straightforward; however, this computation could sometimes be tricky. Notice, for instance, that if we add to this black-box just *one* single input that also can take only two values, as in Fig. 3.2, then according to what we have said so far, the variety of the black box *will not* be eight [i.e., (0,0,0);

(0,1)

(0,1)

Fig. 3.1 A system described as a black box with one input and one output

Fig. 3.2 A system described
as a black box with two inputs
and two outputs – a case of
variety proliferation

(0,1)   (0,1)

(0,1)

(0,0,1); (0,1,0); (0,1,1); (1,0,0); (1,0,1); (1,1,0); (1,1,1)], but sixteen (Beer 1979, p. 54). In this case, the list of all possible states will be the following:

Inputs:	00	01	10	11
	0	0	0	0
	0	0	0	1
	0	0	1	0
	0	0	1	1
	0	1	0	0
	0	1	0	1
	0	1	1	0
	0	1	1	1
	1	0	0	0
	1	0	0	1
	1	0	1	0
	1	0	1	1
	1	1	0	0
	1	1	0	1
	1	1	1	0
	1	1	1	1

The first row corresponds to the state in which for all possible combination of inputs the outcome of the black box is always 0. The last row corresponds to the state in which for all possible combinations of the inputs the outcome of the black box is always 1. The other intermediate states are interpreted in a similar way. The above array is showing the *dynamic behaviour* of the system, that is, its *outcomes* instead of its *outputs* in order to consider the time dimension. Metaphorically, we can imagine that the black box is producing sounds whenever an input comes and an output is produced. What we are observing here are patterns of sound or 'melodies' produced by the black box. In this way we account for its complexity through time.

The distinction between *outputs* and *outcomes* is quite important here; while the former refer to single values at a particular moment in time, the latter refer to patterns of values through time. Suppose, for instance, that the system that is being described as a black box is one depicting a production manager regulating the production process of her company. If she decides to observe the monthly sales as a variable to decide for the future production of her company, certainly she will not concentrate attention on individual values of this variable (e.g., the output of last month) but on the patterns of this variable in time, that is, its behaviour (i.e., its outcome). Therefore, to compute the variety of a system described as a black box we have to take into account all its possible behaviours through time.

In general, it can be proved that the variety of a black box with n inputs and m outputs, each one having two values, follows the equation:

$$V = \left(2^m\right)^{2^n}$$

This is a very fast growing expression in terms of the number of inputs and outputs. If, additionally, each input can take q different values (instead of just two values) and each output can take p different values, then the variety of the black box is:

$$V = \left(p^m\right)^{q^n}$$

This helps us to appreciate the speed at which variety can proliferate in a system.

Suppose that the system of concern is the deliberation process of a jury, which has to decide whether the accused is guilty or not guilty considering 50 different issues in a criminal case where each issue can be interpreted in three possible ways: as incriminatory, as not-incriminatory, or of a doubtful value for the case. In this case, the variety of this system is

$$V = 2^{3^{50}}$$

which is an extraordinary huge value.[5] This is the variety that the jury itself would have to manage in order to come up with a final unanimous decision at the end of its deliberation. In other words, this huge variety has to be reduced to a single value: guilty or not guilty (i.e., a variety of two) within a pre-established time limit. We may expect that the effectiveness of the jury (in terms of a verdict involving the careful and open debate of each issue by all the members) will depend on the mechanisms they use to do this variety attenuation. If they are based on the imposition of the viewpoints of some members of the jury upon others, or just by ignoring the discussion of some issues, the likelihood is a miscarriage of justice.

This example not only illustrates the explosion of variety in a particular situation but also the idea of *variety attenuation* in managing it. This attenuation may be achieved differently depending on the way the situation is organized. We will go

---

[5]The system here is the criminal justice system in a concrete location, where juries face, say, 50 issues with three possible values each; this is their input. On the other hand, the output is a single decision with two possible values: guilty or not-guilty. The variety of the system is, then, the variety of the output (i.e., two) to the power of the variety of the input (which is 3^{50}).

back to this point of variety attenuation in the next chapter, which is about managing complexity (Chap. 4).

Summarising, when we are observing a system from its outside, we may compute its *variety* as the number of possible states of the black box we use to describe it. Its *complexity*, on the other hand, is the number of outcomes (dynamic states) that we can actually distinguish over time. (In our above example, the balance over time of guilty or not guilty verdicts in different situations.) Notice that the focus of our example is on the criminal justice system and not on particular juries.

So far, we have explored the complexity of a situation and the variety and complexity of a system when described as a black box. Now, we would like to use this distinction to study the complexity that arises from our daily interactions as individuals.

Roughly speaking, we may say that there are many occasions in our daily lives when we face a situation that appears to us as complex and we would like to be able to cope with it. For example this is the case when we are driving through a multi lane busy high street in a city centre, or when we are using a computer program to control a production line or when we are facing a particular task in our regular job. In all these situations, one way or another, whether we are aware of it or not, we are dealing with the complexity of the situation (as appreciated by us). According to Ashby's Law of Requisite Variety,[6] only complexity destroys (or absorbs) complexity, which seems to imply that to deal with a complex situation we have to develop our *individual complexity*. At the end of this chapter and throughout the next one, we will see, however, that this is not the only strategy we can follow for effective complexity management. But by now, it seems quite important to understand the process by which our *individual complexity* develops over time in a particular situation.

Let's approach this question by initially considering a simple example of a situation in which we are learning how to perform effectively. Here, to perform effectively means being able to carry out our expectations on the situation. For instance, suppose we are learning how to fly a glider. We take some basic lessons on how to take off and how to land properly before flying alone. During the first flights when we look through the window we will simply observe the clouds. Later on, after approaching regularly some of these clouds and experiencing recurrent strong changes in altitude we may start to distinguish some clouds from others. After a while we may distinguish cirrus from cumulus and those from nimbus. But those *distinctions* are accompanied by corresponding *practices* on flying the glider. In fact, we have learned that by approaching cirrus we will be able to gain in altitude and by passing through a cumulus we will experience some turbulence. In other words, in order to become more effective in this domain of gliding, we have been making new distinctions by which we have developed suitable new practices.

---

[6]Ashby formulated this law originally as 'only variety absorbs variety' (Ashby 1964). Here we are using complexity instead of variety.

We can generalize the example above by saying that the distinctions we are able to make for which we can produce differentiated responses (i.e., practices) define our complexity in that particular domain of action (i.e., a situation). Figure 3.3 illustrates an operational description of the process by which we continuously constitute and re-constitute our complexity in a particular situation (Espejo 2000).

This diagram can be read in the following way. As we interact with others (and with our surroundings) in a particular domain of action, we bring forth incorporated practices in this domain. Often, we may experience some breaks in our moment-to-moment interactions. These breaks are sensed when expectations are not fulfilled. If those breaks are recurrent, we may construct them as new distinctions in language. We could perceive them as breakdowns (i.e., problems) or as breakthroughs (e.g., new, possibly better ways of doing things). In either case, we construe them as issues of concern. If we develop and incorporate new practices to deal with those breaks, we are changing our complexity in the situation. This complexity increases if more new distinctions are made and new practices are incorporated than are lost in a period of time.

It should be clear from this description that our complexity in a situation does not always increase. It is possible that new distinctions may replace old ones or new practices may make others irrelevant. It is also possible that new distinctions may not even be transformed into new practices at all. These distinctions, from the point of view of our performing, that is, from our acting in the situation, are lost. Let us explain this with another example.

It is often said that Eskimos have a much wider lexicon to refer to what we simply call snow[7]: Apparently they ascribe these names to distinguish different kinds of snow depending of what kind of activities they are performing (walking, hiding, hunting, building igloos, etc.). Suppose that you go to Alaska with the aim of learning how to make these distinctions yourself. You choose an Eskimo as your teacher; write down the 11 or so different words for snow with their corresponding meaning

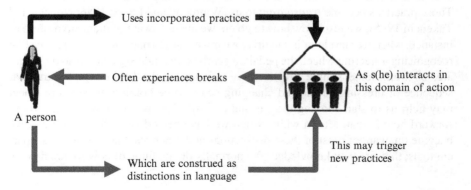

Fig. 3.3 An operational description of the individual complexity in a situation

---

[7]http://en.wikipedia.org/wiki/Eskimo_words_for_snow#cite_note-Pullum.27s_explanation-0

and take your time to understand and memorize them. When you think you have succeeded, you take an exam and pass with honours. Then you decide to go for a walk and soon get trapped in some particular form of snow that you failed to distinguish!

The important point of this example is that in order to perform effectively in a particular domain of action (i.e., the domain of walking in the snow in the previous example) it is not enough to be able to say (or write or explain) the relevant distinctions; you have to develop suitable corresponding practices. Making distinctions in language is fundamentally different to making operational distinctions. As we said before, from the point of view of effective performing in a particular domain of action, new distinctions without corresponding new practices are wasted distinctions.[8]

The previous discussion makes apparent the need to distinguish between our *operational domain* that is the domain of our moment-to-moment interactions, from our *informational domain* that is the domain of our representations and thoughts (Espejo 1994; Pickering 2010). We will see throughout the book that these domains are very useful constructs whenever we approach operational or performative descriptions of phenomena.

Going back to the diagram in Fig. 3.3, it may be clear by now how we explain, by using an operational type of description, the way we dynamically constitute our complexity in a particular domain of action. As a way to summarize this process, we can say that our complexity evolves as we experience recurrent breaks, we language them in our informational domain and incorporate new practices in our operational domain. It can be argued that this process is, in essence, a very basic learning process by which we improve performance in a situation. We will go back to develop this diagram in more detail in Chap. 4 when we approach the concept of managing complexity and its relation to learning.

But by now let's explore a bit more performance and its relation with the concept of complexity. Notice that when we incorporate new practices in a domain of action, over time and as we master them, we start performing them in 'automatic pilot'. Those practices become *transparent* to us (Winograd and Flores 1986; Nonaka and Takeuchi 1995); we just know how to go on, we are not aware of them anymore. For instance, when we start learning to drive a car we learn to make new distinctions like recognising a steering wheel, the pedals, a gearbox, the light signals and so on. There are, as well, some simple practices we develop at the beginning: a particular sequence of pressing pedals and changing gears while holding the steering wheel may help us to start moving the car and so forth. The point we are trying to put forward here is that, after a while, when we have been driving for some time, we become unaware of most of these distinctions and practices, they become transparent to us; they are tacit knowledge. We normally do not think of how we are driving

---

[8]Notice that some authors have recently challenged that Eskimos actually have different names for snow. However, this fact does not affect the point we want to illustrate here. We could use many other examples of cases in which we recognize new distinctions in language but we are not able to make these same distinctions in our practices. We kept the Eskimos case because of its popularity.

a car when we are driving it, we do not think which gear we are in, which pedal we have to push in order to brake and so on. We just drive; in a sense our 'body' is driving. Sometimes even the whole car becomes transparent to us. We can even perform other activities like sustaining a conversation with others while driving the car, something that is quite difficult to do if you are learning to drive.

These distinctions and their corresponding practices that have become transparent to us in a particular domain of action are the *complexity in our operational domain*. This is the *detailed complexity* we manage in that action domain.

There is a subtle difference between our evolving complexity in a particular domain of action and our detailed complexity in the same domain. The latter refers to distinctions and practices that we have *incorporated* in our bodyhood, in other words, we have *embodied* these distinctions in our actions (Reyes and Zarama 1998). We are not aware of them; we have grounded them in the way we act in a situation. The former, on the other hand, refers to the constitution of complexity as part of a learning process. Evolving and detailed complexity constitute our individual complexity.

When the transparency of the detailed complexity is interrupted, for example if our car breaks down, some of these distinctions may become apparent to us again. If we realize, for instance, that we are not able to drive faster than we want and instead our car is slowing down until it stops, then our attention probably will switch from whatever we were thinking of to our gearbox and our accelerator pedal. If we construct this break as a new distinction later on while talking to a car mechanic in a garage, as we learn that the car's sparking plugs got wet when passing over a puddle, we may come up with new possibilities of approaching puddles. These new possibilities will increase the *complexity in our informational domain*. Notice that for as long as we are open to any new practices, this complexity, in terms of new possibilities, is what we have been calling *variety*. This makes apparent the difference and relationship between variety and complexity in a particular situation.

In general, languaging new distinctions helps us to realize possible futures (Espejo 1994). In the context of our interactions with others, realising new possibilities is the outcome of *conversations for possibilities*, this usually implies questioning the assumptions, meanings, values and norms we normally take for granted. This is the process by which we are inventing the world (Winograd and Flores 1986, p. 65). If complexity in our informational domain (i.e., variety) triggers new practices, the complexity in our operational domain will increase whenever they become transparent. New distinctions that do not become embodied practices will be wasted distinctions; recall the example of the Eskimos mentioned above.

Figure 3.3 illustrates the closed interplay between the informational and the operational domain in a situation. The black arrows represent complexity in the operational domain. The grey arrows in between a person and the interactions represent complexity in the informational domain or variety. As we mentioned before, this figure represents the process by which our complexity evolves in a particular domain of action but, of course, we interact in many different domains throughout all our life. So, how is it that the complexity we develop in each of these domains relates to our *individual complexity*?

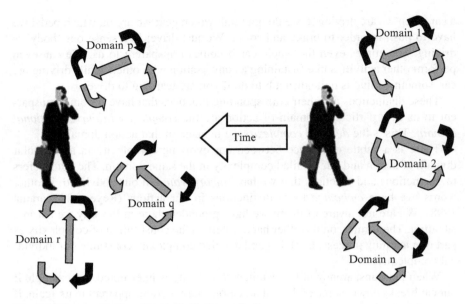

Fig. 3.4 The constitution of our individual complexity

To approach this question let us first point out that despite the differences among the domains in which we have interacted throughout our life, all of them intersect in our bodyhood. Figure 3.4 reflects this fact.

Therefore, we shall define our *individual complexity* as the *current* set of practices that we have embodied for the distinctions that we have made over time in all the multiple domains we have been engaged on. Notice that our individual complexity is not the sum of all the distinctions we have embodied in our history because, as we mentioned before, this is a dynamic process of constitution and re-constitution (construction and de-construction) in which we create new distinctions and practices but we also replace, combine and make irrelevant some others.

Notice that all the distinctions and practices that constitute our individual complexity also constitute our identity in our operational domain. In fact, Fig. 3.4 could be seen as representing the process by which we constantly configure and re-configure our identity through our personal history. It is in this sense that in Chap. 1 we said that we distinguish ourselves as individuals by distinguishing what we apparently are not: the world around us (Varela 1975). The distinctions and practices we have embodied not only allow us to construct a world and perform in it but also to constitute ourselves as particular individuals.

Figure 3.4 also illustrates the process by which our individual complexity evolves in time. An important aspect to recognize in this process is its circularity. In fact, not only the breaks experienced in a situation may trigger a reconfiguration of our individual complexity but also new embodied practices may change the situation itself. This circular process of mutual adjustments is what we referred to in Chap. 1 as *structural coupling*, and the history of all these changes in our bodyhood (i.e., all our distinctions and incorporated practices) is our *ontogeny*. Therefore, we may say that our individual complexity is the outcome of our ontogeny. It is in this sense that we say that we are the outcome of our own history.

Sometimes the last sentence is interpreted as meaning that we are locked (i.e., trapped) in our history. This is true in the sense already explained, that is, we could say that our individual complexity (i.e., the set of distinctions and embodied practices) constrains the way we see and perform in the world. But, at the same time, these distinctions and practices enable us to experience breaks that may open up new possibilities for reconfiguring our individual complexity and, therefore, modifying the course of our ontogeny. Of the many possible futures, or variety, we have had in time and space; we have recognized and incorporated the ones precisely defining our current complexity. We are the outcome of a myriad of contingent selections made throughout our lives (Espejo 2000).

If our ontogeny evolves through even more demanding situations, that is situations in which to perform effectively, we need a larger capacity to make distinctions and a larger repertoire of responses (i.e., practices). Then our development (i.e., ontogeny) implies an increase in our individual complexity. The same argument applies not only to human beings but also to any biological species. This is how we may explain, from this particular framework, the relationship that has been observed between the evolution of a living being and an increase in its complexity (Kauffman 1993).

To summarise, we have offered three concepts useful to study the complexity of us as individuals: the complexity in our informational domain (or variety); the complexity in our operational domain (or detailed complexity); and our individual complexity. Figures 3.3 and 3.4 illustrate the relationship between these concepts and the way by which we continuously constitute and re-constitute our individual complexity.

The argument throughout this chapter has followed so far the following order. We started by approaching the study of the complexity of a situation; then we moved on to approach the complexity of a system, as represented by a black box and, in the previous paragraphs, we considered the complexity of an observer (i.e., an individual). To end this chapter we will go on now to look at the complexity of a collective as its participants become engaged in a Human Communication System, the main type of systems we are interested in this book.

We have said that a Human Communication System (HCS) emerges from people's recurrent interactions. As these interactions produce stable linguistic structures, values and norms, a shared cultural context is emerging. The tacit, culturally grounded distinctions and practices shared among the members of the HCS, to the point where they coordinate their actions transparently, without apparent effort, define the complexity of the HCS (Espejo 2000).

This set of shared distinctions and practices are the outcome of a continuous process of mutual adjustments and learning (i.e., of many structural couplings among the members of the HCS). Figure 3.5 illustrates this process, which can be visualized as a generalization of the process by which our individual complexity is constituted in a particular domain of action.

When individuals in a HCS learn how to communicate effortlessly, almost without the need for channel capacity, they bring forth a social operational domain.

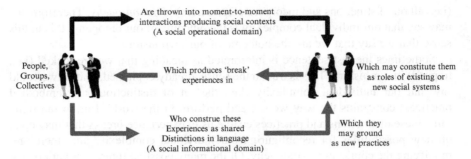

Fig. 3.5 The constitution of the complexity of a HCS

That is, a domain of shared grounded distinctions and embodied practices. Now, in this domain they constitute themselves as roles whose interactions, in turn, produce the HCS. This is again a circular process of mutual constitution.

However, this is not a static process, in fact, when interacting as roles, they may experience some breaks and if in response to them they language new distinctions and learn new practices, they may become part of new emergent Human Communication Systems. In this process they are operating in the informational domain of an existing HCS.

The process described by Fig. 3.5 explains a mechanism for functional differentiation in which people open possibilities for creating new organized collectives. However, these different possible futures are restricted by what they want to conserve of the system they are producing. Here, similar to our discussion about individual complexity, people in a HCS are locked in their social operational domain and again the system's variety is the source for developing the system's complexity.

HCSs are structurally coupled to their milieu and similar to individuals they may unfold a particular ontogeny through time. If the outcome of this structural coupling is towards a further functional differentiation we may experience an increase in the complexity of the system. Of course, it can also happen that as a result of certain breaks, people in a HCS lose already learned practices. We will approach in more detail this structural coupling of a HCS with its milieu in the following chapter (Chap. 4).

By now it should be apparent to the reader that developing this chapter about complexity was, in a way, a complex task. Complex in the sense of the number of distinctions we needed to put forward in order to explain the concept. We distinguished between variety and complexity from the outset and then we differentiated among detailed complexity, individual complexity and the complexity of a HCS.

Some authors distinguish also between detailed complexity and dynamic complexity in a situation. According to Senge (1990) dynamic complexity refers to situations where cause and effect are subtle and where the effects over time of interventions are not obvious. He claims that for 'most people systems thinking means fighting complexity with complexity devising increasingly complex solutions to increasingly complex problems' which, he says, it is the antithesis of 'real systems thinking' (Senge 1990, p. 72).

In our discourse, what Senge calls dynamic complexity is no more than connected outcomes of multiple black boxes that consider both the broader context of our moment-to-moment interactions and the effect of our actions on this context. Indeed, to perform effectively in a situation we need to develop our capacity to become aware of the intended and unintended consequences of our actions.

In our view fighting complexity with complexity is a strategy to tackle problem situations that comes from a straightforward interpretation of Ashby's Law of Requisite Variety (Ashby 1964). However, the metaphor of the boxer fighting the other's complexity with his or her own complexity is a poor one. The Ju-Jitsu metaphor, on the other hand, of fighting the other's complexity with his or her complexity is a much more effective one (Vester and Hesler 1988). This is the case for enabling the self-regulating and self-organizing processes of a collective when attempting to manage it.

But understanding self-organizing and self-regulating principles and using them to approach problem situations from the perspective of individuals and Human Communication Systems is at the core of *managing complexity*; an issue that is at the centre of the next chapter (see Chap. 4).

References

Arthur WB, Durlauf S, Lane DA (eds) (1997) The economy as an evolving complex system II. Perseus Books, Reading, MA

Ashby R (1964) An introduction to cybernetics. Methuen, London

Beer S (1959) Cybernetics and management. English Universities Press, London

Beer S (1979) The heart of enterprise. Wiley, Chichester

Blume L, Durlauf S (2006) The economy as an evolving complex system III. In: Studies in the science of complexity. Oxford University Press, Oxford

Espejo R (1994) What's systemic thinking? Syst Dynam Rev 10(2–3 Summer-Fall):199–212

Espejo R (2000) Self-construction of desirable social systems. Kybernetes 29(7–8):949–963

Gell-Mann M (1995) What's complexity? Complexity 1(1):16–19

Kauffman S (1993) The origins of order: self-organization and selection in evolution. Oxford University Press, Oxford

Kelly K (1994) Out of control. Fourth Estate, London

Lewin R (1993) Complexity: life at the edge of chaos. Phoenix Paperback, London

Nonaka I, Takeuchi H (1995) The knowledge-creating company. Oxford University Press, New York

Pickering A (2010) The cybernetic brain. The University of Chicago Press, London

Reyes A, Zarama R (1998) The process of embodying distinctions: a reconstruction of the process of learning. Cybern Hum Knowing J Second Order Cybern 5(3):19–33

Senge PM (1990) The fifth discipline: the art and the practice of the learning organization. Doubleday/Currency, New York

Varela F (1975) A calculus for self-reference. Int J Gen Sys 2:5–24

Vester F, Hesler A (1988) Sensitivitats-Model. Umlandverband, Frankfurt

Waldrop MM (1993) Complexity: the emerging science at the edge of order and Chaos. Viking, London

Winograd T, Flores F (1986) Understanding computers and cognition. Ablex Publishing, Norwood, NJ

Chapter 4
On Managing Complexity: Variety Engineering

Abstract We, as individuals, are dealing with complex situations, that is, with situations challenging us with a large number of states changing rapidly and unpredictably over time. In all these situations to perform effectively we have to manage the complexity of the situation. This chapter is dedicated to explore principles for managing complexity. We take the view that in general managing complexity refers to our ability to achieve an adequate performance in particular situations of concern. Their boundaries are defined by the purposes we ascribe, implicitly or explicitly, to them. So, in this chapter we explore how we ascribe purposes to situations and why this is important for managing their complexity. The concepts and detailed methods we explain in this chapter are known as variety engineering, which is the key concept that guides our operational design of organizations.

We mentioned in the previous chapter that we could identify many occasions in our daily lives in which we are challenged by situations that appear to us as complex and we would like to be able to cope with them. Daily tasks that we perform in our regular jobs are good examples of those. A general manager that is managing a company, a production engineer that is in charge of running a control system for a production line, a professor who is running an undergraduate course, a doctor who is performing an organ transplant surgery, a politician who is carrying out her political campaign for the next general election, a prosecutor that is investigating a case of multiple bank frauds, a computer programmer that is implementing a visual interface to navigate through the Internet and a child minder who is in charge of managing a local nursery are but a few examples.

These are examples of individuals dealing with complex situations that are challenging to them, with often unpredictable changes over time. In each situation they have to manage the complexity effectively.

Let us start by saying that in general, managing complexity refers to our ability to perform well in particular tasks. We focus our attention on these tasks by ascribing, implicitly or explicitly, a purpose to situations of concern. Let us explore first with more detail how we ascribe purposes to situations and why this is important for managing their complexity.

R. Espejo and A. Reyes, *Organizational Systems*,
DOI 10.1007/978-3-642-19109-1_4, © Springer-Verlag Berlin Heidelberg 2011

We may ascribe tacit purposes to what we do simply by doing certain things and not others. This is what Argyris and Schön (1978) relate to *theory-in-use*. But we may also ascribe a purpose to our actions in an explicit way. This, however, may vary drastically from individual to individual even when referring to the same actions. In his book about Perestroika, Mikhail Gorbachev tells us a relevant story: 'Everything we are doing can be interpreted and assessed differently. There is an old story. A traveller approached some people erecting a structure and asked one by one: "What is it you're doing?" One replied with irritation: "Oh, look, from morning till night we carry these damned stones ..." Another rose from his knees, straightened his shoulders and said proudly: "You see, it's a temple we're building!"' (Gorbachev 1987).

Situations do not have purposes of their own. We, as observers, create meanings as we ascribe purposes to situations of our concern. As participants of shared tasks, while interacting with each other, we ascribe purposes. When we reach agreements about the meaning of a situation, we may concentrate our efforts on producing it by effectively carrying out aligned activities. When there is alignment between individual purposes (i.e., the meaning we ascribe to our actions) and situational purposes (i.e., the purposes we ascribe to a shared task), people feel more committed, their motivation is likely to be stronger and their performance better. Here is when the management of complexity appears as a relevant discipline that can help us in designing and producing effective tasks to pursue our purposes.

In terms of complexity, we often feel overwhelmed by the situations of our concern; there is an imbalance between their complexity and our much smaller individual complexity. In the previous chapter we mentioned that Ashby's Law of Requisite Variety establishes that only complexity absorbs complexity, however, as we also mentioned, this does not imply that to perform well we have to increase our individual complexity to match the complexity of a situation. We have to gather together complexity management strategies that, similar to using a pulley for lifting a load beyond us, allow us to match this situational complexity. Clarifying these strategies is the purpose of this chapter.

Let's use Fig. 4.1 to represent a case of a person in charge of performing a task in a situation. Suppose she has defined a performance criterion as a way to observe her effectiveness. This criterion is, of course, closely related to the purpose she has ascribed to the situation. It is clear that any event that could affect her performance (according to this criterion) should be an issue of concern, that is, is a relevant distinction for her effectiveness. In other words, she needs adequate practices to respond to those events in order to maintain an appropriate performance. We represent these events in Fig. 4.1 by the set of Relevant Distinctions (or perturbations) while the set of Responses correspond to those practices that she has to carry out to perform effectively.

In this diagram the complexity of a situation corresponds to the cardinality of the set of perturbations, that is, to the number of its elements (i.e., 16 relevant distinctions). On the other hand, the individual complexity corresponds to the cardinality of the set of responses (in this case, eight practices). This imbalance of complexities tells us that the individual cannot *control* the situation. In other words, there are

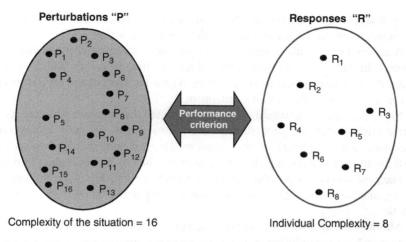

Fig. 4.1 Managing the complexity of a situation – complexity imbalance

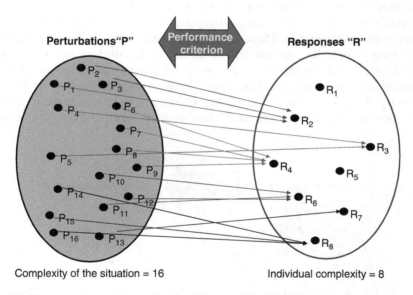

Fig. 4.2 Managing the complexity of a situation – matching complexity

events for which, if they materialize, there will not be an appropriate response. This suggests that the only way to assure adequate performance in this situation (based on the defined criterion) is that the two complexities match; this is precisely Ashby's Law of Requisite Variety that we mentioned above. However, as we suggested before, this law requires interpretation.

Notice that if we redesign practices in such a way that each one can take care of several relevant perturbations we could regain control of the situation as shown in Fig. 4.2. Here, for each perturbation we have an adequate response. On the other hand, responses or practices that do not match perturbations, such as R_1 and R_5 in the diagram, are irrelevant practices in this domain of action.

A closer look at this diagram shows also an interesting consequence of this strategy. In effect, if we group together all relevant distinctions for which we use the same response or practice, then we end up with a partition of the set P. Figure 4.3 shows this new arrangement of elements in P.

Now, because each subset of P is constituted by relevant distinctions (i.e., perturbations) that are not distinguishable in terms of their corresponding responses, the complexity of the situation (i.e., the number of elements of the partition of P) is just six, which is more than matched by the individual's complexity (i.e., the number of practices at hand), which is eight (Fig. 4.3). Not only have we regained a balance of complexities but it is apparent that there are two unused practices.

Although the approach we have used to explain the management of complexity in a situation has been quite abstract, it is useful to illustrate a strategy to deal with this kind of complexity imbalance. This strategy suggests two actions to regain a balance of complexity. First, redesign practices in such a way that each one can take care of several relevant perturbations. Secondly, classify these perturbations to reduce the complexity of the situation. The outcome of the first action is called amplification (of individual complexity); the outcome of the second is called attenuation (of situational complexity). In other words, though we can always manage the complexity of a situation by attenuating the situational complexity and amplifying our response capacity, these are useful strategies only if they permit us to achieve a desirable performance. But in more practical terms what are the meanings of *complexity*

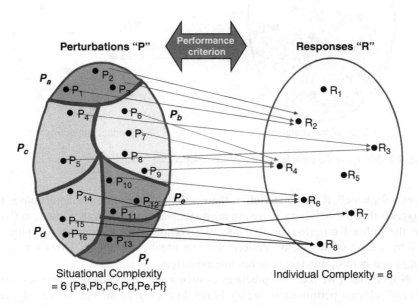

Fig. 4.3 Managing the complexity of a situation – attenuation and amplification of complexity

attenuation and *complexity amplification*? These are key concepts to understand the management of complexity and the rest of this chapter unfolds around them.

Let us start by showing a real-life example of using the idea of complexity attenuation and amplification to redesign an organizational process. In the early 1980s in Bogotá (capital of Colombia) the city's justice system had about 70 courts in charge of criminal cases. One of the crucial activities in carrying out the prosecution of those cases[1] was the 'notification'. Every major decision taken by a court had to be notified to those accused in the case. The practice of notification was considered so important that each court had people with the specific role to do it, the 'notificador'. It is this task that we analyse in terms of the management of complexity.

The purpose of this task was to notify court decisions to those accused within a time limit. These persons normally lived in Bogotá, a large city with about seven million people. A performance criterion was the number of notifications done by a court in 1 month. Typically this number was about 80, an average of 4 notifications per day or a total of about 5,600 notifications per month for all 70 courts. This was the case because every 'notificador' had to reach the personal or working address of the person to be notified. Because the size of city to notify persons living in opposite parts of the city could take several hours going for one point to the other (especially in the rush hours). Soon 'notificadores' were overwhelmed by the complexity of the task (i.e., the number of notifications waiting to be accomplished) and the courts started to accumulate cases because they could not advance them unless notifications were completed. A radical revision of this practice was needed.

The redesign of the practice was based on three ideas. First, all 'notificadores' were removed from the courts and gathered in a single notification office; secondly, the city was segmented into 70 zones, one for each 'notificador'; thirdly, every court decision was classified according to the zone in which the person to notify was living or working. Figure 4.4 shows a sketch of the new practice.

In the new practice every decision by a court was sent to the notification office. There it was classified and located in a pigeonhole. Every morning each 'notificador' took the decisions from his or her assigned place in the pigeonhole and left to the corresponding zone to do the notifications of the day. Because the size of each zone was considerably smaller than the city, performance increased considerably. Now the average number of notifications per day was about 20 per 'notificador', a total of 28,000 notifications per month for all courts. The performance of the task was multiplied by five using basically the same resources as before.

In terms of complexity management, we could see that the idea of dividing the city and classifying decisions according to this segmentation was a mechanism to attenuate the complexity of the situation (notice that in this case the *complexity driver* was the number of decisions produced by the courts). In a similar way, the idea of organizing the notification office and the assignment of a 'notificador' to a

---

[1]At that time in Colombia the prosecution and trailing of criminal cases was in the hands of the courts.

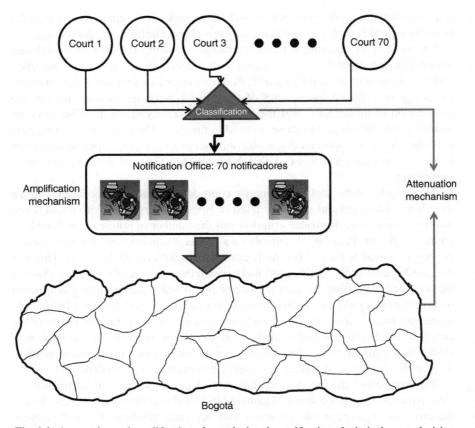

Fig. 4.4 Attenuation and amplification of complexity, the notification of criminal courts decisions

single zone was a mechanism to amplify the notification capacity of each court (now each court had the notification capacity of 70 'notificadores', not just one).

In general, we say that any device, mechanism or procedure reducing the number of states in a situation or the number of distinctions that we need to appreciate in it is an *attenuator of complexity*. So by choosing to pay attention to some aspects of the situation and not to others we are already attenuating its complexity. In fact, sheer ignorance is a huge complexity attenuator (Beer 1979). But how do we decide which factors to pay attention to in a particular situation? Well, by now it should be clear that any aspect that we experience as affecting the performance in the situation is an aspect that we have to take into account when managing its complexity. This is why purpose and performance are important to the management of complexity.

But even if we have criteria to select which aspects are relevant for the management of complexity in a particular situation, we may still make a huge number of distinctions for which we have inadequate complexity attenuators, something which impinges on our performance. In general, as we saw in the notification example, any mechanism of classification of relevant variety acts as a complexity attenuator. This classification may be achieved by means of creating categories or imposing an order to them. For instance, the A-Z map of a big city, such as London, is a good example of a complexity attenuator. In general, it is much better than trying to locate a particular address by intuition or by asking a passerby (two alternative attenuators). In a similar way, postal codes are attenuators of complexity for the task of delivering mail across a city.

On the other hand, we say that any device, mechanism or procedure used to increase our response capacity in the situation constitutes an amplifier of complexity. Broadcasting and the organization of resources (such as the notification office) offer good ideas for designing these kinds of mechanisms. In the rest of the chapter we will present many other examples of complexity attenuators and amplifiers.

In summary, a method to manage the complexity of a situation includes the following steps: first, ascribe a purpose to the situation; second, establish performance criteria and use them to choose relevant aspects of the situation (we shall call these aspects *complexity drivers*); and third, assess, and if necessary design and implement, devices, mechanisms or procedures (in pairs) to attenuate the complexity of the situation and to amplify the response capacity. Notice that attenuators and amplifiers of complexity go in pairs as the notification example illustrates. For instance, it makes no sense to do clever distinctions if they are not used to produce or trigger appropriate actions. In fact, effective management of situational complexity depends on the balance between the set of attenuators and amplifiers we have implemented. We will go back to this point later on. By now, Fig. 4.5 illustrates the concepts we have developed so far regarding a person managing the complexity of a task in a situation.

Let us illustrate with another example the process of designing amplifiers and attenuators of complexity in a particular situation. Consider the case of a professor in

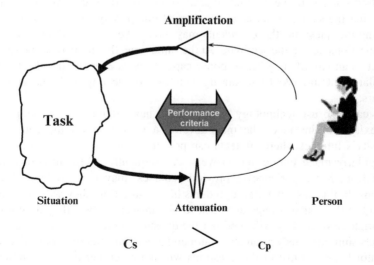

Fig. 4.5 Managing the complexity of a situation

a business school who is running a popular undergraduate course on management cybernetics. She naturally wants most of her students to understand the basic concepts of the course, so students' questions are one of the key aspects she wants to attend to in this situation; questions are an important *complexity driver* in this case.

Given that the number of questions that students may have during the course could be huge, she can set a question time schedule which will act as a complexity attenuator. For instance, she may ask students to formulate questions either during the last 10 min of each lecture or in her office, on Tuesday and Thursday, from 7 a.m. to 8 a.m. Notice that when answering the questions, in the first case the classroom acts as an amplifier of her response capacity because an answer to a specific question from a student will go to all students attending the class. In the second case, when she receives students in her office, she can use a bulletin board or an email service to make her responses available to all students or she may encourage that students talk with their classmates about their learning in these meetings. Therefore, in this way she is attenuating the complexity of the situation (by reducing the number of questions she has to deal with at a particular moment) and she is simultaneously amplifying her response capacity (by distributing each response to most or all students). Notice that making responses available to everybody may also prevent similar questions to be raised in the future; they may have been answered in advanced.

This additional example gives a flavour of the process of *designing pairs* of attenuators and amplifiers for *complexity drivers* (i.e., critical issues relevant to achieving performance criteria) in a particular situation. But there is still much more that we can say about these basic concepts of attenuation and amplification.

Suppose that our academic decides to organize the course in such a way that all students come to a general weekly lecture with her and once a week they also participate in smaller seminars run by tutors. She meets once per week with the tutors to discuss with them which aspects should be stressed during the seminars. Notice that the seminars act as attenuators of complexity from her point of view regarding the questions those students may have. The tutors will answer many of these questions during the seminars. At the same time, the tutors (and the seminars) may act as an amplifier of her response capacity whenever she decides to stress a particular point and asks tutors during their weekly meeting to do the same in the seminars.

She can also use technology to implement new attenuators and amplifiers of complexity. For instance, she may develop a web page for the course in the university's Intranet where students can post their questions at any time and she can regularly make public her answers. A 'frequently asked questions' (FAQ), chosen from her experience in previous courses, may help students deal with questions. In this case, whenever students have a question, they will go straight to the FAQ in the course's page and look for an answer. Only if they do not find an appropriate answer, they will send her the question. In this case, the course's web page acts simultaneously as an attenuator and as an amplifier of complexity. It is an attenuator because most of the questions will not reach her and it is an amplifier because she will use it to communicate her answers to all the students using a single media. With this strategy she is, in fact, promoting that students get their answers by themselves; her concern will be in maintaining the web page updated. This is an example of a self-regulating mechanism.

Another strategy that the professor can use to manage the complexity of her course (taking the number of students' questions as a measurement of the complexity driver) is encouraging students to use a course's virtual discussion group on the web page. If she succeeds in doing this, it is quite possible that students will engage in discussing course topics and many of the questions that they have as individuals may be answered during their discussions. Notice that if this is the case, again she will be aware only of the questions that students themselves are not able to answer. In other words, by promoting the organization of students with the use of the website virtual discussion groups, only part of the questions that they have during the course will reach the professor. We call this the *residual complexity* of the situation, that is, the complexity that the academic has to deal with because it is not dealt within the situation itself (Espejo 1989). This is an example of self-organization. We will come back to this important point later on.

So far we can see that in order to manage the complexity of a situation we have the following strategies at hand: we can design pairs of attenuators and amplifiers of complexity; we can promote or enable the attenuation of complexity in the situation itself; or we can do both at the same time.

Figure 4.6 illustrates a revisited version of the strategies to manage the complexity of a situation using the academic example. We have included here self-organization and self-regulation mechanisms for attenuating the complexity inside the situation itself.

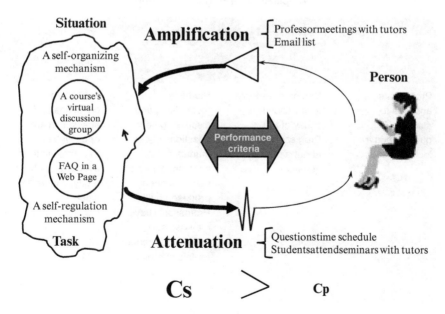

Fig. 4.6 Managing the complexity of a situation revisited

   Both amplifiers and attenuators of variety are *variety operators* that may happen
de facto in our daily lives or in the moment-to-moment operations of an organization, or, may be designed to make more effective the management of the situational
complexity. This is what Beer has called variety engineering (Beer 1979, 1981,
1985). In methodological terms it is necessary to work out first the complexity
drivers for the situation of concern; in our academic example a driver is the number
of questions emerging from the professor's interactions with students. Assuming an
academic situation where there are many questions, it is apparent, as was illustrated
above, that multiple forms of amplification and attenuation of complexity will
emerge in the practice of learning. For design purposes Figs. 4.7 and 4.8 illustrate
the types of variety operators that may be useful to consider for a dynamic and
effective interaction between professor and students.

   For amplification it is necessary to find ways of:

- Strengthening the source variety, that is, making possible one-to-many interactions. The lecture theatre allows the professor to talk simultaneously with many
  students.
- Increasing the resolution of the source variety, that is, using human and technological means to unfold in more detail the source variety. A textbook, and in
  more general terms, a library allow students to see more variety than that
  provided by the professor.
- Creating new variety relevant to the regulatory situation, that is, expanding the
  regulatory situation beyond the professor as the sources variety. The students'

Amplifiers of a Regulator's Variety

Strengthen the source variety	Increase the resolution of the source variety	Create new variety	Make variety time independent
Professor's answers to students' questions in a lecture theatre.	Students' in-depth elaboration in an essay of the Professor's views about a particular question.	Students recognising and discussing new questions about management cybernetics, which have not been proposed by the Professor. They may use self-organizing groups for this purpose.	Publishing questions and answers in an open website, thus making them available 24 hours a day, 7 days a week.

Fig. 4.7 Four approaches for variety amplification

Variety Attenuators of an Academic Situation

Make weaker the situational variety	Reduce resolution of the situational variety	Chop-off aspects of the situational variety	Make situational variety time dependant
Select at random a handful of the students' questions for the Professor's attention.	Summarise and cluster the content of the students' questions.	Focus on questions related to particular topics at the expense of the others.	Reduce academic/ students' interactions to particular periods during the course.

Fig. 4.8 Four approaches for variety attenuation

self-organization in small groups to discuss questions triggered by their interactions with the professor and tutors may generate much new variety not considered by the professor. This spontaneous generation of variety needs alignment with the professor's purposes to be a powerful amplifier of the situational variety. Otherwise it is a source of disturbances.

- Maintaining, as far as possible, the relevance of source variety over time, that is, maintaining the amplification provided by the above mechanisms throughout the length of the course.

For attenuation it is necessary to find ways of:

- Reducing, weakening, the source variety *for the regulator*. This can be achieved in the professor's case by focusing on students' *defined* variety. Asking each student to prepare and submit with anticipation questions and providing a *short time* for debating all of them in the class room reduces the source variety and possibly increases the quality of their interactions.
- Reducing the resolution of the situational variety to develop an aggregated view of a situation. This is a strategy that aggregates situational variety and reduces local resolution. This would be the case when students' questions are generic. The cost is failing to deal with individual nuances. This complexity management strategy, similar to the first one, does not restrict the source variety, which can continue to grow.
- Selecting situational variety according to criteria *defined by the professor* rather than the students. This strategy has the effect of chopping-off aspects of the

situational variety at the professor's discretion. Sorting students' questions according to the professor's experience may help to deal with the most pressing learning issues but may lose opportunities to discover hidden learning difficulties.
• Making situational variety time dependent to critical parts of the course. This strategy may help managing the professor's interactions with students over time; some parts of the course will be supported by intensive interaction, others not. The cost of this strategy may be not to keep situational variety updated over time.

Variety engineering is particularly significant today in our digital society. With the new information and communication technologies it is possible to design complexity management strategies that were unimaginable a few years ago. Variety engineering is at the core of multiple new enterprise complexity models (Espejo 2009) and is tacit to problem solving in general (Tapscott 2009; Tapscott et al. 1998). This chapter offers methodological support for this engineering.

But, beyond complexity management strategies between people and environmental situations, attenuation and amplification of complexity also takes place within people and organizations. Figure 4.9 illustrates three venues in which complexity amplification and attenuation take place: the *cognitive venue*, the *interactive venue* and the *task venue* (Espejo and Watt 1988; Whitaker 1992). Let us explain briefly each one of these venues.

The *cognitive venue* refers to the individual's capacity to create and produce some kind of cognitive order out of the situational complexity. With reference to Chap. 3, this venue relates both to the variety and the current set of practices that we have embodied for the distinctions that we have made over time in the multiple domains we have been engaged on (i.e., our individual complexity). Remember that cognition is not capacity to map environmental situations but capacity for effective action in selected domains of action; in this sense knowing is doing (Maturana and

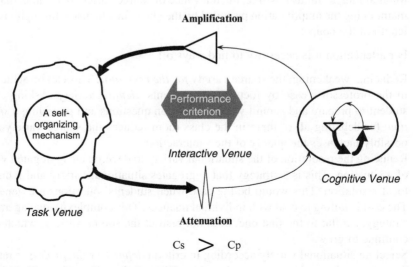

Fig. 4.9 The venues of complexity management

Varela 1992, p. 248). In this venue we develop, through learning, capacity to interact and participate in cooperative work.

Examples of complexity attenuators in the cognitive venue are listening skills, logical thought and conceptualisation (i.e., our ability to make abstractions). On the other hand, instances of complexity amplifiers in this venue are clarity of expression, creativity, systemic thinking and an ability to make a diagnostic use of concepts (Espejo et al. 1996).

The *interactive venue*, on the other hand, is that of our recurrent encounters with others. It is where we negotiate our distinctions, achieve commitments and develop mutual expectations. It is here where relationships are formed as well as self-organization and organizations unleashed. Examples of complexity attenuators in this venue are selection of relevant conversations and most fundamentally the values, norms and shared meanings underpinning our interactions. Instances of complexity amplifiers may be achieving the commitments of others and our ability to generate mutual expectations.

It is in this venue where we need to display our ability to delegate by choosing the 'right' person for a task and getting his or her commitment to carry it out. It is also in this venue where we choose to pay attention to some aspects while ignoring, at least temporary, others. Whereas in the first case we are amplifying our response capacity (through the actions of others) in the second case we are attenuating the complexity we are facing in a particular moment in time. This attenuation can be directed by exercising a personal discipline according to the following heuristics (Espejo et al. 1996): (a) deal first with those things that are important to us and that need to be done urgently; (b) decline, under most circumstances, to commit ourselves to things that may appear urgent to ourselves or to others, but upon reflection turn out to be not important in terms of our priorities, values and long term goals; (c) avoid altogether time-wasting activities that are neither important nor urgent to us; (d) use the time freed by (b) and (c) to invest as long as we can on activities that are important to us but not urgent.

In this same venue we have also to learn how to balance *local* with *distant information* and how to balance *experience* with *observation* (Espejo et al. 1996). Regarding the former let us consider two extreme situations to illustrate the point. In the first place, suppose the case of a manager of a company who is very well known by his ability to engage in communications with the people in his immediate workplace. He manages to get the commitment of colleagues and is kept very well informed on what is going on around the office. However, he does not put too much attention on what is happening outside the limits of his immediate relations. He depends mostly on others in order to have a grasp of distant information and takes little time to corroborate it from direct sources. The outcome of this may be that he will not develop an accurate understanding of relevant contexts that may affect in the near future the effectiveness of his work. It is quite common for people in those situations to be trapped in 'ivory towers' where their close colleagues filter out so much (usually unpalatable but indeed relevant) information to avoid damaging local relations. This could be a recipe for short-term success but long-term disaster.

The other extreme is the case of a manager who spends most of her time grasping and checking what is going on in her "environment" but at the expense of building relations with her immediate colleagues. She will be quite aware of distant threats and possibilities for the company's future but probably will fail in getting people's commitment to take care of necessary local actions. People around her will feel that she is out of touch with what happens in her office and she probably will not understand why, despite all her efforts the company seems to be failing in reacting fast enough to desirable changes.

These are, of course, two extreme cases but reflect the need to be aware of the importance of maintaining a balance between local communications and distant information in our interactive venues when we are engaged in the management of complexity of particular situations. Notice, finally, that this balance applies not only to situations relevant to managers of organizations but also to any role in an organization and even to most of our personal roles in daily lives. Managing local communications helps us to build up strong relations and commitments with our close mates. Being aware of what is distant for the same situations helps us in building a deeper understanding of the context in which these situations are evolving.

Regarding the emphasis in practices (e.g., experience through action) or distinctions (e.g., creativity), we say that we need to learn how to balance the two in particular situations. Let us illustrate the case by considering, again, two extreme situations. In the first, we have a person who is well known as an action-oriented person. When facing any particular issue his immediate reaction will be 'let's do something about it now!' He wants to be involved in the action and disregards discussions, debates and critical thinking as time-wasting activities. The doing is what is important to him and pragmatism is his philosophy of life. It is quite probable that a person like him will fail as a manager because he does not have the capacity to elaborate new opportunities and possibilities for his company: the 'here and now' will obscure the need to take strategic decisions for the future. The chances are that his company will get locked in its well-developed practices and niches and will fail to respond to changes in its relevant environment.

The other extreme is that of a person who, on the contrary, prefers to debate and question almost any aspect that is brought up to her attention. Her main characteristic as a manager is discussing and creating new meanings all the time. She prefers spending time developing theories and models, making more sophisticated distinctions, to understand what is going on at the expense of developing and implementing new practices. Again, her chances of success as a manager are limited; people may find it extremely difficult to work with her and feel that all those meetings, debates and discussions are effectively a waste of time: 'things simply don't happen'.

These two extremes illustrate the need of a middle-way in between as a way to balance our practical experience with our creative and reflective approach to situations of concern. In terms of the management of complexity, while the first example shows a person with little capacity to recognize and create new distinctions, the second shows a person with poor capacity to develop and implement new practices. In both cases the loops closing attenuation (making distinctions) with amplifications (developing practices) of complexity and the other way round are wasteful. This makes apparent, furthermore, that this balance between experience and reflection is not exclusive to managers but to anyone involved in the management of complexity of relevant situations.

Finally, the *task venue* involves the more general organizational context of our interactions where we do things through others and therefore resources are not directly under our control. Complexity attenuation in this venue is directly related to self-regulation and self-organization. This is, perhaps, one of the most powerful ways of managing complexity. This is why, from the point of view of the management of complexity, it is crucial to understand how to enable self-regulating and self-organizing processes in a particular situation. Both are powerful means to deal with complex situations; potentially they reduce considerably the residual variety relevant to managers in the situation. They are means to amplify situational complexity at the same time of attenuating the complexity reaching management. We will go back to develop this concept with more detail in Chap. 6.

This discussion suggests that managing the complexity of a situation requires a balance between attenuators and amplifiers of complexity in the cognitive, interactive and task venues. Remember that, in general, to deal with residual variety each attenuator has a corresponding amplifier. For instance, in approaching a particular situation it is not enough to be skilled at building up abstract models (i.e., attenuating complexity in the cognitive venue) if we fail to make a diagnostic use of them (i.e., complexity amplifier in the same venue). We should recall here what we said in the previous chapter about complexity; in general, for the purpose of effective action, distinctions without corresponding practices are wasted distinctions.

Summarizing so far, the purposeful management of complexity in a situation implies carrying out two main actions: making explicit performance criteria; and designing and implementing pairs of attenuators and amplifiers of complexity vis-à-vis these criteria. Notice that this is a very general approach to manage the complexity of any situation similar to the ones we mentioned at the beginning of this chapter. In other words, to perform effectively in a particular domain of action we have to keep an appropriate balance between pairs of attenuators and amplifiers of complexity. But as we have said before, contrary to what intuitively we may think, this does not mean that our response capacity has to match the complexity of the situation. Only the complexity that is not absorbed by the situation itself through self-regulation and self-organization should be filtered out by appropriate attenuators and matched by our response capacity, which once properly amplified, will affect back the situation.

This is a learning mechanism that usually is adjusted as time goes by as we observe our performance in the situation. If the performance is not what is expected we may modify our sets of attenuators and amplifiers of complexity. Similarly, if we change the performance criteria probably we will have to adjust the attenuators and amplifiers of complexity again. Normally, as we mentioned in the previous chapter, more stringent performance criteria implies an increase on the number of distinctions that all those involved need to do in a situation (i.e., to increase the resolution capacity of the attenuators) and a corresponding increase in their response capacity (i.e., increase the action capacity of the amplifiers). However, it is perfectly possible and moreover it is desirable, that ingenuity helps to bridge, in an increasingly effective fashion, the complexity gap between regulators and their relevant situations. In practice this may imply that one response is capable of dealing with a large number of distinctions.

In this learning cycle we can identify four steps as shown in Fig. 4.10. The person *observes* the situation and uses performance criteria to do an *assessment* of his or her effectiveness in the task. If the outcome is not what is expected, then they can *design* and *implement* new mechanisms to affect back the situation. If this circular process goes on, we say that the person is engaged in an individual learning loop (Espejo 2000). Notice that our capacity to observe and assess the performance in the situation (i.e., to make distinctions) is directly related to the resolution of the attenuators in place. On the other hand, the impact over the situation (i.e., the developed practices) depends on our ability to design and implement appropriate amplifiers of response capacity. Again, achieving desirable performance requires balance between attenuation and amplification of complexity.

An imbalance of complexity in any of the venues may be experienced as a break in our expectations (vis-à-vis the purpose ascribed to the task) that may need to be resolved. As we mentioned in the previous chapter, breaks in our expectations may trigger 'problem situations' or *issues of concern for us as the performers in the situation*. By referring to Figs. 4.9 and 4.10 we may identify four types of problem situations regarding these imbalances. The focus for this discussion of problem situations is on us as the performers, however, their trigger is often an inadequate *task performance*, that is, inadequate interactions of those producing the task with agents in the environment. We will come back to this point later in the chapter when

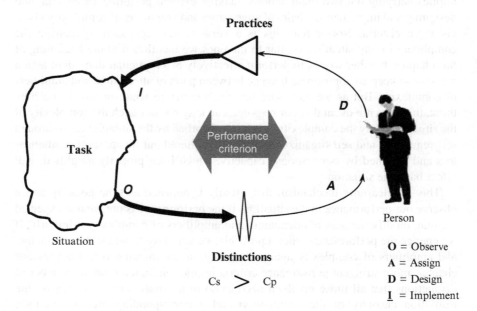

Fig. 4.10 Complexity management and individual learning

we will expand the individual management of complexity to the organizational reality.

The first types of problems are called *identity problems*. They refer to breaks in expectations triggered by a lack of clarity in the purposes and boundaries ascribed to the situation itself. This may happen when we do not explicitly ascribe a purpose to the situation or when the ascribed purpose is not aligned with the purposes ascribed by other relevant agents. Resolving these problems usually depends on the effective orchestration of *conversations for possibilities with other relevant agents*, in a context of communicative action (Habermas 1979), in order to reach aligned purposes for the situation.

These type of problems may highlight the issue of boundary judgments (Ulrich 2000). They arise in situations where it is seen as necessary to clarify the performer's task venue, in which local and distant (even unborn) stakeholders may be relevant. One common example of this situation happens when a production manager of a company is not aware of the ecological impact of his plant. This lack of awareness is tacitly showing the purpose (e.g., meaning) that he is ascribing to the task. However, if other relevant stakeholders like some of the workers in the plant and local people in the community have an increasing concern about this environmental impact, the likelihood is that an identity problem will arise sooner or later.

On the other hand, *response problems* derive from an imbalance between attenuators and amplifiers of complexity in favour of the first. In other words, the distinctions made by the individual do not have a corresponding effective response because the amplification capacity is poor. An example of this may happen if our professor invites all her students to email questions directly to her but she does not have enough time and resources to answer them.

Discrimination problems also come from an imbalance between attenuators and amplifiers of complexity but in favour of the latter. Here the individual is unable to distinguish disturbances that may be relevant for the effective management of the situation. Although amplification capacity may be enough, there is no good attenuation (i.e., the resolution of the attenuators is poor). Of course, sheer ignorance of what is relevant is the extreme case of these kind of problems and in our business course example this problem may occur if instead of leaving students to make questions freely the professor designs a form asking students to choose from a set of questions. This will act as an attenuator of the questions students can ask, however, the questions left aside could have been more important to their understanding of the course concepts, which is a performance criterion used by the professor in this situation.

Finally, *cognitive problems*[2] may occur in the cognitive venue of the performer. This is the case when individuals fail to do enough distinctions although the resolution of the attenuators (in the task and interactive venues) may be adequate, or they fail to produce effective responses although their amplifiers have enough

---

[2]Cognitive in this context relates to a person's capabilities for making distinctions and also acting upon them; cognition is not only a mind activity, it is a total body activity.

capacity in the interactive and task venues. An 'incompetent' professor, that is a professor whose performance is regularly underrated by their students and external reviewers, in a context in which most professors are assessed as competent, may be a simple example of a cognitive problem.

Although these four types of problems have been presented as separate items, it should be noticed that they might all be perceived in the management of complexity of a single situation. In fact, when we are performing in a situation the three venues usually intertwine; what happens in one may affect what happen in the others. Drawbacks in our cognitive venue may affect our interactive venue; drawbacks in our task venue may affect our interactive venue and so on.

It should be clear by now that managing the complexity of a situation is neither a reactive process nor a static one. It is not a reactive process because our actions may modify the situation itself. We may act now to prevent things going out of control in the future. On the other hand, it is not static because all venues are varying over time. New distinctions may be realized, new actions may be produced, new sets of attenuators and amplifiers of complexity may be designed and implemented and different criteria for performance may be set.

This dynamic, mutual interaction between us and the situation of concern is best depicted as a dance, or co-development, in which we coordinate our actions in an ongoing process of mutual adjustments. In this process of co-development we change and are changed by the situation; we are structurally coupled with it (Maturana and Varela 1992). Performing effectively in this context means maintaining stability in the situation far from equilibrium (Prigogine and Stengers 1984). Stability criteria emerge from our interactions. Whether these stability criteria are aligned with the purposes we ascribe to our actions in the situation is a complex organizational matter that we discuss in Chap. 6. For now we can say that the stability emerging from our structural couplings implies far more complexity than the performance criteria we ascribe to a situation; it implies the stability of people's interactions beyond particular measurements. Structural coupling is in the operational domain of the people involved, performance is in the informational domain of the performer and related customers.

This structural coupling is, as we mentioned before, a learning process. We learn over time, for instance, which are the aspects (i.e., distinctions) to which we must pay special attention and that need highly selective responses. They are our *critical success factors or complexity drivers* in this particular situation (Espejo et al. 1996; Rockart 1979). We will go back to this point when considering in more detail the management of complexity in the context of organizations in Chap. 6.

It is important to notice also that performance criteria relate to the individual's role in the task and not to the person. It is perfectly possible for a person to have adequate competencies for a task in a context where the assessment of the overall task's performance is not good. This would be the case of a person who knows how to improve task performance but is unable, because of contextual/structural difficulties, to steer related processes in the right direction. Therefore individual performance is the outcome of the interplay of all three complexity management venues and not of the individual's actions in isolation. These reflections imply that in addition to problems of individual concern there are problems of organizational concern and that these two types of problems are intertwined (cf. Chap. 11).

Notice that if the professor in the example we have used in this chapter is engaged in an individual learning loop, she probably will develop new pairs of attenuators and amplifiers of complexity to increase her performance each time she runs the course. However, this may be only an individual learning if she fails to incorporate the distinctions and practices she has developed into the organizational context of the school where the course belongs to. On the other hand, if she operates in an enabling organizational environment, where courses in the school are supported by learning aids such as internet for virtual discussion groups, tutors to discuss case studies in smaller workshops, supporting colleagues and so forth, the tutor and the school will engage in an organizational learning loop. Here the balance of complexity is not only between individual academics vis-á-vis their courses but between the *role* of a professor and the courses they are in charge of. We are moving from the individual to the organizational context.

This shift is necessary because as we normally experience in our daily lives, our capacity to cope effectively with complexity is very limited. In this sense, we are often in a state of insufficient response capacity to deal with the complex situations we are facing (Espejo and Howard 1982). Organizations, in fact, enable us to perform tasks that are inherently beyond our personal capacities. But, at the same time, this implies that in this context we always rely on others to carry out the tasks for which we are accountable. This is precisely the dilemma that modern managers face all the time; they are accountable for the management of tasks that are inherently more complex than their own individual complexity. Being aware of this dilemma is what, in our view, makes relevant the discourse we have been developing so far. A popular aphorism says that variety is the spice of life, but we think we should add: 'if and only if we have requisite variety to cope with it' otherwise, life could be a nightmare. But then we have to extend the discourse on complexity management from the individual to the organizational context. This is the purpose of the rest of this chapter.

An organization co-develops with agents in its environment, such as customers, competitors, suppliers, neighbours, etc. This environment is largely beyond the knowledge and control of the people within the organization; they simply cannot take for granted the actions of the environmental agents, let alone know everything about every aspect of the world within which they operate. Similarly, managers cannot take for granted the people working within the organizational system, let alone know everything about every aspect of the organization that they manage. People may not only be unpredictable but also may defect if so they wish. However, if the organization is to maintain *viability* within its environment, and management is to steer the organization, then the Law of Requisite Variety, as we have studied in this chapter, suggests that the variety of organizational responses should at least equal the relevant challenges emerging from its environment, and also, the variety of managerial responses should at least equal the relevant challenges emerging from the organization they manage (see Fig. 4.11).

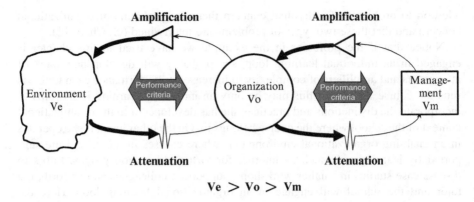

Fig. 4.11 Managing complexity in an organizational context

Yet, as established above, the variety of the environment is far larger than that of the organization, which in its turn is far larger than that of management, so, it would appear, these varieties couldn't equate. But organizations maintain viability in their environments and managements steer, more or less effectively, their organizations. Both develop one way or the other strategies to cope with the much larger variety of the opposite side.

These mismatches are resolved by recognising that of all the environmental variety, only part of it is relevant to the organization; namely that part producing the disturbances that the organization has to respond to in order to maintain viability according to the ascribed performance criteria. Also it is not necessary for people in this organization to deal with all this relevant variety since agents within the environment may perform much of this activity for the organization. For example, a car dealership network performs this service for the car manufacturer. A volume car manufacturer could not hope to deal with each individual customer buying a car; instead, the dealer sells the cars and passes on orders to the manufacturer. Thus the massive variety of the actual and prospective customers' requirements is absorbed by the dealership network, which then passes block orders to the manufacturer.

The organization as a system striving for dynamic stability in its relevant environment can only respond to a relatively small number of states in this environment, but uses agents in this environment to respond indirectly to the rest of relevant states. It is this capacity to collaborate with others and support action in the shared environment that allows the organizational system to deal with a much larger variety than otherwise would be the case. How much of the environmental variety is relevant depends on performance requirements. More competition implies higher performance requirements, which in turn increase the number of states that are relevant to the organization.

The above argument suggests that it is possible to match more variety (i.e., achieve more) with less variety (i.e., fewer resources). This implies using more of the capacities of the environmental agents in support of the organization's performance. In our example of the car manufacturer, dealers in the environment deal with most of the relevant variety. However, the *residual variety* that is not dealt with by these environmental responses must be met by the organization itself. The orders from the car dealers to the manufacturer make up the *residual variety*, to which the manufacturer responds by producing the required number of vehicles.

The same relational pattern occurs between *management* and the other participants within the organization. To say that management controls the organization (i. e., that maintains dynamic stability with others in the organization) does not mean that the varieties of both are the same, but that the residual variety left unabsorbed by the processes of self-organization and self-regulation within the organization has to be absorbed by management. Complexity is again dealt with by the use of management amplifiers (e.g., delegation, people's commitment and training) and attenuators (e.g., exception reporting, modelling and selective conversations).

However, it is a common occurrence for amplification and attenuation processes to creep out of balance: the promises made by the sales people cannot all be fulfilled due to lack of adequate delivery channels (i.e., the attenuation of customers' requirements as expressed by accepted orders cannot be matched by delivery of products; there is not enough amplification capacity, leading to the system's underperformance), or the market segmentation in use does not offer distinctions (attenuation) that the organization's response capacity could deal with if it only knew about them; they treat varied groups of customers as if they were all the same (poor attenuation leads to waste of amplification capacity). These are instances of response and discrimination problems that arise out of imbalances between attenuation and amplification of complexity that we saw before but now we are seeing them in the organizational context.

Figure 4.12 shows this balancing of variety between the environment, the organization and its management. A test for effective management is achieving this balance at a minimum cost to the organization and management. In this figure we find that of the seven environmental critical success factors, CSFs, (the seven lines to the left of the figure) four are matched by response capacity in the environment itself (the circular arrow, which absorbs the variety of four critical

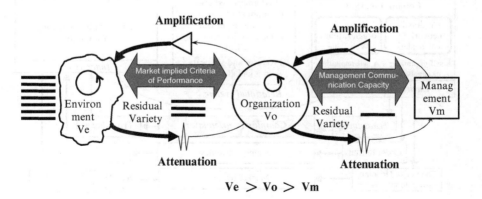

Fig. 4.12 Residual variety in an organizational context

success factors) and three by organizational responses (the three lines to the left of the organization). It is apparent that increasing the variety absorption capacity of environmental agents, to the point where say, they absorb the variety of five CSFs would make possible a leaner organization, requiring capacity to deal directly with only two CSFs rather than the three shown in the figure. The same argument applies to the interactions between management and the organization, where the more self-regulation and self-organization takes place locally within the structure the less management is required for a similar level of performance.

There is a general format that can be used to design the management of complexity either in the individual or in the organizational context according to given performance criteria. In both cases, once we have ascribed either the purpose of the task or the purpose of the organization in focus, we can identify self-regulating or self-organizing processes in the situation or in the environment respectively. For the residual variety that is left unattended by these internal mechanisms, we should design pairs of attenuators and amplifiers of complexity in order to achieve an adequate performance. Figure 4.13 shows this scheme. This Figure is a variation of Beer's homeostatic loop (Beer 1985, p. 147) that he proposed to check his four principles of organization (Beer 1979, 1985), and is the basis for his idea of variety engineering. In our version of the homeostatic loop, based on the idea of residual variety, the key for this variety engineering are the processes of self-organization and self-regulation on the high variety side, which reduce the relevant variety that the organization and management have to deal with in the environment and the

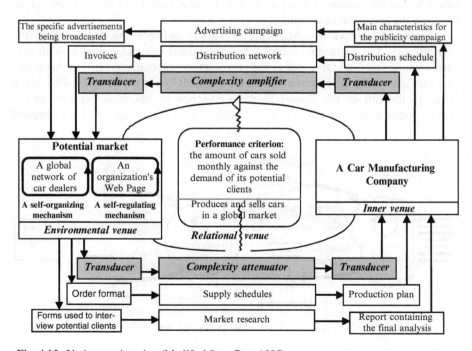

Fig. 4.13 Variety engineering (Modified from Beer 1985)

organization respectively. For these residual varieties it is necessary to work out amplifiers and attenuators of variety, as well as transducers, as proposed by Beer.

To illustrate the use of the scheme we are considering as an example the case of a car manufacturing company. Let's suppose that this company produces and sells cars in a global market. A criterion for effective performance of this company in its environment could be given by the cars sold monthly against the demand of its potential clients. Therefore demand constitutes the main complexity driver for this criterion of performance.

We could differentiate three venues related to the structural coupling of the company with its environment in the following way.[3] The *organizational processes*[4] supporting the company's production of cars constitute the *inner venue*. The relations sustained between the company with its clients and suppliers constitute the *relational venue*; and the relations taking place in the environment that have a direct effect in the complexity drivers of the company (for the established performance criteria) constitute the *environmental venue*.

As we mentioned before, a global network of car dealers manages the huge complexity of millions of potential customers and car owners in the market. This network acts as self-organizing mechanisms that attenuate the complexity in the company's *environmental venue*. Dealers are small companies on their own that are part of this environment. They are dealing with individual customers, supporting them in their purchasing activities and the maintenance of their cars afterwards. They purchase cars in large quantities and in this way they reduce the complexity that the car manufacturer has to deal with directly; the environment's residual variety is that much less challenging. These complexity operators in the environment make possible for the manufacturer to reach individual customers globally. Notice that an independent web page with a section of FAQ about cars' characteristics and performance will act in the same venue. Using it, potential customers may themselves deal with inquiries about new models, services and other relevant information regarding getting a new car. This is an example of a self-regulating mechanism.

In their turn these dealers and the manufacturing company need attenuators and amplifiers of complexity in their interactions; this is their *relational venue*. Indeed, on the one hand, dealers need to negotiate *supply schedules* (an instance of attenuators) based on their understanding of their local markets, on the other hand, the manufacturer has to set up a *distribution infrastructure* (an instance of amplifiers) to match the performance requirements implied by the negotiated schedules.

In the same venue, *market research* carried out by a specialised firm on behalf of the manufacturer is an example of a complexity attenuator that helps reducing, by classification, the multiple options of future cars expected by potential clients.

---

[3]These are similar to the three venues explained for the case of individual management of complexity.

[4]These are processes that allow the company to create, produce and regulate its own tasks. We will develop in more detail this concept later on in Chapter 6.

An *advertising campaign* through an appropriate agency offering the new models produced as a result of the market research acts as a corresponding amplifier of complexity (i.e., one product for multiple requests) in the same relational venue. Another example of an attenuator of complexity in this venue could be an Internet site in which, using the same software interface, multiple clients' requests are received and processed. Again, the logistics involved in the delivery of the cars sold in this way is the corresponding amplifier of complexity (i.e., the same procedures and structure is used to reach different clients' requests). Notice that attenuation does not necessarily mean chopping off environmental complexity; it may mean a more sophisticated set of distinctions that increases the enterprise's understanding of its market.

On the other hand, amplifiers and attenuators of complexity in the inner venue are related to the organizational processes of the company. We will explore them with more detail in Chap. 6.

But before finishing this chapter, there is an element in this scheme that has not been explained yet. It is the concept of a *transducer*. Conceptually, a transducer represents encoders or decoders of a message that crosses a boundary between two systems (Beer 1985, p. 53). A transducer is more than a translator in the sense that it not only translates information from one system to another, but it is a different mode of expressing the message.

The forms used to interview potential clients during the market research and the report containing the final analysis of this research are instances of transducers related to one of the attenuators of complexity mentioned in the example of the car manufacturing company (Fig. 4.11). The form is a transducer between the environment (i.e., the potential clients) and those doing the market research (i.e., the attenuator of complexity in the relational venue); the report is a transducer between this attenuator and those in the inner venue (e.g., marketing specialists in the car manufacturing company). On the other hand, a document containing the main characteristics that the publicity campaign should present to the public and the specific advertisements being broadcast are instances of transducers of the corresponding amplifier of complexity. Namely, the former is a transducer between, for example, the public relation specialists in the inner venue and the advertising company doing the campaign in the relational venue (i.e., the amplifier of complexity for the car manufacturing company) while the latter is a transducer between the advertising company amplifying the car manufacturing products and the potential customers in the environment.

Notice that so far we have assumed that there is always an imbalance of complexity between the situation and the individual or between the environment and an organization. However, this certainly may not be the case. For instance, when a new organization is formed, it has to create its market for the products or services it wants to offer.

Marketing is the natural way of producing environmental complexity but again, this has to be done in such a way that it does not overwhelm the response capacity of the organization. If this happens the organization may experience some of the response problems we mentioned before. An interesting case happened during 2005 when a new mobile company was created in a Latin American country to exploit a new communication technology. In order to get part of the market, the newcomer started an aggressive marketing campaign offering discounts of 50% in calls per minute if made between company mobiles. The campaign was so successful that in 4 months they had taken about 40% of the market share. The company was not prepared for growing so fast and soon their communication channels collapsed, 5 months later the company was absorbed by one of its rivals. This real-life case alerts us to the importance of maintaining a balance of complexity right from the beginning.

The concepts and the method we have explained in this chapter are known as variety engineering. The management of complexity is the key concept that guides the operational design of organizations. It constitutes the building block of the viable system model as we will see in Chap. 6. But before going there, we need to formalize the concept of an organization and its difference to collectives and institutions. This is the goal of the next chapter.

References

Argyris C, Schön D (1978) Organizational learning: a theory of action perspective. Addison-Wesley, Reading, PA

Beer S (1979) The heart of enterprise. Wiley, Chichester

Beer S (1981) Death is equifinal. Society for general systems research 25th annual meeting. Toronto, Canada

Beer S (1985) Diagnosing the system for organizations. Wiley, Chichester

Espejo R (1989) The VSM revisited. In: Espejo R, Harnden R (eds) The viable system model: interpretations and applications of Stafford Beer's VSM. Wiley, Chichester, pp 77–100

Espejo R (2000) Self-construction of desirable social systems. Kybernetes 29(7–8):949–963

Espejo R (2009) Performance management, the nature of regulation and the Cybersyn Project. Kybernetes 38(1/2):65–82

Espejo R, Howard N (1982) What is requisite variety? A re-examination of the foundation of Beer's method. Working Paper Series: 242. Aston University, Birmingham, UK

Espejo R, Watt J (1988) Information management, organization and managerial effectiveness. J Oper Res Soc 39(1):7–14

Espejo R, Schuhmann W, Schwaninger M, Bilello U (1996) Organizational transformation and learning. Wiley, Chichester

Gorbachev M (1987) Perestroika: new thinking for our country and the world. HarperCollins, London

Habermas J (1979) Communication and the evolution of society. Beacon Press, Boston, MA

Maturana H, Varela F (1992) The tree of knowledge. Shambhala, Boston, MA/London

Prigogine I, Stengers I (1984) Order out of chaos. Heinemann, London

Rockart JF (1979) Chief executives define their own data needs. Harv Bus Rev (March–April):81–93

Tapscott D (2009) Grown up digital. McGraw-Hill, New York

Tapscott D, Lowy A, Ticoll D (1998) Blueprint to the digital economy: creating wealth in the era of e-business. McGraw-Hill, New York

Ulrich W (2000) Reflective practice in the civil society: the contribution of critically systemic thinking. Reflective Pract 1(2):247–268

Whitaker R (1992) Venues for contexture: a critical analysis and enactive reformulation of group decision support systems. Research Report UMADP –RRIPCS, Department of Administrative Data Processing /Informatics. Umeå Universitet, Umeå, Sweden

Chapter 5
On Organizations: Beyond Institutions and Hierarchies

Abstract In this chapter we argue that organizations emerge when members of a collective produce a closed network of recurrent interactions or *relations*. Interactions can be direct communications, such as everyday conversations, or indirect communications, such as when people coordinate their actions as an outcome of sharing a context or culture. A closed network, or 'closure', means that the collective has decision rules and mechanisms to make up their own minds about relevant issues and produce, through their actions and decisions, a whole that maintains a separate existence. We also make a clear distinction between collectives, institutions and organizations. As for organizations the focus of this book is on viable systems. These organizations have recursive structures of autonomous units within autonomous units where organizational cohesion is achieved by the willing alignment of individuals' purposes, which recognize the synergistic advantage of their coordination. In line with the concepts introduced in Chap. 2, control means to a large degree, enabling the self-regulation of autonomous units. In this chapter we introduce concepts to deal with recursive organizations. In the next chapter we develop this approach in full by explaining the Viable System Model, which is a model that balances autonomy and cohesion.

People may get together for many different reasons such as interests of all kinds, ecological concerns, security, pleasure and challenges in general. But meeting regularly although it is a necessary condition to form an organization it is certainly not a sufficient one. For instance, when a group of persons gathers regularly every Sunday to attend to a football match, they form a collective. With time they may become a football club and may be recognized as such by governmental agencies and by people in general. What conditions should be met in order for a collective to become an organization? What are the invariants that allow us to recognize the same organization even though people constituting it may change over time? Is there any difference between an organization and an institution? These are the questions that the present chapter seeks to answer.

We claim that an organization emerges when members of a collective produce a closed network of recurrent interactions or *relations*. Interactions can be direct communications, such as everyday conversations, or indirect communications, such as when people coordinate their actions as an outcome of sharing a context or culture. Through interactions people co-ordinate their actions and ascribe meaning to them. A closed network, or 'closure', means that the collective has decision rules and mechanisms to make up their own minds about relevant issues and produce, through their actions and decisions, a whole which maintains a separate existence. Through these rules and mechanisms, for instance, people know who does and who does not belong to the organization that is being formed.

This *closure* is needed in order for a consensual domain of interactions to emerge as an organization with its own identity. This identity is produced when a particular set of organizational *relationships* is formed and therefore particular norms, values and meanings emerge as shared distinctions and practices that mediate individuals' recurrent interactions. The set of *relationships* formed triggers what an observer may identify as, for instance, the University of Lincoln or the Barcelona Football Club. Notice that this emergent identity, as an outcome of recurrent interactions, has a different ontological status (a much stronger 'grounded meaning') than conversations agreeing an identity for the University of Lincoln or the Barcelona Football Club, even if carried out by people deeply involved in the day-to-day life of these organizations.

From this definition it is clear that the *identity* of an organization is independent of the particular individuals involved in these interactions; these can be any as long as they satisfy these relationships. For instance, the identity of a university is defined, in part, by the relationships between students and academic staff, between administrative staff and academics, and between lecturers in processes of teaching and researching. In all these cases, there is no reference to particular individuals. Therefore, we can see that as long as the relationships are preserved, the identity of an organization will remain the same, even if the individuals involved in producing these relationships change. Conversely, if the relationships change then the identity changes and a new organization emerges, even if the individuals involved in constituting these relationships remain the same.

Notice that we are differentiating between organizational *relationships* and individual *relations*. While relations are concrete recurrent interactions realised by particular individuals with particular resources and in a particular place and time, relationships are abstract but grounded (i.e., operationally stable) *forms* of interaction independent of the individuals involved in their constitution. They are produced and re-produced by concrete relations among individuals over time. Therefore, the same organizational relationships can be produced by a variety of different relations.

An old Chinese game called Tangram can be used to illustrate how identity and relationships intertwine. The game consists of getting different shapes using the same components. Figure 5.1 shows three of these shapes: a square, a cat and a house. Clearly we are using exactly the same geometrical components; however by changing the spatial *relationships* of the components we get very different outcomes. The shape we distinguish is its *identity* that emerges from the pattern of the spatial *relationships* of the components.

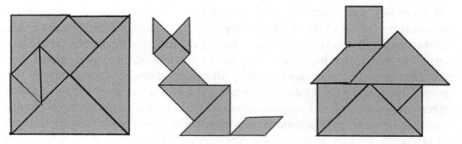

Fig. 5.1 Different shapes formed by the relationship of seven components

Relationships are formed when particular distinctions are grounded and shared by a group of individuals through recurrent interactions.

As for experiencing relationships in the constitution of organizations, notice that in making distinctions about relationships we identify two *aspects*, although both are intricately interwoven in knowledge and practice: distinctions support the constitution of *meaning* and are closely connected with *sanctions*. Indeed, the *semantic* aspect of distinctions refers to the discursive and tacit meaning that actors ascribe to their recurrent interactions and context. The *normative* or regulative aspects of distinctions refer to the appropriate or legitimate manner in which activities may be carried out, as well as to the positive and negative sanctions which are applicable to them. The knowledge of these implicit distinctions generates mutual expectations that exert an influence on individuals' behaviour. The expectation of others' expectations is a platform for actors' co-ordination of actions (Luhmann 1995). But expectations not only tend to constrain individual behaviour, as illustrated by Foucault's panopticon and the fear of sanctions (Foucault 1977), they are also the motor for social change through learning, as is discussed below.

Therefore, because of the semantic and normative aspects of distinctions, relationships convey a particular set of meanings, norms and values that underpin our day-to-day interactions and culture. In other words, changing the culture of an organization means changing the relationships underpinning individuals' interactions in that organization. Furthermore, the stronger the cultural links between organizational members (i.e., the stronger their relationships) the larger the capacity of the communication channels supporting their conversations (Conant 1979). An example will clarify this point. When we interact with others in language we are following certain grammatical rules and, normally, we are speaking within a particular context of expectations. The shared knowledge of these rules and context between us, as speakers, and others as listeners, makes the messages transmitted more predictable. This 'predictability' is what Shannon called *redundancy* (Shannon and Weaver 1949).[1] It is this redundancy that allows us to have stable

---

[1] Shannon estimated that the syntactic and grammatical rules of English accounted for a redundancy ranging between 50% and 75%.

conversations with others in noisy surroundings. In this sense, the redundancy provided by the structure of the language (i.e., its rules) and the context of the conversation effectively increases the channel capacity of the conversations. Similarly, the shared meanings, values and norms constituting the organizational relationships amplify the channel capacity of organizational conversations. A few simple words and gestures may be enough to express a wealth of information that otherwise would require a massive investment in communication resources. In this sense, and contrary to the common view of redundancy as a waste (i.e., duplication) of resources, we may recognize the importance of redundancy in the structure of organizations. In fact, the communications producing an organization depend to a significant degree in the redundancy built into their structure (Beer 1979, 1981).

But how do we define an organization's structure? To begin with, we say that the basic components of organizations *are not* people but interacting *organizational roles* (Espejo 2000). Notice that people are constituted as roles (for instance as members of a football club) only as they are actively involved in its production. With this in mind, we claim that the particular roles and resources constituting organizational relationships at a particular time and in a particular context define the *structure* of the organization (Espejo 1994, p. 205). In the case of a university, the concrete teaching groups, committees, support groups, services, and so on, in existence at a particular time and their interactions constitute the university's structure. This implies, of course, that different structures may produce the same class identity. In other words, what differentiates two universities with similar relationships is precisely their structure. In addition, this also means that we may change an organization's structure without changing its identity.

An *organization's structure* is often understood as the formal hierarchy of functionally based reporting relations among people as shown on the typical organization charts. In our definition, however, structure emerges from stable forms of communication, or *mechanisms*, which permit the parts of an organization to operate together as a whole. These parts, as we mentioned before, are *organizational roles* embodied in persons or in *units* such as teams, departments, business units and so forth. These organizational roles are resourced by all kinds of materials, tools and technologies. This point suggests the relevance of understanding both the contribution of technology and other resources to organizational processes and the influence of structure in the design of communication and information systems.

Summarising so far, organizations arise in consensual domains of action when people's interactions produce a closed network of relations. The underlying organizational relationships constitute the organization's identity that is realized, at any moment in time, through particular relations among organizational roles and resources that constitute its structure.

Now, let us make a distinction between organizations and institutions. By now it should be clear that organizations are constituted dynamically by people's recurrent interactions and not by *formal agreements* of members of a collective, though these agreements can be catalysts for organizations in the operational domain. Therefore the fact that an institution, such as an enterprise, is legally created does not imply that it is constituted as an organizational system.

Formal institutions often are not organizations because they depend on decisions of external agents to achieve closure and their cohesion is hindered by uncommitted components, which in general have the option to defect. If educational establishments, for instance, fail to create their own policies, and only reproduce the central government's policies, they are failing to achieve organizational closure and therefore they are not organizational systems individually. Equally, a collective without regulatory capacity may fail maintaining the cohesion of the collective's members and therefore fail to achieve organizational closure.

On the other hand, in many instances the collaborative efforts of several institutions are necessary to achieve closure. This would be the case for a national education system, where its organization may emerge from the interactions among people creating policy through national and regional educational authorities, regulating these policies through regulatory bodies and producing education in a myriad of schools and other formal and informal educational bodies.

Notice that when a collective is constituted as an organization, their members are not only creating but also producing collective meanings. These produced meanings are the collective's purposes and values-in-use, which may be different to the purposes and values that they *create* and espouse. No doubt, members of a collective, by agreeing purposes for their action can align their efforts better. However, if conversations concerning purposes are inadequate or are poorly grounded in people's every day actions, the collective's purposes-in-use may become out of phase with their individual or group espoused purposes, suggesting lack of coherence (i.e., people not walking the talk) and possibly lacking alignment with the interests and requirements of customers and other agents co-evolving with them in their environment. In other words, it is only when resources for the *creation, regulation and production of a social meaning* come operationally together that an organizational system is constituted.

The *creation* of social meanings (e.g., policies) feeds onto implementation activities, which *produce* social meanings (e.g., products and services for customers/ stakeholders), which feed back to those creating the meanings bootstrapping production and creation in processes of operational closure. Therefore achieving closure (i.e., developing a capacity to create, regulate and produce social meanings) is what determines whether a collective may become an organization or an institution.

Let us now elaborate upon these definitions and explore their consequences. In particular, we would like to unfold the consequences of *closure* as a necessary condition for an organization to emerge and the consequences of defining its structure in terms of relations. But in order to do this, we need to develop a bit further the concepts of *informational* and *operational domains,* mentioned in the previous chapter, in the context of organizations.

We said in Chap. 3 that the informational domain is the domain of *detached reflection* about on-going interactions, whereas the operational domain is the domain of these interactions (which, of course, include *participative reflection*). Therefore, given a particular domain of action, its operational domain is produced by the participants' interactions in that domain. On the other hand, its informational domain is produced by the descriptions (i.e., distinctions) made of that domain by any observer regardless of being an external observer or an observer-participant in that domain of action. A few examples may help to clarify these ideas.

Suppose that the domain of action we are considering is that of a football match. It is clear that the movements of the players, the thinking of options, the kicking of the ball and the passing shots during the match are all instances of actions carried out in the operational domain of the football match. It is clear also that the conversations and shouts of spectators in the stadium while watching the match are actions carried out in the informational domain of the match (though these shouts may influence the players' behaviour). You may wish to reflect whether the instruction during half-time and the shouts of the coaches from the pitch line during the game belong or not to the operational domain of the match; are they a constitutive part of this domain of action or not?

It is clear that the conversations of these same coaches while debriefing a past game or planning a future game belong to the informational domain of those matches. However, notice that these same conversations belong to the operational domain of coaching if coaching is defined as the domain of action here.

The point of the previous discussion is that informational and operational domains are concepts that make sense only in regard to particular domains of action. Once these domains of action are made explicit, we may distinguish the two domains. In the context of a company, for instance, planning exercises with external facilitation are likely to be activities that belong to its informational domain. On the other hand, creating and producing a mission and vision through the set of relationships grounded in individuals' recurrent interactions, belong to its operational domain. Notice that the specific domain of action in this case is the company's doing in its environment (i.e., medium). With these clarifications lets go back to explore the implications of closure for organizations.

An organization has closure in its operational domain, in other words, it is *operationally closed* in its medium; otherwise it would not constitute a distinction in that medium. However, it must be open in general to resources (i.e., energy) and what we usually call information; otherwise it would not be sustainable and adaptable. Resources are necessary to maintain the components' interactions over time and information is necessary for the co-evolution of the organization and its components with environmental agents. In-formation, in this context, is not understood as messages representing the environment within the organization but as external disturbances that are accommodated within it, as was explained in Chap. 1.

An implication of having closure is that organizations are *structure-determined*. In Chap. 1, we said that structure-determined systems are systems whose behaviour at any moment in time is determined by their own structure. External perturbations may trigger structural changes and corresponding responses but they, alone, do not determine these changes and responses.

In the context of organizations this means that change is the outcome of a closed network of multiple adjustments taking place in the operational domain of participants as they adjust through their interactions to external perturbations. This makes apparent that the concept of information is not enough to understand organizational change. Change may be triggered by information but not determined by it. In other words, organizations do not 'pick up information' from the environment nor do they 'respond' to external 'information', as it is often said. This view may be useful in the informational domain of an observer who is describing the interaction of the organization with its environment as if it were a black box. However, in the operational domain of the organization what happens is exactly the opposite. It is the structure of the organization that specifies which patterns of the environment are perturbations and what changes will be triggered by them (Espejo 1993a). This fact has important consequences for designing change processes in organizations. In order to be effective, changes in organizations do not only have to be *culturally feasible* (Checkland 1981) but also *systemically feasible*, that is, recognized and supported by the organization's structure (Espejo 1993b, p. 85).

Closure implies also a distinction between the organization and its medium. The medium is the *substrata*, or *ecology*, in which an organization is constituted. It is a concept that belongs to the operational domain of the organization; its focus is on the instant-by-instant communications between each and every one of the organizational actors and stakeholders in this medium. The fundamental aspect here is that an organization is the outcome of relationships between *actors* who achieve a degree of cohesion vis-a-vis their medium. The engine to achieve this cohesion is the tension produced over them by environmental *agents* (or external stakeholders) with some expectations. Without the tension between actors, producing the organization, and agents stretching it, there is neither organization nor a medium. They are mutually constituted.

An organization's medium is constituted by its external stakeholders (suppliers, customers and interveners). Relations with these stakeholders account for most of the organization's resources. Those stakeholders are the source of complexity that organizations have to manage as suggested in our discussion of management complexity at the end of Chap. 4. In the chapter about Naming Systems (see Chap. 7) we will study a particular tool to drive discussions about an organization's medium or ecology.

Notice that, on purpose, we talk about an organization in its *medium* and not about an organization in its *environment*. As we anticipated in the previous chapter, we make a clear distinction between the two. Whereas medium belongs to the operational domain of an organization, environment belongs to its informational domain (Espejo 1993a). The organization's environment refers to external circumstances as well as trends and issues perceived by an observer as relevant to the organization's success. It is a strategic concept and its focus is planning response strategies, based on intelligence information gathered by relevant people in the organization. Thus, *strategies* may also pertain to the informational domain of the organization. In some sense, an organization's environment entails possible future variations in the organization's medium. An emphasis on environment is an emphasis on information and strategy from the position of an observer; an emphasis on medium is an emphasis on actors' relations, co-ordination of actions and communication processes.

These distinctions suggest that the idea of only a few individuals concerned with the organization's environment, namely those working out its strategy and plans, risks taking them out of organizational processes. This idea should be replaced by everyone being responsible for the organization's communication with its medium. Every single participant should appreciate how his or her actions, as members of the organization, affect the medium (Espejo 1993a, p. 78; Espejo and Stewart 1998).

Dealing with the environment in the informational domain of corporate staff alone risks decoupling them from organizational processes. At the individual level people are thrown into action (their operational domain) at the same time that they construe this action in their informational domain. This is characteristic of our capabilities for reflection and self-reference. This self-reference poses an additional demand on organizations where managers need to learn to match their informational and operational domains in a collective rather than a personal action domain. For them their operational domain is role defined and implies interacting with the organization's medium through the actions of other people. In this case their individual reflection and self-reference should encompass these other people. The quality of this reflection (in the informational domain) is influenced by both the quality of their interactions with these people (producing their relevant operational domain) and the quality of their interactions with those producing the organization's overall meanings (in the organization's operational domain).

The consequences of poor interactions are not only poor individual management, but also a mismatch between the organization's informational and operational domains. The organization's ascribed purposes and values will not match the meanings it produces in its medium. When managers engage themselves in producing strategies and plans for the organization without managing people's capabilities and interaction, that is, configuring effectively the organization's resources (Eisenhardt and Martin 2000; Teece 2008) we may expect inconsistent informational and operational domains. This is a typical situation where managers lose reference for their actions. They will start thinking for others, thus invading their domains of action or start acting without adequate reflection about these actions and therefore not taking responsibility for them or both. As their informational domain loses touch with their operational domain they put themselves in a non-learning situation.

Making the organization's operational and informational domains coherent requires managerial roles construing realistic models of necessary interactions and communications in the organization and being aware of their operational contribution to the organization. The organization's model about itself, emerging from actors' interactions, is the anchor for managers to produce realistic models about their own action domains and to align their informational and operational domains. This reflection suggests that a calculus for self-reference, to relate managers to the organization, is necessary (Varela 1975).

We normally expect that a successful company will have well developed strategic planning methods and sophisticated information systems. However, it is perfectly possible to encounter successful, viable companies with apparently limited strategic planning and not much evidence of sophisticated corporate information systems.[2] Such organizations have tacit distributed information and planning systems built into their organization structure. There is dynamic stability in the organization's structural coupling with its medium; its members are engaged in effective interdependent task-loops, which enables their organizational units to absorb disturbances. In such cases, centralised strategic plans and information systems may be redundant.

An emphasis on the structural coupling of an organization with its medium seems to be the formal underpinning of ecological management. A *responsive* organization is one sensitive to its medium rather than one focused on an observer constructed environment (Espejo and Reyes 1999). In other words, the *responsive organization* is aware of far more complexity than the *strategic organization*.

The other consequences of our definition of organization follow from our understanding of the organization's structure. Let us recall that we said that the structure of an organization is not the formal, usually hierarchical and functionally based, reporting relations that appear in any organization chart. Instead, we said that roles and resources constituting the organizational relationships produce an organization's structure. What we would like to explore now are the consequences of looking at the structure of an organization in this way.

To begin with, we may say that individual relations form mechanisms, that is, stable forms of interaction that allow the individuals to operate as a collective whole. Therefore, understanding the structure of an organization means studying the mechanisms of interaction that constitute that organization. We will reflect upon two different ways in which these mechanisms can be constituted: one is normally called *hierarchical* structure; the other is what we call *recursive* structure.

In the past hierarchy was praised as a good structure for getting work done in large organizations (Jaques 1990). Perhaps the genesis for this belief comes from the hierarchical structures commonly used by early military and religious organizations. Today, while not many organizations espouse hierarchical structures many constitute such structures.

The implication of this traditional dogma is that as we go higher in a managerial hierarchy, the individual managers deal with an increasing complexity because the time horizon of their respective problems increases as well. Therefore, the complexity managed by top managers – dealing with problems of a long time horizon (e.g., 10–20 years) – has to be larger than that managed by foremen on the shop floor – who are dealing with problems of a short time horizon (e.g., days or weeks). So it is quite natural that the actual design of tasks in these organizations is made in such a way that lower structural levels deal only with the short term while the long term is left as the responsibility of the higher levels only. Figure 5.2 illustrates this case (Espejo et al. 1996, p. 97).

The pitfall of this assumption is that it conflates *individual* and *organizational complexities* two concepts that we differentiated early in Chap. 3. First of all, notice

---

[2]A particular example is cited by Espejo (1993), while discussing Sir John Harvey-Jones troubleshooting activities (Harvey-Jones 1992).

Senior Management

Bottom level

Fig. 5.2 An illustration of a hierarchical structure in terms of complexity management

that whatever the capacity and commitment of a top manager might be, he or she will always be limited by his or her biological response capacity. Therefore people, whether they are the Chairman of the corporation or a foreman in one of the plants, share similar potentials for managing complexity (that is both are constrained by their essentially similar neuro-physiological capacity). Secondly, it is clear that the organizational complexity relevant to the general manager is much larger than that relevant to people in the shop floor. The problem arises because the hierarchical strategy to manage complexity reduces the problem solving capacity of people at lower structural levels in order to relieve senior managers' overload. The paradox is that by not fostering autonomy at lower structural levels, a much larger 'individual' residual complexity is left to the attention of the general manager, producing the *control dilemma* (see next chapter). Then clearly not only does the organization as a whole lose out (by creating conditions for less organizational complexity) but individuals are likely to feel less committed to the organization and managers are likely to feel overloaded by demands beyond their control; individuals' own purposes are less likely to be aligned with those ascribed by managers to the organization. A syndrome of hierarchical structures is top managers overloaded with large quantities of information and low-level managers under loaded by limited responsibilities.

By contrast, the assumption in what we call *recursive* organizations (or an organization with a recursive structure) is that people, at all structural levels,

Senior Management

Bottom level

Fig. 5.3 An illustration of a recursive structure in terms of complexity management

have the potential to deal with more or less the same complexity; they share the same biology. Figure 5.3 illustrates the point. Therefore, by distributing responsibilities and accountabilities throughout the organization, recursive structures promote the use of individuals' talents and a more even distribution of complexity. Thus, recursive structures enhance problem solving at all structural levels by enabling individuals to develop their complexity to the full, promote organizational complexity by encouraging autonomy at all structural levels, and ensure that each autonomous unit at each structural level is fully aware of the short, medium and long terms. In recursive organizations, therefore, although the organizational complexity relevant to the general manager can be very large, the residual complexity that he or she has to deal with can be much smaller. This is a good example of a strategy to deal with complexity by promoting self-organization and self-regulation as we explained at the end of Chap. 4.

In a recursive organization, the differentiation between structural levels is not brought about by lines of authority but emerges from the fact that the total tasks of those at lower structural levels are *encompassed* by the total tasks of those at higher structural levels. Notice that in a recursive organization tasks at lower structural levels are autonomous and strive for their viability in the same way as those at a more global level. Since the variety of our world is very large indeed the complexities that managers at global and local levels can see is similar (they are constrained by similar physiologies). A key issue is the degree to which local complexity is constrained by the use of power by those in more global positions.

There is a close connection between the structure of an organization and the establishment of power relationships. Let us explore it.

The exercise of power depends upon the access that organizational actors have to resources, the knowledge they have about them and their practices in using them. Exercise of power can be unilateral and coercive or enabling and emancipating. The grading between these extremes depends on the use of influence mechanisms or structures enabling their actions. In some interactions it is quite possible that actors have access to similar resources and therefore that they can achieve a sort of equality of arms, or symmetry, in their interactions; power is balanced between the interacting actors. However, the usual case is an asymmetrical distribution of resources and relations in organizations; this is the situation where effective structural mechanisms can help redressing the imbalance. This structural underpinning of power is discussed in the next chapter.

However, from the perspective of identity an asymmetrical distribution of resources and relations among actors shapes the organizational relationships; power relationships are formed and maintained. Along with *semantic* and *normative* aspects, *power* is a constitutive element of *organizational relationships*. All these three aspects of relationships are mutually interconnected and are separable only for analytical purposes.[3]

The relation between power and the semantic aspect of relationships may be appreciated, for instance, in the use of accounting systems in the majority of today's organizations. Though standardization of accounting procedures is useful, if these systems impose a particular framework of categories upon individuals in the organization, such that their actions may be interpreted and evaluated only in those categories, local flexibility is lost. The framework establishes what shall and what shall not count as significant and valid within an organization. This particular relation between the power and semantic aspects of relationships is analogous to Foucault's discussion of the relation power/knowledge (Foucault 1972).

At a more basic level, an asymmetrical distribution of resources provides some individuals in an organization with more flexibility to create new distinctions and categories, while others will interact in situations that have been defined for them. This circumstance will 'propel them into a fixed, 'objective' world in which they have no option but to construe it as implied by the distinctions made by those in power' (Espejo 1994, p. 207). This 'objectivity' can be created, for instance, when the standards imposed by the accounting profession interferes with the creativity of local structural levels. The recurrent use of these standards may

---

[3]Giddens calls these three aspects *Signification*, *Legitimation*, and *Domination* respectively (Giddens 1984).

reinforce relationships of dominance throughout society. We debate this point further in the next chapter with reference to the VSM's Coordination Function.

This closed connection between the semantic aspects of relationships and power helps understanding the concept of *empowerment* in a rather particular way. Indeed, empowerment in organizations is necessary to give individuals, whatever their roles or location in the organization structure, the opportunity to invent their own distinctions and ground them in their operational domain for those aspects that are aligned with the organization's purposes. What normally happens in today's organizations is that only those at the corporate level have the means to enact organizational distinctions which may unfairly restrict the autonomy of other members of the organization. Structures that promote the effective empowerment of individuals should be a characteristic of socially responsible organizations. This is one of the characteristics of a recursive structure.

Recursive structures imply having autonomous units within autonomous units where organizational cohesion is achieved by the willing alignment of individuals' purposes, which recognize the synergistic advantage of their coordination. Control to a significant degree means self-regulation of autonomous units that have emerged out of the synergistic relations of autonomous units at a lower level of recursion. This is the complementarity between control and autonomy, as we will show in more detail in the next chapter.

In the organizational context, the focus of this book is on recursive organizations. In this chapter we wanted to introduce the concepts necessary to deal with this way of looking at organizations. In the next chapter we will develop this approach in full by explaining the Viable System Model (Beer 1979, 1981, 1985); a model for recursive organizations that balances autonomy and cohesion.

To understand this model let us remember that the *interactions of individuals* constituting organizational roles, and not the individuals, are the building blocks of an organization. As people's relations, that is, their stable forms of interaction, produce, and are produced by mechanisms of communication, it is important to keep in mind the nature of communication processes as explained in Chap. 2, along with the related idea of control. These ideas are fully applied as we discuss the Viable System Model.

This chapter has highlighted through the operational and informational domains both the significance of the operational and black-box descriptions of organizations (see Chap. 1). In particular we have discussed identity from the perspective of relationships and not of the organization's doing. However, for observers it is this doing (that transforms inputs into outputs) that makes apparent what an organization 'is', albeit in a much less precise form than this proposition suggests. Observers construct different meanings for these transformations. Operational descriptions are particularly important to understand how an organization works; black box descriptions, are relevant to measure the complexity of a transformation from a particular viewpoint. This point is discussed throughout Part II of this book.

From the black-box perspective an organization's identity emerges from the recognition it receives from others; it is not just the outcome of its inner working regardless of others. Recognition influences the way we see ourselves (Taylor 1989).

It is in our relationships with others that we construct meanings for our actions. Our identities emerge from the extent people care about what we do and respect this doing. An organization's identity evolves from its relationships with context providers, external stakeholders in general. Lack of recognition from these stakeholders implies for the organization weak or non-existent relationships, that is, weak or non-existent identity. From an operational perspective, relationships, structure and identity define each other in an organization. In other words certain structural forms would be impossible to realise unless certain relationships emerge. For instance the emergence of autonomous units within autonomous units is possible if global managers are prepared to accept the self-determination of local managers, and without this self-determination there is no *recursive structure*. Identity – the meanings ascribed to what the organization does – evolves from these relationships. There is duality between 'isness' and doing. Relationships constituting an organization as a recognisable whole in its environment are identified in the Viable System Model in the next chapter. Doing, as recognition from others, is discussed throughout Part II.

References

Beer S (1979) The heart of enterprise. Wiley, Chichester

Beer S (1981) Brain of the firm, 2nd edition. Wiley, 2nd edition Chichester

Beer S (1985) Diagnosing the system for organizations. Wiley, Chichester

Checkland P (1981) Systems thinking, systems practice. Wiley, Chichester

Conant R (1979) Communications without a channel. Int J Gen Syst 5:93–98

Eisenhardt KM, Martin JA (2000) Dynamic capabilities: What are they? Strateg Manage J 21(21): 1105–1122

Espejo R (1993a) Domains of interaction between a social system and its environment. In: Tsivacou I (ed) A challenge for systems thinking: the Aegean Seminar. University of the Aegean Press, Athens, pp 97–104

Espejo R (1993b) Management of complexity in problem solving. In: Espejo R, Schwaninger M (eds) Organizational fitness: corporate effectiveness through management cybernetics. Campus Verlag, Frankfurt/New York, pp 67–90

Espejo R (1993c) Giving requisite variety to strategy and information systems. In: Stowell F, West D, Howell D (eds) Systems science addressing global issues. Plenum, New York, pp 33–39

Espejo R (1994) What's systemic thinking? Syst Dyn Rev 10(2–3 Summer–Fall):199–212

Espejo R (2000) Self-construction of desirable social systems. Kybernetes 29(7–8):949–963

Espejo R, Reyes A (1999) Responsive accounting: a grounding of the informational domain in the operational domain of an organization. In: Heylighen F, Bollen J, Riegler A (eds) The evolution of complexity: the violet book of 'Einstein meets Magritte'. Kluwer, Dordrecht, The Netherlands, pp 307–325

Espejo R, Stewart N (1998) Systemic reflections on environmental sustainability. Syst Res Behav Sci 15:483–496

Espejo R, Schuhmann W, Schwaninger M, Bilello U (1996) Organizational transformation and learning. Wiley, Chichester

Foucault M (1972) The archaeology of knowledge. Tavistock Publications, London

Foucault M (1977) Discipline and punish: the birth of the prison (trans. Sheridan). Allen Lane, London

Giddens A (1984) The constitution of society: outline of the theory of structuration. Polity Press, Cambridge

Harvey-Jones J (1992) Trouble shooter 2. BBC Books, London

Jaques E (1990) 'In Praise of Hierarchy'. Har Bus Rev (January–February): 127–133

Luhmann N (1995) Social systems. Stanford University Press, Stanford, CA

Shannon C, Weaver W (1949) The mathematical theory of communication. University of Illinois Press, Urbana, IL

Taylor C (1989) Sources of the self. The making of the modern identity. Harvard University Press, Cambridge, MA

Teece JD (2008) Technological know-how, organizational capabilities, and strategic management: Business strategy and enterprise development in competitive environments. World Scientific Publishing, London

Varela F (1975) A calculus for self-reference. Int J Gen Syst 2:5–24

Chapter 6
The Viable System Model: Effective Strategies to Manage Complexity

Abstract In this chapter we build on the concept of organization as a closed network of relations having identity to explain in detail the Viable System Model (VSM). This model offers a systemic form of observing collectives and institutions in today's societies. The VSM clarifies the quality of the strategies used by a collective to manage the complexity of its self-defined tasks and is a particularly helpful instrument for organizational diagnosis. This chapter develops complexity management strategies for policy-making and policy implementation and explains processes to maintain the organization's cohesion and support its adaptation in a problematic environment. Though the Viable System Model is used most commonly as a tool to observe and describe organizations it also supports, most importantly, the design of effective communication structures.

In Chap. 5 we developed the concept of organizations as a closed network of relations having identity. We also made a clear distinction between collectives and organizations. In this chapter, we explain a systemic model that allows us to observe and describe organizations as human communication systems; this is the Viable System Model (VSM) (Beer 1979, 1981, 1985).

The VSM offers a systemic form of observing collective behaviours in today's societies. Its history goes back into the 1960s when it was developed by Stafford Beer in the context of the earlier work in cybernetics by Wiener (1948), McCulloch (1989), and Ashby (1952, 1964).

The VSM allows us to diagnose the structural mechanisms of an enterprise and use them as a platform for organizational design. This chapter shows the VSM as a powerful tool to steer interactions in directions that produce effective organizational processes. Organizational design has to go beyond tinkering with local improvements in the direction of improving resource allocation and relationships to produce enterprises capable of creating, regulating and producing espoused purposes and values. Most current approaches (see for instance Galbraith 2002) used in designing or re-structuring organizations run short of braiding business and value chain processes with a myriad of organizational processes producing together with them the emergent organization. We need a holistic framework to relate value creation, business processes and organizational processes as well as local and global processes. This is what the VSM is all about.

The VSM helps diagnosing the actual bounding of people's interactions in closed networks of relationships or *shared communication spaces for knowledge creation* (Nonaka and Konno 1998), whether real or virtual. Often these shared communication spaces are populated by people with uneven power that produce hierarchical structures, which become the media to constitute interactions with uneven distribution of power. This is a social structure that leaves in the hands of the few most of the influence to produce knowledge and disregards the huge knowledge creation capabilities of the most. As we discuss below these are relational problems in organizations, which imply a poor management of complexity or bad cybernetics. The declarative power of the few can be seen as responsible for the creation and development of our enterprises. This distribution of power has fundamental consequences in the constitution of responsible enterprises.

The VSM provides a means of observing the structural context constraining people's communications as they experience problem situations. A lack of awareness of this context often produces both *unintended consequences* and *performance problems* (Beer 2009). The VSM offers through diagnosis a framework to assess these risks and through design a framework to ameliorate them. Too often we tackle problem situations without establishing this necessary condition for effective action. The VSM is above all about enabling connectivity and structuring the system to facilitate the healthy development of relationships and ultimately effective performance.

Finally, in this chapter we explore how organizations can release the potential of people, enabling them to handle autonomously their problems, thus providing enterprises with the flexibility they need to survive in complex and rapidly changing environments. An effective enterprise produces simultaneously global cohesion and local autonomy. The first is a requirement to achieve synergy; the second is a requirement to achieve flexibility and distributed creativity.

Viable systems are those that are able to *maintain a separate existence*. Such systems have their own knowledge creation and problem solving capacity. If they are to survive, they need not only the capacity to respond to familiar events such as customer orders, but the potential to respond to unexpected events, to the emergence of new social behaviours and even of highly improbable occurrences (Taleb 2008). The latter capacity is the hallmark of viable systems; it gives them the capacity to adapt to changing environments. While the emergence of the improbable may throw the viable system off balance, the fundamental characteristic of viability lessens its vulnerability to the unexpected, making it more adaptive to change.

In the previous chapter we highlighted that the hierarchical organizations, which in spite of all the management developments of the 1980s and 1990s still dominate management practice, structure enterprises as pyramids, with decisions about policy being taken at the top and implemented through their lower structural levels. According to this practice an enterprise's total task is broken down into smaller and smaller fragments, leading to an increasingly narrow definition of tasks and an emphasis on centralized control.

We said that the VSM works on a different principle, one that is derived from studying biological systems: hierarchy is replaced by *structural recursion*. Living (viable) systems, from the most elementary cells to human beings, are self-organizing and self-regulatory. Evolution is responsible for their increasing complexification, where cells' functional differentiation and connectivity may produce more complex living systems, without cells losing their self-organizing and self-regulatory characteristics. This produces viable systems within viable systems, at increasing levels of complexity. Each component maintains its autonomy vis-à-vis its environment, but contributes to the production of a larger also autonomous viable system. It is like picturing Russian dolls within Russian dolls, only that there is not only one within each of the larger dolls but potentially many, which most importantly, for social organizations, can defect. All autonomous components amplify the complexity of their embedding wholes and share their structural and management requirements to remain viable. This is a recursive structure with huge complexity amplification capabilities, where components are functionally differentiated but share an invariant structure. This structure is a powerful strategy for complexity management; most of the complexity is managed locally in each of the components and only a small residual variety is required to align them with the functional requirements of higher levels of evolutionary complexification.

Social systems may evolve from the simple to the more complex, but often we experience the opposite process; a collective of people with some sense of what they want but unclear functional differentiation find themselves without the requisite structures to carry out something that is still not well defined. They interact, try to find their common path and hope for the best; if the ride is difficult some of them may defect if that is at all possible, the ones left behind fight, suffer and eventually may generate some degree of cohesion and collective viability. It is in this scenario that collectives may strive for an improved viability, beyond survival. They can learn from biological systems how to create conditions for local viability without unnecessary fragmentation of the global task. Now we are opening the Russian dolls, and learning how it is that autonomy within autonomy can be enabled; we are unfolding the enterprises' complexity. Naturally we can also encounter examples of organic growth, where individuals or small cohesive units develop synergistic relations with other previously independent people or units and produce new organizations. Of course, we may find many other forms of complexification where new organizational forms emerge. Regardless of whether the process is bottom-up, top-down or of any other form, in all cases we find that there is complexity unfolding.

The unfolding of complexity of a collective is more often than not the outcome of local processes of self-organization, rather than purposeful design. The formal organization chart bears little resemblance to the organic processes of communication and control in use within, say, an enterprise. In order to reduce the pain and cost that is often involved in processes of self-organization the challenge is to learn, both from past social experiences and also from nature, strategies to manage connecting processes leading to successful composite viability. This means producing cohesion of adaptive components while respecting their autonomy. For collectives, as meaning producing social systems, this implies aligning the meanings produced locally by small teams with the purposes they collectively ascribe to their joint enterprise. The better is this alignment, we will argue, the more effective is the enterprise's organization.

A balance should be achieved between the actions *producing* collective purposes and the actions *creating* these purposes and *enabling* their production. In the extreme, if all actions went into production there would be neither capacity to support connectivity and cohesion nor capacity to challenge the already ascribed purposes. This is a crucial distinction; we call those actions producing these purposes *primary activities* and those enabling them *regulatory/support functions* (Espejo 1989c). Viable systems emerge from the connectivity (i.e., communications and interactions) among primary activities and regulatory functions (see Chap. 9 for a detailed account of this connectivity). However, for collectives, whether an action is primary or regulatory is in the eye of the beholder; it depends among other aspects on the awareness that observers have about the collective's purposes and their own individual or group purposes. It is common to find that what keep collectives together are relationships rather than explicitly shared purposes. Often members of a collective strive for their own, rather than the collective's purposes, but are not prepared to defect. In practice this produces conflicts as different groups ascribe different unaligned purposes to their collective's actions.

The activities carried out by the library in a university, for instance, would normally be taken as regulatory/support activities. Academics and students may see them as an important support for their research and learning goals. However, if people working in the library see themselves as part of a unit whose purpose is keeping the state of the art in their traditional collections (books and journals) independently of the changing interests of lecturers and researchers, then it is likely that conflicts will arise. As a regulatory activity, the purpose ascribed to the library should be aligned to the purpose ascribed to the primary activities it supports, in this case research and teaching. In practical terms this means that the criteria to choose collections should be heavily loaded towards the interests of researchers and lecturers.

Producing a transformation in the environment (e.g., offering a successful service to customers, or increasing people's aesthetic awareness) is a highly complex relational process that depends on the collective's purposes. In a way these purposes are the 'problems' they want to solve in their surrounding or environment. Complexity emerges from the collective's relations with environmental agents, which may be the trigger for an organization. Demanding environments can stretch the collective and put pressure on their ingenuity. This stretching may transform the collective into a cohesive organization with problem solving capabilities.

The organization needs to find ways to amplify its own variety to match the variety of a demanding environment and ways to attenuate, but not 'kill', the environment's relevant variety to cope with it, hopefully making 'more with less' (i.e., reducing residual variety). This is a driver for problem solving and ingenuity. A powerful way to achieve amplification is to enable individual and teams' autonomy within the organization. Autonomy releases individuals' creativity and increases the organization's flexibility to deal locally with environmental variety. As for attenuation, the environmental complexity is not completely chaotic; it has structure itself. It comes, for instance, in chunks of connected customers and suppliers, or chunks of geographic needs or chunks of time in which services are required and so forth. These are the complexity drivers we mention in Chap. 4. An effective organizational structure maps these chunks of complexity (for a methodological recognition of these chunks see Chap. 8). How people in the organization chunk their environmental complexity is a matter of ingenuity. For instance, some may exploit creatively the difficulty to see connectivity in the light of their strategic intent and the technologies-in-use. Some may develop new technologies altogether. Whatever are the chunks they visualise and decide to respond to, the organization's structure should map them. This mapping is a consequence of Conant and Ashby's theorem that states 'every good regulator of a system must be a model of that system' (Conant and Ashby 1970).

An interesting case of a practical application of this theorem in a complex institutional set up took place in Colombia as part of a project to redesign the auditing processes of the National Auditing Office (NAO) (Espejo et al. 2001; Reyes 2001). The main purpose of NAO was to guarantee the transparency, efficiency and effectiveness of the resources used by public institutions in the country. In other words, for the State's organization this was a support/regulatory function. On the other hand, the State provides public goods and services to the population like education, health, justice, defence and so on. Over time institutions of different kinds have been created to produce these services: state industries, public universities, public hospitals, airports, schools and so forth. As we can see there is a natural way to group these institutions regarding the production of public goods and the Conant and Ashby's theorem tells us that NAO's structure should map the State's unfolding of complexity, as a regulatory function of the State's primary activities; in other words it should map these structural chunks that reflect the organization of the State.

Since, in general, individuals cannot cope in isolation with these chunks, organizations foster structurally their collaboration to form *autonomous units*, accountable for chunks of environmental complexity; these are the organization's primary activities. Each of these autonomous units is functionally specialised in producing an aspect of the organization's purposes. If, as an outcome of a learning process, they find that a number of these autonomous units could beneficially collaborate with each other to map a bigger chunk of environmental complexity, they are now recognising a larger autonomous unit embedding a number of autonomous units. Equally they may find the need to break an existing autonomous unit, say their total organization, into several units to produce some form of desirable functional specialisation and thus map better their relevant environmental complexity. Further structural unfolding may happen within each of the newly formed autonomous units or primary activities, suggesting even further specialisation. These are all learning processes, dynamically producing the organization's structure (see Chap. 8). These processes of *complexity unfolding* are at the core of how collectives structure the management of their purposes (see Fig. 6.1).

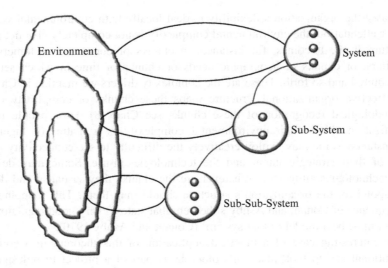

Fig. 6.1 Unfolding of complexity

The organization's total transformation is thus produced by the synergistic communications of multiple autonomous units. Whether these autonomous units are designed or are the outcome of self-organizing processes sensitive to the structure of the environment's complexity, is a complex question that requires empirical observations. However, some form of complexity unfolding happens in most complex situations and the challenge is to hypothesise alternatives that increase the organization's fit to the, to some degree, self-created environment; considering existing, available and new technologies.

The potentially large number of autonomous units or primary activities within the organization, structured in whatever form, define the organization's performing complexity. They produce its products and services. The exact number of structural levels and the number of autonomous units at each level is an empirical issue; however a good appreciation of the environment and also of the technologies available to cope with its complexity may help to anticipate successful structures, making the learning more effective. In all cases the structure is of autonomous units within autonomous units within autonomous units and so forth (see Fig. 6.1). And all autonomous units experience the same challenge, that is, to solve an often self-constructed problem, in a situation where their complexity is much lower than that of the relevant environment. The requisite structures to enable autonomy and cohesion are common to all of them; these are *recursive structures*. When the identification of autonomous units is directly related to a clarification of the purposes ascribed to an organization we name them primary activities.

Achieving the cohesion of primary activities within an organization requires regulatory capacity, which is produced by regulatory/support functions. The more regulatory capacity is kept at the level of small autonomous units, the smaller is likely to be the residual variety left to the attention of higher levels of administration and management. But, how much decentralization do members of the collective want and are prepared to accept? This is often a political, but also technological, social and cultural question. A highly centralized structure can be viable, but only at a high cost of coordination and support activities (see details in Chap. 9).

An autonomous unit is desirable if the collective gives a positive answer to the question: Do we want to make this unit viable? Answers to this question define an organization's espoused purposes. In a diagnostic mode it is possible to observe the actual organizational forms or structures matching the environmental complexity implied by these espoused purposes; if there is a mismatch it is possible to diagnose a dysfunctional organizational structure (see identity and structural archetypes in Chap. 12).

Functions such as personnel, finance, marketing, information services, etc. tend to fall in the category of *regulatory or support* functions. They produce the regulatory functions giving cohesion and adaptability to the primary activities and are crucial to the viability of the overall organization and of each of its embedded autonomous units. Regulatory/support functions are performed at different levels depending on the balance between centralization and decentralization accepted within the organization. Functions such as quality assurance and human resources management may need to be devolved in one form or another to each primary activity. Also, functions like finance and research and development may be kept more centralized. Making decisions about centralization/decentralization define the interactions between regulatory functions and primary activities. These decisions are central to the type of emergent organization, and the VSM is used to assess this emergent structure. This suggests that in any viable system there is, in one form or another, a complementarity between cohesion and autonomy. The challenge is to find design criteria to make this complementarity effective (see Chap. 9).

The concept of a recursive organization suggests that all autonomous units in an enterprise have (should have) a structure that gives them the capacity for meaning creation (i.e., policy making), regulation (i.e., management and services) and meaning production (i.e., implementation). It is not unusual to find that some of these capabilities are not embodied in the primary activities of modern enterprises. Unfortunately, these enterprises remain hierarchical in nature, in spite of all claims to the contrary. This implies an unnecessary restriction of people's autonomy and therefore a reduction in performance complexity. Autonomous units, to maintain a separate existence in their environment, need to create their own meanings (i.e., policies) as well as implement them. Etymologically autonomy means to govern oneself, but in this context autonomy means also to produce one's products.

From natural systems we learn that structurally there are two key mechanisms for viability. One is the mechanism that keeps the components together as a cohesive whole; this is the cohesion mechanism. The other is the mechanism that supports the organization's co-evolution with agents in its environment; this is the mechanism for adaptation. In what follows we will describe how these two mechanisms operate. For the sake of simplicity in the presentation, we will refer, for the most part, to the operation of these mechanisms for an enterprise; however, it must be remembered throughout that the same principles apply to all viable systems, at whatever level of structural recursion they find themselves.

For a collective to become an organization they need to achieve cohesion (see Chap. 5). Cohesion requires aligning individual and collective interests. This alignment does not imply that individuals and their collective have the same interests and purposes, but that however different these might be, the implementation of individuals' purposes produces the purposes collectively ascribed to the organization. Of course we may expect that organizational purposes constitute individual purposes in a cycle of mutual production and constitution. The cohesion mechanism explains how to achieve structurally this alignment at the same time of respecting autonomy. In other words, it explains the kinds of stable forms of communication that increase the chances of articulating the autonomous units' programmes with the organization's purposes. For the purpose of explaining this mechanism we distinguish between those resources and relations *producing* the organization's purposes, we call them the *implementation function*, and those resources and relations *steering* the implementation function in the direction of the collective's purposes; we call them the *cohesion function*.

All primary activities, whether real or virtual, formal or informal, *producing* the collective's purposes constitute the implementation function. It is not unusual to find out that the units that develop autonomy in a collective are not consistent with the collective's purposes. This discrepancy suggests that there is a distinction between their espoused theory and their theory-in-use (see archetypes in Chap. 12). In this situation the collective either adjusts its espoused purposes or creates the conditions for the emergence of desirable autonomy and the elimination of undesirable autonomy.

It is common that these discrepancies are the outcome of a series of contingencies in the historic development of the collective. They can also take many different manifestations. For instance the National Registry of Colombia (NRO) is a public institution with three primary activities: keeping records of the population (births, civil status and deaths); giving national identification cards (identity cards to people younger than 18 years old and citizen cards to people older than 18); and organizing public general elections (presidential, parliamentary, municipal and others). The identity espoused in the law and written in the official documents and strategic plans of the NRO were consistent with these three primary activities. However, there was an emergent fourth primary activity that nobody at this level had recognised.

Indeed, because the NRO kept records of all citizens, including fingerprints, other institutions were regularly asking for the identity records of people they were dealing with. For instance, the police needed to know the identity of a person whose fingerprint had been found in a crime scene; banks requested fingerprint checks of some customers and so on. Failure to respond to these requests accurately and in time could have undesirable consequences (e.g., letting a criminal offender go). Eventually the NRO found that it was dedicating significant resources (people, technology and money) to these requirements. The effect of this was that a primary activity had emerged de facto making the purpose-in-use of the NRO different to its espoused purpose. However, this espoused purpose remained unchallenged and unchanged for many years, affecting the autonomous development of this *unseen* primary activity and most importantly affecting the proper debate about its legitimacy.

Managing the coherence of established policies and their implementation is the purpose of the *cohesion function*. The cohesion function is constituted by resources whose purposes are, first to negotiate programmes and resources with its embedded primary activities or autonomous units in order to make local policies coherent with the organization's global policies, second to monitor the development and performance of these programmes over time to ensure that the local and global understanding of policies remains aligned and third to contribute to the definition of the organization's policies (see mechanism for adaptation below). Its fundamental concern is the organization's internal complexity, that is, the 'inside and now' (Beer 1979), of which it has to be an effective attenuator and enabler. It is pivotal in constituting a *cohesion mechanism*. For this the cohesion function needs an accurate appreciation of first the achievements and capabilities of primary activities, and second, their coordination potentials and requirements. In this sense the cohesion function is a *form of control* that respects and enables the autonomy of primary activities in the organization.

Unfortunately, as introduced earlier in this chapter and discussed in Chap. 2, control is a loaded term often related to hierarchical relationships and structures, which reduce the knowledge creation of an organization. Here we explain why this type of relationships is so prevalent and then we explain the cohesion mechanism, which is the VSM's response to this inadequate management of complexity.

Cohesion managers and people in primary activities often experience the *control dilemma* (Espejo 1989c): managers, having less variety about implementation activities than the people in the primary activities they control, cannot possibly maintain awareness of all that is going on with them, particularly if these units are increasingly challenged by environmental complexity. There is a natural 'information gap' between cohesion managers and people in primary activities; but managers know they are accountable for any loss of control. The information gap often leads to a feeling of discomfort and uncertainty on the part of management (questions such as, 'what is going on down there?' 'How do I know whether they're telling me the truth?' are likely to emerge in the context of their traditional hierarchical upbringing). This anxiety to know more tends to increase demands for information and reports and the undertaking of more investigations to keep 'in control'. However, in reality these demands and instructions only serve to reduce the response complexity of people in primary activities, making them less flexible, as they struggle to fulfil increased management requirements at the expense of responding to their local environmental demands. At the very time that these autonomous units need more flexibility to respond effectively to environmental pressures, managers' behaviour is reducing this flexibility. However, the Law of Requisite Variety asserts itself and managers in the cohesion function cannot win with this type of control strategy. This strategy reduces the complexity of implementation units, hindering their autonomous development and performance, and at the same time it increases the residual complexity that managers need to deal with. This kind of relationship is the hallmark of hierarchies and bureaucracies.

Sometimes this control dilemma is very difficult to observe. The general manager of the City of Bogotá's Audit Office (CAO) decided to support a new discourse about control, one based on the idea of self-regulation; he sent a memorandum to his subordinates telling them to inform managers of the City's institutions about this new policy. Each institution had to run a self-diagnosis at the end of the year to report its main drawbacks. By the end of the first year CAO's general manager, pressed for results by the political party that had appointed him, started to get nervous. This party wanted to build a case against the City's Mayor who belonged to the opposite party. CAO's general manager decided then to send another memo to all managers of local public institutions asking them to include in their reports a form with some additional information. This form had over 250 variables, most of them of no use whatsoever for the management of each individual institution. However, being an official requirement from the auditing office, they had to assign resources to fill in the form. Of course they did not believe in CAO's self-regulation discourse anymore. On the other hand, at the end of the reporting period people in the CAO received so much information from the 50 regulated public institutions that they did not have the capacity to process and check it all. At the same time, quite naturally these public institutions were increasingly challenged by more demanding customers. The quality of CAO's report produced out of all this was heavily questioned. Managers of the 50 public institutions realized this lack of processing capacity and increasingly carried out their activities concealing information. Of course people in the CAO realized that as well and started to check all information in detail. After all these cat and mouse exchanges people felt that there were two main lies in the auditing practices. The first lie was what auditors used to say when they first visited the manager of a public institution: 'Sir/Madam we are here to serve you'; the second lie was the answer of the manager: 'You are very welcome!'.

Control games with negative effects are common phenomena in these circumstances. These are interpersonal games in which, on the one hand, senior management uses the allocation of resources as a means of exercising control power, and on the other, local management uses its better knowledge of implementation to manipulate senior management into unchecked decisions. Most of the time, these games are not the outcome of deliberate actions, but simply of poor interpersonal interactions.

In summary, as primary activities feel the pressure from agents in their environment to become more flexible and sophisticated, managers sense larger information gaps and respond with traditional control strategies that reduce flexibility and produce larger bureaucracies, precisely when there is a need for greater flexibility. A proliferation of control games is the likely result.

From the perspective of complexity management strategies the challenge is how to achieve the cohesion of primary activities despite corporate managers experiencing these unavoidable information gaps. Or more precisely, how is it possible to match effectively the desirably large amplification complexity of autonomous primary activities with the unavoidable low variety of management? Indeed, autonomy is a requirement to make units more responsive to agents in their relevant environment, and the low variety of managers is in their very fabric as human beings. This question leads to another question, how to reduce the residual variety that is relevant to management at the same time of increasing the organization's response capacity. Indeed, the more local problem-solving is enabled within autonomous units the less implementation variety is left unattended by those close to the task, and therefore the smaller is the residual variety left for the attention of management. The VSM gives us advice for this purpose; the design of the *cohesion mechanism*, which assumes that the collective has evolved into a number of primary activities, embedded in the collective enterprise, itself a primary activity at a more global level (e.g., the industry). This design is driven by three guiding principles (Espejo 1989c).

1. *Negotiate operational programmes minimising the use of direct commands*

Figure 6.2 shows the operation of the cohesion function in relation to three primary activities (e.g., operational divisions in an enterprise), which are to a greater or lesser extent interdependent by virtue of the fact that they belong to the same organization. Indeed, defining primary activities and working out their inter-dependences challenge the ingenuity of the cohesion function. Primary activities may interact operationally, by one providing inputs to another, or through the environment, for example through an overlap in the markets they serve, or through sharing technologies or through any other ingenious form of seeing them as part of the same whole. A key role of the cohesion function, as its name suggests, is to achieve a degree of cohesion among these primary activities by fostering their self-regulation and self-organization through these overlaps.

The central vertical channel between the cohesion function and the management of each of the three primary activities (e.g., divisions in a company) is the communication channel through which senior management negotiates programmes with

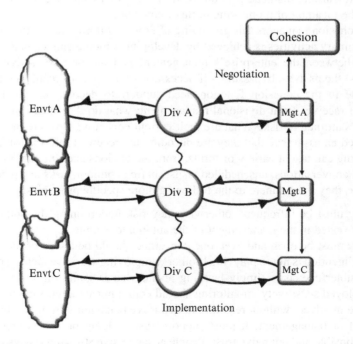

Fig. 6.2 Negotiation of resources

divisional management. Also, it is the channel through which performance reports are passed and corporate intervention takes place (e.g., issuing safety policies in the company). As we have seen above, however, overloading this channel, confusing it with a command channel, only leads to control dilemmas. No doubt, one way of reducing direct commands is making use of 'exception reporting', common in most organizations today, and equally 'management by objectives' that avoids too much interference and helps management to 'see the wood from the trees'. Yet these devices are not in themselves sufficient to bridge the communication gaps between managers at different structural levels. They may deal with information overload but not with communication problems of maintaining organizational cohesion and developing synergy among autonomous units. The next two 'design criteria' address these issues.

2. *Use sporadic monitoring – with discretion*

The communication problem emerges from primary activities at two different structural levels; the enterprise and the autonomous divisions, trying to communicate with each other. Enterprise and divisions as autonomous units have their own structural determination. Neither side can assume that the other assigns the same meanings to the information they share. Making this assumption would deny the autonomy of the other, which of course is what happens with lower level units within hierarchies. Giving meaning to the shared information requires its contextualisation and this implies crossing sporadically the boundaries of the autonomous units, and learning firsthand the context from which they produce the information. This is the meaning of monitoring in this framework.

For cohesion managers this grounding of flowing information in the operations of the primary activities is achieved by developing a monitoring channel that runs *directly* between the enterprise's management and the primary activities (e.g., divisions) themselves, bypassing – if necessary – their management (see Fig. 6.3).

People in the cohesion function need support to decode the accountability reports it receives from divisional management; what do they mean? What is the division's attitude to risk? What are their current concerns? How are they coping? They need an assurance that they are decoding the received information properly. Monitoring can take a variety of forms, from the obvious auditing programmes, to informal conversations, unscheduled visits, sharing common tasks and many more. However, they must adhere to the following more specific principles:

(a) They must be infrequent, otherwise they risk undermining the authority and trust vested in the management of the autonomous units.
(b) They must be open and everyone concerned should be aware of these events. The intention is not to play 'big brother', employing secretive tactics and games of subterfuge; it is simply learning about what is going on at first hand. If employed sensitively, monitoring should communicate a message of caring to those involved, without resulting in defensive behaviours from the 'by passed' level of management. It must support trust building processes that produce responsible and not naive trust. People at successive structural levels trust each

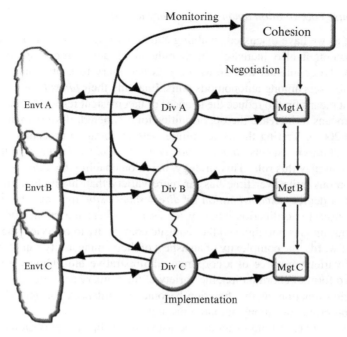

Fig. 6.3 Monitoring of primary activities

other because they are communicating and through these communications they are assessing the competence and sincerity of each other.

(c) In general, it must happen only in between successive structural levels. Monitoring activities at several levels below, like the traditional 'management by walking around' of senior managers not only by-passes several levels of management, which is a poor strategy to manage complexity, but more significantly may inhibit necessary communications in between. However, it may be necessary when local structural levels experience situations that go beyond their own management and therefore need the attention of higher levels of recursion; these exceptions are Beer's algedonic signals (Beer 1979).

Negotiation of programmes and their monitoring are the two sides of the same coin, that is, two sides of the same cohesion function.[1] One without the other is meaningless. Programmes for which there is no negotiating capacity are not negotiated. 'Negotiation' without understanding the other side is gaming and not negotiation. *Trust between negotiating partners is what monitoring should bring into the cohesion function* (Espejo 2001).

---

[1]In Beer's terminology the Cohesion Function is System 3 and monitoring is System 3*; in our view these two systems are the two sides of the same coin and therefore treating them as independent of each other is an inadequate fragmentation.

3. *Maximise coordination among the primary activities*

While, as we have discussed, enabling autonomy improves the flexibility of the viable system, it also increases the likelihood of units producing inconsistent responses. To counteract this drawback it is necessary to enable and if possible design stabilisers among autonomous units. Enabling their *lateral communications* is indeed a means first to reduce the chances of inconsistent responses and second it is also a means to increase the opportunities for a coherent development (see also Galbraith 2002). Sharing the same culture, setting common procedures and standards in all those aspects *that are not central to the primary activities' own purposes* can play this role. This strategy, based on enabling the *mutual regulation* of autonomous units over time has far more variety than hierarchical regulation. Naturally, a degree of *coordination by direct supervision* may also be necessary. This is a useful coordination strategy for aspects where the connectivity among autonomous units is not high and the requisite complexity to overview them is low, or in other words, the complexity of an aspect of their connectivity can be contained by a low variety resource of a corporate administrative unit. Otherwise, being a centralized form of coordination, the variety of the primary activities may overload the cohesion function, as this function becomes a bottleneck for unresolved communication problems among autonomous units.

Whether we are talking of mutual adjustments or direct supervision an organization depends on a *coordination function* to enable autonomy. It is a critical function to enable connectivity and therefore cohesion. The stronger is the coordination function the less residual variety is left for the attention of the cohesion function, and the more space primary activities have to assert their autonomy. The coordination function provides a common language that facilitates lateral communications among autonomous units and thus enables local problem solving. Coordination by mutual adjustment takes place in the moment-to-moment actions of people, and as such it may absorb far more complexity than any formal device to coordinate people's actions from above.

Unfortunately, it is not unusual for those operating in traditional hierarchies to perceive the setting of standards as bureaucratic interference with their personal freedom. This is partly because standards appear as instructions coming down the line ('Here we go again, management throwing its weight around!') instead of lateral support, designed to make their lives easier in the longer term. However, if people in regulatory (support) functions can learn to enable people's coordination, communicating their purposes with greater clarity, they may begin to change this attitude; and if such guidelines are clearly couched in a language different from that of direct commands and instructions, their acceptance may increase.

Summing up, the *coordination function* is a powerful, high variety function: the stronger it becomes, the greater the space for self-regulation within the *implementation function*, thus reducing the residual variety that needs attention of the *cohesion function* and the greater the autonomy exercised by the lower structural levels. Together cohesion, coordination and implementation constitute the *cohesion mechanism* (see Fig. 6.4).

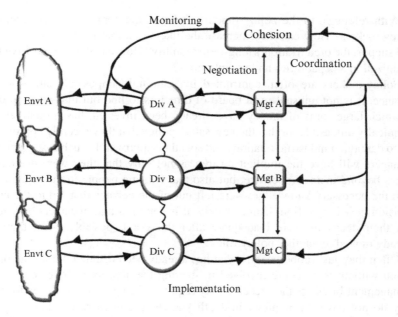

Fig. 6.4 Cohesion mechanism

The cohesion mechanism is a mutual control strategy, in the sense of achieving a dynamic but stable relationship between corporate managers and primary activities at a high level of performance.[2]

But it is not enough for the collective to become a cohesive whole to maintain viability; in addition this cohesive whole must be *adaptive* to changes in its environment. This is the hallmark of viability and a necessary condition to transform the collective into an organization. An effective enterprise is one that not only 'does things right' but is also able to find the 'right things to do'. Moreover, a *responsible enterprise* is one that finds ethical means to do the right things. Capacities for adaptation and sensitivity to the eco-system are normally associated with the enterprise's normative and strategic levels of management.

The three types of resources involved in adaptation are: first, those focused on the 'inside and now', that is those constituting the cohesion function; second, those focused on the 'outside and then' (Beer 1979) and third, those giving closure to the organization. These last two are referred to as the *intelligence function* and *policy function* respectively. These resources together with their relations constitute the *mechanism for adaptation*. In what follows we discuss the complexity management strategies and structures required for adaptation.

---

[2]Earlier versions of this model (Espejo 1989c) talked about the monitoring-control mechanism; however the socially negative connotation of control suggested the convenience to talk about the cohesion mechanism. What is apparent is that the above discussion has offered a *control strategy* that is very different to the hierarchical, coercive strategy.

With reference to the policy function, what is the appropriate contribution of policy-makers? How can they increase the likelihood that their vision and values will support the organization's long-term viability? How can they be sensitive to the organization's capabilities and potentialities?

Policy-makers are often confronted by seemingly impossible situations. For instance, it is not unusual for a board of directors to find out that a new product, in which large sums of money have already been invested, has no market, or is technically unfeasible; or that the new salary policy that they recently approved has led to damaging industrial relations and social disapproval. In such cases, hopefully managers will have the implicit awareness not only that they were deciding on issues beyond their competence, but also that existing people in the organization, with the necessary knowledge, were left out of the debates that led to the critical decision now in question. Unfortunately, it is common that managers only realise that their decisions were inadequate after the event, possibly when they have already moved to another policy role.

Often they just rubber-stamp what has already been decided within the organization without them being involved in steering the appropriate debates. Also the management briefings they receive may require judgments about issues for which they do not have the required in-depth knowledge. In these conditions, policy-makers may either abdicate their responsibility completely by blindly following internal advice, or they may take a 'strategic decision' (i.e., a leap in the dark), and hope for the best.

If policy-makers are often in the invidious position of deciding issues that are beyond their competence, either because of the inadequate processes followed in their study or because their content is too complex for their scrutiny, how can they keep control of these policies? In other words, how can they be accountable for the organization's policies?

Quite naturally the complexity of policy-makers to deal with policy issues is much lower than the organization's complexity focused on these issues, therefore, they must have effective attenuators to reduce this complexity and bring it within range of their limited response capacity. In practice this means that most of the complexity has to be absorbed within the structure only leaving a small residual variety for their attention.

In broad terms there are two main sources of complexity for policy-makers: that of the inside organization now, or its *internal environment*, and that of the outside organization challenging its longer term viability, or its *problematic environment*. The former is concerned with the conditions occurring within the organization; the quality of its structure, the configuration of its capabilities and in general all those aspects that ground policies in operational realities. The latter is concerned with the 'outside and then' of possible future environmental opportunities and threats; it is concerned both with the turbulences likely to make bumpy the organization's gliding in its environment, and the corridors for free and exhilarating flying. We have referred to these two structural attenuators of complexity as the organization's *cohesion* and *intelligence* functions (see Fig. 6.5).

Fig. 6.5 Adaptation
mechanism

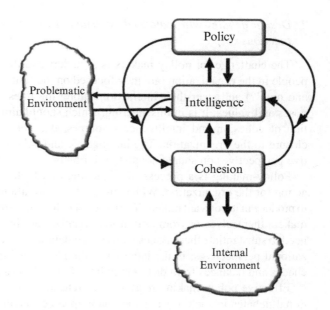

These functions exist in one form or another in any *viable* organization, but are not necessarily related to well-defined entities in the organization chart: it is perfectly possible, for example, that one department within an enterprise has both intelligence and cohesion functions, and that in a small organization one individual fulfils both functions. The essential question is how to relate these resources in order to make policy-making more effective? The basic principles are as follows:

1. *Reduce the residual variety relevant to policy-makers*

There is no need for policy makers to be 'experts' either in their industry or the technologies they use. In a way, it can be argued that policy-makers should avoid meddling with content; the details of organizational issues are complex enough to be beyond their personal attention. The likelihood is that the study of options and related checks and balances need the participation and contributions of many people within the organization. These people are the ones in the end offering the options for policy-making. Policy makers should provide clarity about the overall direction, values and purposes of the organization, as well as design, at the highest level, the conditions for organizational effectiveness. Whether their understanding of technical issues is good or otherwise, they will not have time to go deep into them. Their appreciation of these issues should be sufficient to maintain an informed communication with intelligence and cohesion resources, after these resources have gone through the necessary checks and balances among themselves to articulate options. Policy makers should only manage the residual variety left unattended by the interactions between cohesion and intelligence resources. Indeed, to remain in control of the policy processes the briefings reaching them need to make limited demands on their attention, consistent with their contextualised response capacity.

2. *Design debates with balanced contributions of the cohesion and intelligence functions*

The challenge for policy-makers is to understand the systemic contributions of people in the organization (are they focused on the 'outside and then' or the 'inside and now'?) and steer their interactions along the lines of the organization's purposes and values. It is in this steering, which should aim at the balanced contribution of cohesion and intelligence resources, that selecting among options gives closure to the organization. The intelligence and cohesion functions offer alternative perspectives on shared adaptation problems.

Policy-making is a process, the outcome of which is the choice of courses of action for the organization. Which are the transformations the organization intends to produce in its relevant milieu? The issues of policy concern may stem from the policy-makers themselves or from within the organization. In the former case, there is a need to substantiate these issues with further detailed research from different organizational perspectives; in the latter case, the ideas need to be subjected to detailed checks and balances from different points of view *before* they reach policy-makers.

Effective policy-making requires the orchestration and monitoring of organizational debates in such a way as to enable people to contribute to the best of their abilities to organizational adaptation and survival. This is the meaning of the arrows that start from the policy function and go to the arrows that relate the intelligence and cohesion functions in Fig. 6.5. It follows from this point, and the concept of structural recursion that the policy-making process should happen not just at the level of the global enterprise but also within all primary activities, at all structural levels. Extensive debates within the organization among different and opposing viewpoints should produce informed conclusions and improve the quality of policy briefings. Policy-makers should only be exposed to issues and alternatives that have been properly examined in this way.

A lack of balance in the intelligence and cohesion resources for a policy issue damages the performance of the policy function. For example, if intelligence produces issues of policy relevance at a higher rate and detail than the cohesion function can cope with, then policy-makers will receive views of external possibilities unchecked by on-the-ground management; or if all the issues reaching policy are concerned with matters of internal efficiency, vital signals from the wider external problematic environment may be overlooked. Decisions over-influenced by either of the two functions are likely to be both costly and ineffective.

3. *Make intelligence and cohesion highly interconnected*

The effectiveness of the intelligence and cohesion functions depends not only on purposeful and balanced debates *among managers* or senior people *representing* the 'inside and now' and the 'outside and then', but more to the point by the on-going interactions and communications of *all* people constituting the cohesion and intelligence functions. These are the resources, for instance, doing research and development and monitoring of primary activities. The allocation of resources for these purposes and their balanced interactions also influence policy-making.

If communications between these resources were weak then policy-makers would not only be receiving unchecked information independently from both sides, but they would be in the invidious task of having to make the checks and balances themselves. The policy-makers would be the main communication channels between two separate sets of people, which, in enterprises of any size, deal with far more complexity than the policy function itself could possibly hope to cope with.

This situation may sound far-fetched, but how many enterprises have established centralized research and development departments far removed from those managing their current affairs? And how often is manufacturing brought into discussions on new product development as an after-thought, when the marketing and technical teams have already defined all the characteristics of the new product? Indeed, current information and communication technologies offer a hope in overcoming these structural problems.

Both functions, therefore, need to be highly interconnected at the operational level. This is the meaning of the arrows that relate the intelligence and cohesion functions in Fig. 6.5. When this is the case, most of the issues emerging from each side can be crosschecked with reference to the other at multiple levels before reaching the stage of policy options for the attention of the policy makers.

In the light of the above considerations, the role of policy-makers, or leaders at all levels of the enterprise, may be elaborated as follows: first, by identifying key issues of organizational concern; second, by recognising the contributions that different people and groups of the organization can bring into the policy-process (i.e., to form working teams containing a balanced representation of the intelligence and cohesion functions, and for this they need good models of how the organization structure works with reference to the organization's purposes); third, by monitoring the interactions of all those constituting these functions as they debate, cogitate and appreciate issues and structure options in the light of the organization's purposes and values. This is the mechanism for adaptation, which of course is far more chaotic and complex than the above description may suggest (Fig. 6.5).

We have now completed our discussion of complexity management strategies for the organization's cohesion and adaptation, now we will relate them to offer a view of the Viable System Model.

Figure 6.6 shows how the two main mechanisms for viability – those of adaptation and cohesion – are combined to define the organization structure of a viable system. Figure 6.7, in turns, shows these mechanisms taking into account the unfolding of complexity. This figure makes apparent the principle of structural recursion; this is the complete model, which shows a simple structure of an organization with two primary activities, each of which contains two primary activities. For the purpose of a more detailed study, a separate VSM can be drawn for each of the primary activities at each structural level, using a simple labelling system to relate the models to the unfolding of a complexity model.

The key proposition arising from our study of viability is that in truly viable systems, policy, intelligence, cohesion, coordination and implementation are distributed at *all* structural levels (Beer 1979, 1985). In complex environments, people's limited capacity to handle variety makes recursive structures a necessity rather than

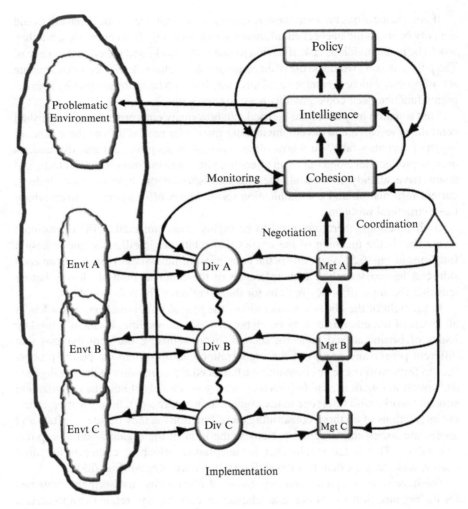

Fig. 6.6 The viable system model for one autonomous unit

an option. If all autonomous units within an organization are designed to contain these self-managing properties, then the organization's capacity for adaptation and learning is widely enlarged.

The Viable System Model is primarily a tool to observe an organization's strategy to manage complexity and to support the design of effective control and communication structures. As a problem-solving tool, it provides a common language to help groups within an organization to learn and interrelate more effectively. The use of the VSM as a framework for diagnosing and design has been extensive (Espejo 1989b; Espejo and Reyes 2001; Reyes 2001; Christopher 2007; Perez Rios 2008). It has been applied in a wide variety of organizational problem-solving contexts. This range has been from large private companies and public institutions to small companies and NGOs in many different countries. This

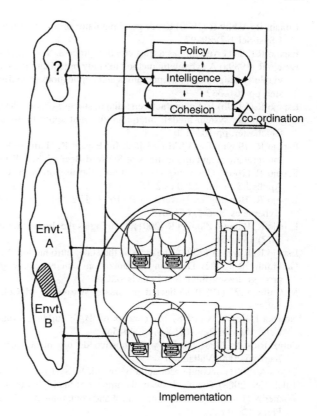

Fig. 6.7 A recursive organization

extensive application of the model and their supporting concepts has allowed us to recognise a group of recurrent problems that we identify as archetypical (Espejo 2008). These archetypes are explained in Chap. 12.

On the other hand, explaining in detail how to use the VSM as a diagnostic and design tool for effective management is the purpose of the Viplan Method (Espejo 1989a; Espejo et al. 1999). The following chapters explain this method.

References

Ashby R (1952) Design for a brain. Wiley, New York

Ashby R (1964) An introduction to cybernetics. Methuen, London

Beer S (1979) The heart of enterprise. Wiley, Chichester

Beer S (1981) Brain of the firm, 2nd edition. Wiley, Chichester

Beer S (1985) Diagnosing the system for organizations. Wiley, Chichester

Beer S (2009) The culpabliss error: a calculus of ethics for a systemic world. In: Whittaker D (ed) Think before you think: social complexity and knowledge of knowing. Wavestone Press, Charlbury, Oxfordshire, pp 233–247

Christopher WF (2007) Holistic management: managing what matters for company success. Wiley, Hoboken, NJ

Conant R, Ashby R (1970) Every good regulator of a system must be a model of that system. Int J Syst Sci 1(2):89–97

Espejo R (2001) Auditing as a trust creation process. Syst Pract Act Res 14(2):215–236

Espejo R (1989a) A cybernetic method to study organizations. In: Espejo R, Harnden R (eds) The viable system model: interpretations and applications of Stafford Beer's VSM. Wiley, Chichester, pp 361–382

Espejo R (1989b) PM manufacturers: diagnostic use of the VSM. In: Espejo R, Harnden R (eds) The viable system model: interpretations and applications of Stafford Beer's VSM. Wiley, Chichester, pp 103–120

Espejo R (1989c) The VSM revisited. In: Espejo R, Harnden R (eds) The viable system model: interpretations and applications of Stafford Beer's VSM. Wiley, Chichester, pp 77–100

Espejo R (2008) Observing organizations: the use of identity and structural archetypes. Int J Applied Systemic Studies 2(1/2):6–24

Espejo R, Bowling D, Hoverstadt P (1999) The viable system model and the viplan software. Kybernetes 28(6/7):661–678

Espejo R, Bula G, Zarama R (2001) Auditing as the dissolution of corruption. Syst Pract Act Res 14(2):139–156

Espejo R, Reyes A (2001) The state of the state: introduction. Syst Pract Act Res 14(2):135–137

Galbraith JR (2002) Designing organizations: an executive guide to strategy, structure and process. Jossey-Bass, San Francisco, CA

McCulloch W (1989) Collected papers of Warren S. McCulloch. Intersystems Publications, Salinas, CA

Nonaka I, Konno N (1998) The concept of 'BA': building a foundation for knowledge creation. Calif Manage Rev 40(1 spring):40–54

Perez Rios J (2008) Diseño y diagnostico de organizaciones viables: un enfoque sistemico. Iberfora 2000, Valladolid

Reyes A (2001) Second-order auditing practices. Syst Pract Act Res 14(2):157–180

Taleb NN (2008) The black swan: the impact of the highly improbable. Penguin, London

Wiener N (1948) Cybernetics: or control and communication in the animal and the machine. MIT Press, Cambridge, MA

Part II
Viplan Method

Chapter 6 is the platform to explore the issue of how to study the viability of organizational systems in complex environments. Our main concern in the following four chapters is exploring a method to study an organization's strategies to manage this complexity. This is the Viplan Method that is offered as a heuristic useful for decisions to improve the *performance* of an organization.

The purpose of the Viplan Method is to diagnose and design organizational structures (Espejo 1988; Espejo and Bowling 1996; Espejo et al. 1999). It has been used to highlight structural shortcomings but also to support organizational design. Diagnosing is like producing a snapshot of structural relations at the time observations are made. Designing is the more interesting mode of application of the method; it is not producing a blueprint to achieve a desirable organization. It is an on-going learning process in which actors use the VSM as a performative tool; they make decisions using this model as a heuristic and assess in real-time the consequences of their actions and the organization's performance. Since the environment's complexity is exceedingly large there is no point to aim at a target as if it were fixed. Designing is the ongoing reconfiguration of resources to achieve an adequate and sustainable performance. The implication of design as a problem solving approach is the focus of Part III of this book.

The method is developed in the next four chapters.

Chapter 7 discusses *naming systems* as a tool to explore an organization's identity. We relate this identity to purpose and explain Beer's dictum that 'the purpose of the system is what it does' (Beer 1985). Naming systems pays particular attention to this doing.

Chapter 8 discusses producing *technological and structural models* and uses them to hypothesise the organization's *unfolding of its complexity* or *structural recursion. Technological and structural models* are elaborations of the organization's transformation. Viplan guides the user to work out the chunks of complexity necessary to perform this transformation in the organization's environment. These chunks are the components of technological and structural models at different levels of aggregation. Some of these chunks can be hypothesised as *primary activities* of the organizational system. Others can be considered support activities or indeed contracted out to third organizations. Those interrelated chunks that are accepted as primary activities provide the template *for* the organization's strategy to cope with environmental complexity. On their turn, chunks within chunks can be hypothesised as primary activities at more detailed structural levels. Primary activities at different structural levels define the organization's *unfolding of its complexity.*

Chapter 9 is focused on the last two steps of the method and is complemented by Chap. 10, which offers a detailed discussion of business, organizational and information processes and in doing so it offers an approach to assess performance and discuss the organization's *variety engineering.* Chapter 9 maps the organization's resources onto *the Recursion-Functions table.* This table maps the primary activities that are contained within primary activities and the *functional resources* that support their cohesion and adaptation. The table is a model for the configuration of the resources creating, regulating and producing the organization and its primary activities. These resources may be centralized or decentralized according to the enterprise's strategy to deploy its resources and available technology. In particular the table makes apparent the enterprise's strategy to distribute complexity. Resources are then mapped onto the VSM's systemic functions – policy, intelligence, cohesion, coordination and implementation – and the mechanisms for cohesion and adaptation. The organization's performance is the acid test for the adequacy of its strategies to manage complexity. A method to assess this performance is the focus of Chap. 10.

References

Beer S (1985) Diagnosing the system for organizations. Wiley, Chichester

Espejo R (1988) A cybernetic methodology to study and design human activities, PhD Thesis Management centre. University of Aston, Birmingham

Espejo R, Bowling D (1996) Viplan learning system: a method to learn the viable system model. Syncho, Ltd., Birmingham (www.syncho.com)

Espejo R, Bowling D, Hoverstadt P (1999) The viable system model and the viplan software. Kybernetes 28(6/7):661–678

Chapter 7
Naming Systems: Tool to Study Organizational Identity

Abstract Organizational systems are the main object of observation and study in this book. This is the first chapter of four that build up the Viplan Method to study organizational systems. This method is a heuristic, useful in taking decisions to improve an organization's effectiveness. VIPLAN stands for viability planning. It starts by addressing questions such as: What does the organization do? Who are its stakeholders? How can we differentiate this organization from others? These questions point to the discussion of the organization's identity as an issue regarding its description. In this chapter we focus on these questions using a tool called naming systems. We explain the use of naming systems as a suitable methodological tool to guide identity workshops in this regard. We also introduce the notion of the enabling viewpoint as the viewpoint using the Viplan Method to facilitate the modelling of this organization. A concrete output of this initial step of the method is a set of appropriate names describing the organization in focus in terms of a value added transformation process involving a set of relevant participants. Each of these names can then be used as an input for the next two steps of the method; technological and structural modelling and the unfolding of complexity.

At the end of Chap. 5 we made the distinction between an operational and a black box definition of identity. Though identity emerges from stakeholders' relationships, for observers it is the organization's doing that makes this identity apparent. This is a black box perspective of an organization's identity, which emerges from the recognition it receives from others. Similar to individual identity, organizational identity also depends on recognition; organizations are exceedingly complex and observers work out their identities by ascribing meanings to what they do. In particular it is *stakeholders* that ascribe meanings to this doing from their own viewpoints. Lack of stakeholders' recognition implies for the organization weak or non-existent relationships, that is, weak or non-existent identity. At the same time, in a duality of mutual dependence, operationally identity relates to closure, wholeness, self-reference and relationships. Stafford Beer emphasises closure and cohesion. 'Closure is the snake that is eating its own tail ... Closure stops the entire system from exploding in shattered fragments to the ends of the universe ... Closure is the talisman of identity' (Beer 1979, p. 260). Identity is what allows us

R. Espejo and A. Reyes, *Organizational Systems*,
DOI 10.1007/978-3-642-19109-1_7, © Springer-Verlag Berlin Heidelberg 2011

to see an organization as a whole rather than just as a set of unrelated parts (Beer 1979, p. 418).

The black box definition of identity focuses attention on the organization's transformation of some inputs into some outputs, which is the platform we use to measure an organization's complexity in this part of the book. This is done using the Viplan Method.

The Viplan Method addresses questions such as: What does the organization do? Who are its stakeholders? What meanings do stakeholders ascribe to this doing? How can we differentiate this organization from others? What are their boundaries? These questions point to the discussion of the organization's identity and its description. In this chapter we answer these questions using a tool called *naming systems*.

Our interest is producing debatable descriptions for organizations, which implies making apparent the relevant observers that produce these descriptions. If we are talking about a hospital, for instance, I may observe and produce some descriptions of the hospital but if I do not have any relation with this hospital, it is quite possible that these descriptions will not affect at all what the hospital does. However, if I am currently a patient of the hospital it is possible that my observations and descriptions may have some relevance to what the hospital does, at least in the immediate services I get at the moment of my observations (e.g., complaints). Of course the quality and relevance of an individual's observation may differ enormously from one person to another. We could imagine the differences in the descriptions of a hospital produced by its general manager, or by a group of general practitioners in the community where the hospital is located, or by a doctor who is regularly carrying out surgeries there, or by a group of nurses attending cancer patients, or by a visiting auditing group from the Department of Health or by a patient that has been treated there regularly during the past 6 months. All of them, if asked, may produce descriptions of their observations regarding this particular hospital. They are what we call different *viewpoints* of this hospital. In what follows we will examine the importance of viewpoints in naming organizations.

As we mentioned in Chap. 1, different observers may see (i.e., distinguish) and produce different descriptions of the same situation. A very popular way to illustrate this is by looking at the following picture (Fig. 7.1). Take a few seconds to observe it. What do you see?

You may see a young fellow with a cowboy-type of hat, wearing a handkerchief around his neck and looking toward the right hand side of this page. If you do not see him, do not worry, perhaps what you are seeing is an old man wearing a similar type of hat instead. If you are able to see both of them it is quite nice but if you are not able to see any of them then you may worry about the quality of your sight.

In the following two versions of the same picture we have stressed some of the parts of the picture to facilitate making these distinctions. Try again. Now, do you see both images? (Fig. 7.2)

If we now ask you, what is really depicted in Fig. 7.1, what would your answer be? Is it a young man or is it an old man? The point is that these are not valid questions; it could be both; you may describe it either as an old man or as a young man (or both) if you are able to do the distinctions. In fact, when you ask a group of

Fig. 7.1 An example of different viewpoints[1]

Fig. 7.2 A revised version of 'my husband and my father-in-law' drawing

people what do they see when they look at it you will find that some of them are able to see the young, some others (usually fewer) will see the old man and even fewer will see both. Different viewpoints will see different things in a situation. Here a group of people sharing the same source for their observations and descriptions constitutes a viewpoint, so in this example we may have three different viewpoints.

---

[1]Drawn by Jack Botwinick under the title of 'My husband and my father-in-law' http://www. google.com/images?hl=en&rlz=1G1GGLQ_ENUK317&q=Jack+Botwinick&um=1&ie=UTF-8&source=univ&ei=jLLaTPnoDZO7hAe_iLnPAg&sa=X&oi=image_result_group&ct=title&resnum= 1&ved=0CCkQsAQwAA

Let us consider another example. Take some minutes to examine the following picture (Fig. 7.3). What do you see?

Do you see the Indian looking towards the left? Notice that if you do, the dark area of the picture is part of the figure you see, indeed, it *is* the dark hair of the Indian. However, it is possible that you can also see an Eskimo in this drawing. Look carefully, the Eskimo is facing backwards and is wearing a white coat. In this case, the dark area of the image is *not* part of the figure we are now distinguishing (i.e., the Eskimo). In fact, if we remove this part from the drawing it is quite easy to see the Eskimo (Fig. 7.4).

Therefore, another characteristic of different viewpoints is that they *construct* their distinctions differently. In other words, by looking at a situation, different viewpoints recognize some parts as belonging to the distinction they do while others reject them as parts of their own distinctions, as the example of the Indian-Eskimo illustrates.

Fig. 7.3 Another example of different viewpoints

Fig. 7.4 The Eskimo

Fig. 7.5 A change in perspective may alter a description

One last example is shown in Fig. 7.5. If you look at the figure on the left, you surely may agree that it corresponds to a frog, whereas on the right you will see a drawing of a horse. However, if you look again carefully, you may notice that by rotating the figure 90° anticlockwise on the left, then you will get exactly the other one. Again this nicely illustrates how a change in perspective may alter the description produced by an observer in a particular situation.

In an organizational context the perspective of a viewpoint is determined by both its particular ontogeny (see Chap. 1) and by the relations it sustains with others in the organization. In Fig. 7.6 we illustrate this point.

Here we have two viewpoints referring to what an organization does. The first one may just see the production of cars as the outcome of a factory while the other may see principally environmental pollution. Although both may be looking apparently at the same organization (i.e., the same network of closed relations), their own concerns, values and histories impinge on them to ascribe different purposes. So, what is, at the end, the purpose of this organization? Well, asking this question is similar to ask what is really in Fig. 7.3, an Eskimo or an Indian?

Of course, we can have at least as many different purposes ascribed to a particular organization as there are different viewpoints observing it. So, what can we do? Our claim is that in methodological terms, to answer this question and the ones at the beginning of this chapter, relevant viewpoints need to be ascribed to the organization. For instance, producing cars within acceptable environmental standards could be a shared purpose of relevant viewpoints of the car factory depicted in Fig. 7.6.

But who are these relevant viewpoints? We claim that those that have a stake in the organization; its *stakeholders* are considered as relevant viewpoints. Let us stress that a person or a group may have one or several viewpoints about a particular organization.

Fig. 7.6 Viewpoints may ascribe different purposes to an organization (Espejo et al. 1996)

We distinguish five main types of stakeholders: first, those carrying out the work of the organization (its *Actors*), that is, those producing its products or delivering its services; those providing the resources needed to produce its products or services (its *Suppliers*); those who receive these products or services (its *Customers*); those responsible for steering and adapting the organization (its *Owners*) and finally those with an influence on the context in which the organization operates (its *Interveners*). In short, the stakeholders are not just the owners and employees of the organization but also those who provide resources, receive products and services and challenge/influence its outcomes.

Remember that in Chap. 5 we said that the identity of an organization is what this organization *is* in the sense that this identity is constituted in the operational domain of its stakeholders by the relationships they recurrently produce and reproduce. From our perspective these relationships reflect the stakeholders' management of complexity. Purposes-in-use[2] are the meanings stakeholders experience in these

---

[2]Purpose-in-use as opposed to espoused purpose is a distinction mentioned in a previous chapter following Argyris and Schon (1978).

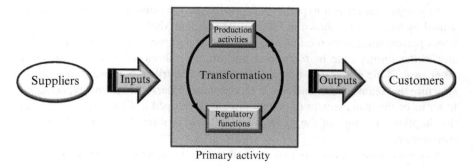

Fig. 7.7 An organization as a primary activity

relationships. They experience the organization's doing in its adaptive performance. However, studying the organization requires a viewpoint ascribing purpose to the organizational system and using it to work out an effective management of complexity using the VSM as a performative model. If internal stakeholders (i.e., actors and owners) fail aligning their actions with the ascribed purpose, their management of complexity will not match the performative requirements of the VSM, thus implying the need to revise the ascribed purpose or to reconfigure resources to make possible the required alignment. In other words, the internal stakeholders' alignment with the ascribed purpose allows them to focus on the same *complexity chunks*, which as we discuss below define the organization's *primary activities*.

Ascribing purpose to the organizational system makes possible using a black box type of system description as shown in Fig. 7.7. Indeed this is simpler than an operational description of the organizational system but one that permits debating *macro strategies* for complexity management. More detailed strategies are required to discuss particular relationships between stakeholders, which we will only touch briefly in this book.

In this case the 'black box' is a short hand for what we called a *primary activity* in Chap. 6, that is, a set of *production activities* and *regulatory functions*[3] that transform certain inputs into products and services, and overtime, into the *meanings* or outcomes experienced by customers. This transformation adds value to the supplied resources to produce products or services. Notice that in this diagram we are explicitly showing some of the stakeholders mentioned before: the suppliers and the customers. The actors and owners who perform the production activities and the functions in charge of their regulation are implicit in the primary activity itself.

---

[3]Activities are production activities if they produce the organization's purposes. Production activities are structured as primary activities when they are hypothesised as autonomous units and therefore produce the organization's unfolding of complexity. Activities are clustered as regulatory functions when their purpose is regulating, supporting or servicing production activities.

Any organization is a hypothesised primary activity and as such can be represented by the diagram shown in Fig. 7.7. The Viplan Method studies the organization's performance with reference to an ascribed purpose or a purpose-in-use. The aim in the former case is *diagnosing* performative shortcomings; the aim in the latter case, if the purpose-in-use is different to the ascribed purpose is *designing* a structure that learns about, and adapts to, the stakeholders' values and expectations. In terms of the management of complexity, as developed in Chap. 4, in either case this implies working out the main complexity drivers for the organization in its surroundings.

So far we have pointed out two main sources of complexity for an organization: its customers and its suppliers. But of course, there are other relevant complexity drivers. For instance, if the organization we are considering is a company like Coca-Cola, other companies that share the same market, like Pepsi-Cola, are relevant for managing its performance. In general, competitors are a relevant source of complexity for organizations. In a similar way, but in different domains of action, other organizations or institutions may affect the performance of a given organization. For instance, a popular ecological organization (like Greenpeace) may have an impact on the performance of a strong organization like Shell UK.[4] Similarly, an institution like the Bank of England may impact the banks' businesses by changing its interest rates policy. In general, we label as *interveners* all those *environmental agents* challenging, providing opportunities, threatening and regulating the organization's performance. These are external agents affecting today's and tomorrow's performance of the transformation process of a given organization.

Graphically, we may represent the relation between an organization and its environment, in terms of complexity management (see Chap. 4), as in Figure 7.8.

In Chap. 4 we said that appropriate sets of pairs of attenuators and amplifiers of complexity should be in place for each complexity driver identified. Those complexity drivers are the main source of perturbations that have to be taken into account for an effective performance of the organization. In other words, given a particular transformation carried out by the organization-in-focus we always can work out who are its Customers, Suppliers and Interveners. One way to do this is by taking the following questions as guidance.

- For the Suppliers: Who provides the inputs needed to make the transformation possible? Notice that inputs here are products that are not only necessary to perform the transformation but are *primary* to their activities. Thus, for instance, though energy supplies are necessary for most activities, in general energy is a *secondary* input to most primary activities, but not to aluminium production.
- For the Customers: Who receives the products or services produced by the transformation? The same products and services may be produced with different added value by transformations at different structural levels in an organization.

---

[4]Shell UK's abandoning of the deep sea disposal of a storage and loading buoy in the North Atlantic as a result of continuous pressures from Greenpeace during the 1990s see http://pa. oxfordjournals.org/cgi/pdf_extract/51/3/397

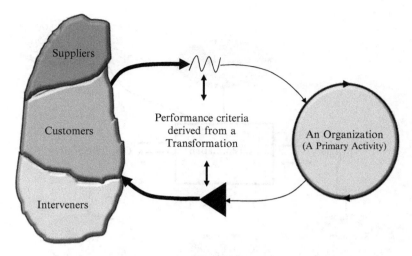

Fig. 7.8 Relevant complexity drivers for an organization in its milieu

This makes apparent a differentiation of customers for different primary activities, in line with the centralisation/decentralisation of resources

- For the Interveners: Who defines in the environment the context for the transformation? In other words, interveners are those who can affect the scope of the transformation because they are competitors, collaborators, regulators or are concerned with some of its side effects, like innovation, ecological impact or other aspects of the inputs and outputs of the transformation. Notice that because the number of interveners could be large, generally only the most significant ones need to be identified.

Let us remember that in this framework the role of Clients, Suppliers and Interveners could be played among many options by a person, a group of persons, a collective, an organization, a group of organizations, an institution or a group of institutions. Figure 7.9 shows the stakeholders of a given organizational transformation.

Operationally, an organization relates to its stakeholders by developing tacitly or explicitly stable forms of interaction in its relational venue (Chap. 4). Notice that since the 1980s, especially with the boom of the Total Quality Movement, it has been clear the importance of the 'client's point of view' to improve the organization's performance.[5] For instance direct communication channels with clients are

---

[5]For instance aspects like Customer Relationship Management have grown in significance, see Best Practice Adoption by Forrester Research 2008 http://www.forrester.com/rb/Research/crm_best_practices_adoption/q/id/44179/t/2

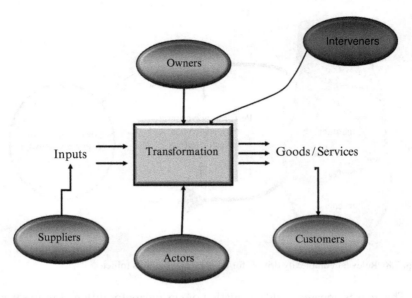

Fig. 7.9 Stakeholders of an organizational transformation

common today and a special care is taken for nurturing and preserving a hopefully long-term relation.[6]

Similarly, companies have realized the importance of developing a transparent, fair and enduring relation with its main suppliers. Not only the quality of raw materials is a precondition for the quality of the products produced but also the timing in delivering such inputs is quite important for achieving client's expectations. The literature about 'just-in-time management' has stressed the importance of the relation with suppliers (Womack and Jones 2003). In some cases this relation could develop in such a way that the supplier is even participating in the costs and profits of the related organization.

Nowadays, if the importance of developing enduring relations with customers and suppliers is part of the 'common-sense' of managing organizations, the concern for some stakeholders affected by the organization's externalities and interveners – leaving aside competitors and direct regulators that are an obvious matter of preoccupation – is still not very well understood. These operational descriptions of complexity, including ecological issues are growing in importance for some industries (like, for instance, cellulose production and oil exploitation) but often organizations do not take seriously the long-term effects of the strategies they decide to pursue. These issues are triggering many ethical considerations that are

---

[6]The development of data warehousing and data mining techniques to learn about client's buying habits and expectations is a good example of the importance that organizations are currently giving to this relation (the Amazon retail website is a prime example); also the establishment of schemes such as the mileage programs on airlines and customer cards with bonus points in retailers, is another example of this trend.

related to corporate social responsibility and corporate citizenship (Cortina 1996; Waddell 2000; Organ et al. 2006). This point, from the perspective of managing complexity, is that these long-term effects may be major threats for the future viability of organizations; trying to develop appropriate responses at a later stage could be simply too late. Reducing or preventing the impact of these side effects are perhaps a more reliable choice; recognizing the relevant stakeholders and establishing their relations with the organization is the starting point.

From what we have said so far, it should be clear that specifying in a precise way the transformation of an organization is crucial to appreciate the complexity of its milieu (i.e., environment). One way to describe this transformation process is by using the following canonical form (Checkland 1981):

The organizational system does X by means of Y with the purpose Z.

X stands for the products, services and externalities that the organization is producing; Y stands for the business model and in particular the technology that the organization is using to produce its outputs; and Z stands for the purpose ascribed to the organization's doing from a particular viewpoint.

In a sense, this canonical form is answering three main questions regarding the organization in focus: What's the organization doing? How does it perform the transformation? With what purpose? Any answer, of course, is done from a particular viewpoint. You may have noticed that in strategic planning a similar set of questions are put forward. However, the emphasis of the Viplan Method is establishing what the organization does rather than what it claims it wants to do. *Vision* is usually taken as the long-term direction where the organization wants to go; whereas its *mission* states a desire that (usually) corporate managers want to achieve.

Methodologically we have made the distinction between *ascribed purpose* and *purpose-in-use*. The latter emerges from the actual deployment of resources and the related structures. From our perspective the idea is to align the purpose-in-use with the agreed purpose as ascribed by relevant stakeholders' to the organization.

The operational identity of an organization, on the other hand, as we established in Chap. 5 is defined by the relationships between those roles constituting the organization. In this chapter we are showing, through a black box description, how we can identify these roles (i.e., the stakeholders, that is, the customers, suppliers, actors, owners and interveners) and how they can make explicit the meaning of the organization's doing (i.e., by using the canonical form of the transformation presented above). This shows the difference between vision, mission and identity.

In methodological terms we need a tool that helps these stakeholders to articulate their viewpoints in order to reach agreements and align their purposes to coordinate their actions. This tool is called *naming systems* (Checkland 1981; Wilson 1984; Espejo 1994) and is used in a conversational process by stakeholders negotiating their viewpoints about the organization in focus to align their purposes.[7]

---

[7]In Chap. 11 we offer a methodologically focused discussion of naming systems and their role in dealing with problematic situations. Here the focus is on identity statements.

The outcome of this process is one or more *declarations of identity* that can be used as hypotheses to explore their structural consequences in further steps of the method. We will see these steps in the following chapters. By now, let us exemplify the process of naming systems.

A declaration of identity is a name that we give to a system that we distinguish by looking at, in this case, a particular organization. It is expressed in one or more paragraphs where the *transformation*, constituted by *chunks of complexity*, is made explicit as a platform to identify the *stakeholders* relevant for this transformation. Again, notice that each declaration of identity reflects a particular viewpoint. Let us consider some examples.

The following is a declaration of identity for a particular prison from the point of view of its governor.

> This prison is an organization that provides a service to the community by receiving and maintaining as inmates people convicted by a criminal court, for as long as established by their sentence, in order to protect the community from their wrong doings. We have a group of well-trained administrative staff and guards who carry out this service under the regulations of the HM Prison Service.

In this declaration of identity we may identify the six elements mentioned before. Certainly, the transformation is realized by taking as an input convicted people and 'transforming' them into people with completed sentences. The actors who carry out this transformation are mainly the administrative staff and guards; the community is its main customer; the criminal courts are their primary suppliers (to distinguish them from secondary suppliers of raw materials needed to run the prison, like food and surveillance equipment); Parliament and the Justice System are the main interveners and the prison's governing body is, of course, the body responsible for the overall transformation.

One way to remember the basic elements of a declaration of identity is by using the mnemonic *TASCOI* where T stands for the canonical form of the *T*ransformation, A stands for the *A*ctors performing the transformation, S stands for the *S*uppliers, C stands for the *C*ustomers, O stands for the *O*wners and I stands for the *I*nterveners.[8] Notice that what we call 'owners' here are those persons or bodies in the organization that have an overview of the transformation and have the responsibility for adjusting performance to meet some criteria of effectiveness. In this sense they 'own' the transformation.

---

[8]TASCOI is a tool related to naming meaningful *chunks of complexity* in the world, on the other hand Checkland's (1981) CATWOE is a tool related to naming ideas that might be relevant in the world (ideas to think about the world). In TASCOI the T stands for inputs that are transformed into outputs via a technological transformation process (e.g., raw materials into finished products), in CATWOE the T often stands for changes of actors' appreciations (e.g., persons without appreciation about a situation to persons with an appreciation of this situation). CATWOE is coherent with a view that systems are mental constructs of possibilities in the informational domain; on the other hand TASCOI is coherent with the view that communications produce or might produce performative systems in the world, in the operational domain.

By using this mnemonic we can synthesize another possible declaration of identity for the prison. But this time let us do it from the point of view of one of its inmates. Suppose that this person has been in prison three times for the last ten years always for participating in car robberies.

- Transformation: taking a person convicted for regular crimes and improving his or her criminal techniques by providing time and space for learning from the most experienced prisoners.
- Actors: the most experienced inmates.
- Suppliers: the criminal courts.
- Customers: regular inmates with, probably, shorter sentences.
- Owners: indirectly (and perhaps unaware of it), the governor of the prison.
- Interveners: the staff of the prison, particularly the guards.

It is interesting to note in this example – originally taken from a real interview to an inmate in a South American prison in the 1990s – that the prison is viewed (and used) by some of the inmates as a centre to update their criminal techniques and to develop new contacts to improve their 'businesses' whenever they go out to the streets again. This is, of course, a totally different viewpoint of a prison than the one produced above by the governor of the prison.

This example also illustrates the importance of recognizing the stakeholders of an organization. In the first one, the inmates are seen as 'inputs' to the transformation and not as relevant customers. Remember, in the first case the customers are members of the community, not the inmates! This implies that it is quite possible that the viewpoints of the inmates are not being taken into account for the organization of the prison and, therefore, the unintended (and certainly undesirable) consequences of the operation of this prison, as stated by the inmate in the second declaration of identity, will be totally blurred for the staff and the governor. We will go back to this discussion about the relevant stakeholders towards the end of this chapter.

Naming systems, in general, is a process to facilitate open and structured debates among different relevant viewpoints regarding an organization's identity. It should be stressed here that each one of the declarations of identity produced in this process is an articulated statement of a *grounded* idea in a reality (Espejo 1994). The viewpoint is describing the organization 'as it is'; indeed, he or she is *naming a system*,[9] that is, a Human Communication System (see Chap. 1). Root definitions, on the other hand, as a methodological tool offered by Soft Systems Methodology (Checkland 1981) are used to explicitly name *insightful* ideas, that is, to show new possibilities; to offer holons.

---

[9]Perhaps it is useful to remember here our distinction between systems and holons that we made in Chap. 1. While a system is a *distinction* that brings forth a set of parts non-linearly related exhibiting *closure*, a holon is a mental construct, an idea or a hypothesis of a whole triggered by observations in the world, regardless of whether it has as a referent a closed network of interacting people.

Naming systems, for as long as the purpose is managing complexity, are also useful to discuss an organization 'as it could be', 'as it ought to be', or 'as it should be'. It is in this sense that they are useful not only to orchestrate conversations for action but also for possibilities.

One methodological question that triggers the above comments is who should participate in these conversations or debates? The straight answer to this question is, of course, that representatives of the organization's stakeholders should be the participants. However, you may have noticed that there is a sort of a circularity implied by this answer. Indeed, the stakeholders are implied by the declarations of identity that are produced by the same conversations being orchestrated. To sort this out we distinguish the *enabling viewpoint* from all the other relevant viewpoints of the situation under consideration. The enabling viewpoint (that could be a person or a group) is the one who is using the Viplan Method to approach a particular issue of concern. In this case it is the one that enables these debates to happen. This viewpoint starts by producing a name for the organization in focus (i.e., a TASCOI) as an initial *hypothesis*. If this enabling viewpoint can be considered a stakeholder of the organization in focus it may have enough appreciation of the situation as to produce this hypothesis straight away; otherwise it would need to gather some information (perhaps through interviews) before producing this initial declaration of identity. In any case, this initial statement is used to identify the stakeholders for the first of iterative debates about the organization's identity.

These iterative debates are run normally as workshops facilitated by the enabling viewpoint. They will act as a learning mechanism regarding the organization's identity. This learning implies an increased appreciation of the situation and possibly a more insightful recognition of stakeholders. A very important issue of these discussions is to have an open debate to consider who are and who ought to be the main stakeholders of the organization. Notice that this consideration relates not only to the purpose stated in the transformation but also to the values held by the people participating in the debates. As we said in Chap. 1, drawing borders for social systems is more than the outcome of a logical proposition; it is making boundary judgements (Ulrich 2000).

In the case of the prison system mentioned above, for instance, we could ask why local schools and universities are not considered as relevant stakeholders of this organization. They could provide teaching material, advice and even some services to allow the prison to offer a permanent and specially oriented learning opportunity to some (probably most) of the inmates. Notice that behind this consideration is the judgment that prisoners, in most cases, are persons that, after having being found guilty for breaking the law, need additional support to rejoin society as productive individuals after recovering their freedom. Training and learning in socially relevant aspects may provide this additional support. If this question is raised during any of the debates regarding naming the prison system, it may produce an agreed performative change in the declaration of identity. The reader may find it useful to produce this new name for the prison and to compare it with the two offered above.

These debates or *identity workshops* stop at the point where the participants reach stability in the names (one or more) they produce. *These names are taken in*

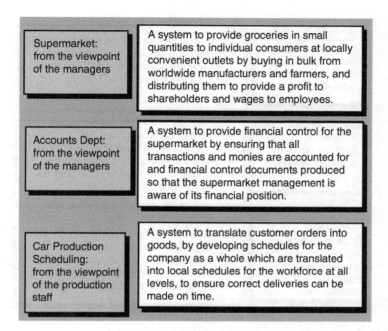

Fig. 7.10 Naming three types of systems in an organization (Espejo and Bowling 1996)

the following chapters as hypothesis to study their structural implications, that is, their implications for managing complexity. We start discussing these implications in the next chapter with reference to the *unfolding of complexity.*

But before we finish this chapter, let us clarify the scope of the tool. We presented naming systems as a way to explore the identity of an organization from relevant viewpoints. It follows that, in general, it could be used to explore the identity of any primary activity. However, it can also be used to name *regulatory functions*, like auditing or planning in a company, or even to name transversal processes, like quality control or any logistic process. The following diagrams exemplify these different applications.[10]

In Fig. 7.10 we can see the names produced for three different organizational systems. The first one describes the transformation process of a supermarket (a primary activity) from the point of view of the managers. The second is the transformation of the Accounts Department of the supermarket (a regulatory activity) as described by the same managers. The third example is the description of the transformation process of a Car Production Scheduling (transversal process) from the point of view of the production staff. In all these cases we can distinguish the three components of the canonical formulation of the transformation. (What is produced? How is it produced? What is its purpose?)

---

[10]These examples are taken from the Viplan software (Espejo and Bowling 1996).

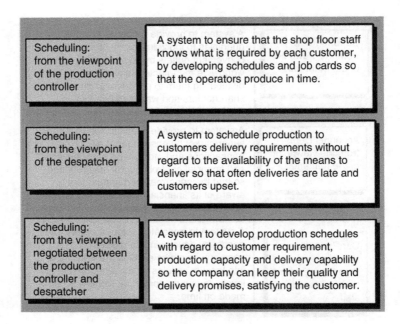

Fig. 7.11 Naming a scheduling process from different viewpoints

Sometimes, as we mentioned before, there are differences in the descriptions provided by several viewpoints. Figure 7.11 shows three names for the scheduling process (a regulatory function) of Trident, a metal-mechanic company within the engineering industry. The first one was elaborated by the production controller whereas the second was formulated by the dispatcher. Disagreement on this name may undermine the coordination of activities among these roles and suggests the need to get an agreement. The third name was the outcome of a discussion process that implied changes in the tasks of the people involved as well as in their relations (Bowling and Espejo 1993).

For each name it is possible to identify all relevant stakeholders using the mnemonic TASCOI. Figure 7.12 illustrates this again for Trident (Espejo and Bowling 1996). Figure 7.13 identifies the stakeholders derived from a name for the tool room of Trident, which is a regulatory function in that case. In Fig. 7.14 we can see the participants of the scheduling process agreed by the production controller and dispatcher of Trident in Fig. 7.11.

The purpose of this chapter has been to introduce the method and explain the process of naming systems as its first tool.

Summarizing, we have claimed that naming systems is a tool to visualize the complexity of an organization by identifying its transformation and stakeholders, as implied by the ascribed purpose to the organizational system. We will see that in particular the actors producing the transformation and the suppliers and customers shaping it are the sources of complexity building up the organization's business model to solve its self-defined environmental challenges. These names are platforms

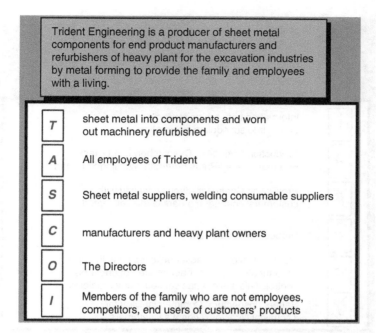

Fig. 7.12 Naming Trident, an autonomous company within the engineering industry (Espejo and Bowling 1996)

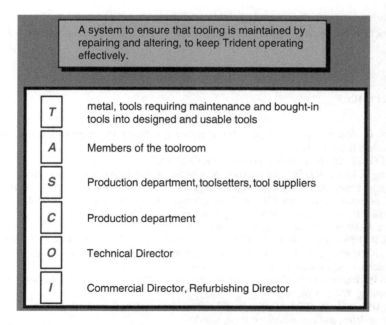

Fig. 7.13 Naming the activities performed by the tool room of Trident (a regulatory function) (Espejo and Bowling 1996)

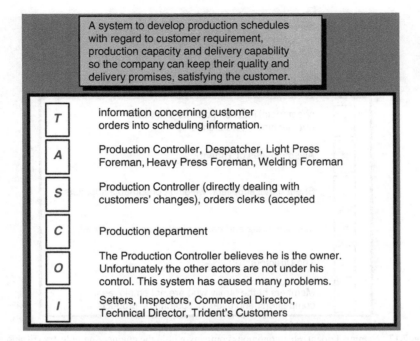

A system to develop production schedules with regard to customer requirement, production capacity and delivery capability so the company can keep their quality and delivery promises, satisfying the customer.

T	information concerning customer orders into scheduling information.
A	Production Controller, Despatcher, Light Press Foreman, Heavy Press Foreman, Welding Foreman
S	Production Controller (directly dealing with customers' changes), orders clerks (accepted
C	Production department
O	The Production Controller believes he is the owner. Unfortunately the other actors are not under his control. This system has caused many problems.
I	Setters, Inspectors, Commercial Director, Technical Director, Trident's Customers

Fig. 7.14 Naming scheduling (a transversal process) of Trident (Espejo and Bowling 1996)

for diagnosing organizational systems and designing performative structures. This connection between purpose and structure is at the core of the next chapter.

References

Argyris C, Schon D (1978) Organizational learning: a theory of action perspective. Addison-Wesley, Reading, MA

Beer S (1979) The heart of enterprise. Wiley, Chichester

Bowling D, Espejo R (1993) An intervention with the cybernetic methodology in regent engineering. In: Espejo R, Schwaninger M (eds) Organizational fitness: corporate effectiveness through management cybernetics. Campus Verlag, Frankfurt and New York, pp 299–330

Checkland P (1981) Systems thinking, systems practice. Wiley, Chichester

Cortina A (1996) Etica de la empresa. Trotta, Madrid

Espejo R (1994) What's systemic thinking? Syst Dynam Rev 10(2–3 Summer–Fall):199–212

Espejo R, Bowling D (1996) Viplan learning system: A method to learn the viable system model. Syncho, Ltd., Birmingham, www.syncho.com

Espejo R, Schuhmann W, Schwaninger M, Bilello U (1996) Organizational transformation and learning. Wiley, Chichester

Organ DW, Podsakoff PM, MacKenzie SB (2006) Organizational citizenship behavior: its nature, antecedents, and consequences. Sage, London

Ulrich W (2000) Reflective practice in the civil society: the construction of critically systemic thinking. Reflective Pract 1(2):247–268

Waddell S (2000) New institutions for the practice of corporate citizenship: historical intersectoral, and developmental perspectives. Bus Soc Rev 105:323–345

Wilson B (1984) Systems: concepts, methodologies and applications. Wiley, Chichester

Womack JP, Jones D (2003) Lean thinking: banish waste and create wealth in your corporation (revised and updated). Harper Business, London

Chapter 8
Unfolding of Complexity: Modelling the Transformation's Complexity

Abstract Showing how to carry out the second and third steps of the Viplan Method is the purpose of this chapter. We assume that the organization in focus can be described in terms of a transformation process needed to produce the products or services implied by its ascribed name. Our concern now is finding the activities, and their relations, that are necessary to carry out this transformation process. These activities (and their relations) can be described or designed by using *technological models*. Each activity is a chunk of complexity including highly interconnected sub-activities. Together they offer a strategy to manage the complexity of the organization's value adding transformation. But not only technology drives the way in which an organization chunks its complexity. The organization may have to take into consideration the localization of its activities; does it matter whether they are close or distant to their markets? Does it matter to differentiate between customer and product segments? How do time factors influence the structure of their technological activities? These are all complexity drivers for grouping their activities. Producing these *technological and structural models* is the second step of Viplan. The third step is studying the organization's *unfolding of complexity*. This activity is at the core of working out an organization's recursive structure. This chapter offers a discussion, supported by a wide range of examples, of the convenience and necessity of enabling autonomy or *primary activities* within the organization. This study is driven by the technological and structural models. This chapter debates the organization's strategy to manage the complexity implied by its stated name.

In the previous chapter we saw how a set of relevant stakeholders can produce different names (i.e., declarations of identity) for an organization in focus. We explained and exemplified the use of *naming systems* as a suitable methodological tool to guide *identity workshops* in this regard. We also introduced the notion of the *enabling viewpoint* as the viewpoint using the Viplan Method to facilitate the modelling of this organization.

The purpose of this chapter is to explore possible structural consequences of these declarations of identity for a given organization-in-focus. Each name specifies for an existing organization what it does and who its stakeholders are. In some way each one defines a particular complexity management strategy. Additionally, beyond working out what *are* these complexity management strategies (in Mode I, diagnosis) we discuss what *could* these strategies be (in Mode II, design) as a consequence of redeploying and developing organizational resources (Teece 2008).

From the definition of an organization's structure in Chap. 5 and the discussions of identity in Chap. 7 we can say that this structure is defined by the resources and relations creating, regulating and implementing the *transformation* it produces. This transformation is a short hand for a black box description of an organization's complexity. In this chapter we use this description as a platform for an *operational (autonomy based) description* of this complexity (see Chap. 1). The transformation is chunked into components to visualize *how* inputs are transformed into outputs for customers. Once done, this visualization is used as the platform to work out the organization's primary activities, that is, the resources and relations that support an operational description of organizational autonomy as developed in Chap. 6.

In this chapter we discuss first the breaking or chunking of a transformation into smaller tasks; we refer to this chunking as the production of *technological and structural models* and second we use these models to work out the *unfolding of the organization's complexity*. These are the second and third steps of the Viplan Method. But before we illustrate these steps let's understand their epistemological underpinnings, which are grounded in the discussions of Chap. 3.

Let's consider a black box with eight inputs and one output (see Fig. 8.1). Each input has two possible states (e.g., ON/OFF) and the output also has two possible states. The variety or number of possible states of this black box is 2^{256} (Beer 1979). This variety is unknowable (Pickering 2010) suggesting that any attempt to know

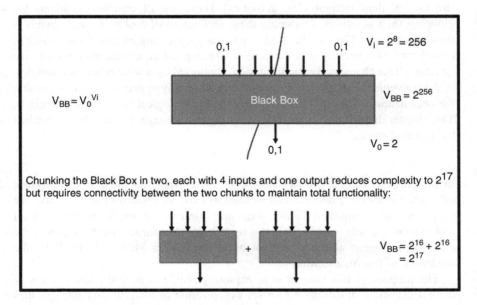

Fig. 8.1 Chunking strategy to manage complex situations

about such a situation makes it necessary to reduce its variety to a knowable and manageable level. A complexity management strategy that we use is chunking its variety; for instance in Fig. 8.1 we have reduced the overall complexity of the situation to two chunks each of four inputs and one output, with a total variety of 2^{17}. If we leave them that way we have simply fragmented the situation.

However, if we are chunking an organization we can appreciate that two chunks reduce its variety in orders of magnitude but leaves the variety in between them unattended. For some form of cohesion a higher order regulator embedding them is necessary; hence the relevance of structural recursion. In fact by necessity we chunk the variety of situations to make them more manageable, however, this chunking has to be thought through. We have to avoid fragmenting where strong connectivity is necessary.

Often the chunking is inadequate, putting too much demand on the higher order regulator, which finds it necessary to restrict the chunks' internal connectivity reducing their ability to cope by themselves with environmental demands (see the bank example at the end of the chapter). In relative terms, a situation that relies on autonomous chunks to manage complexity generates far more response variety than a situation that fragments them to the point where it depends entirely on central control to achieve situational cohesion (compare Figs. 8.1 and 8.2). This is the reason we have autonomous units within autonomous units. Autonomous components absorb more variety internally and decrease the demands on those overviewing them, allowing a larger, more complex, organizational system. On the other hand not enabling autonomy in situations where there are large environmental demands makes it extremely demanding the functional requirements to maintain cohesion. The challenge is making an ingenuous chunking of this variety; one that contains

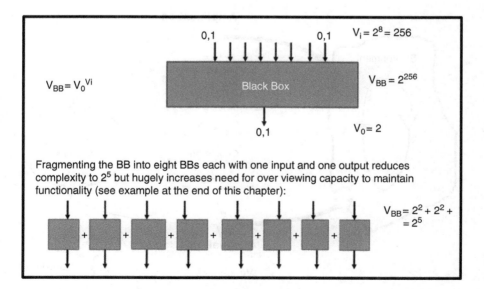

Fig. 8.2 Fragmenting strategy to manage complex situations

highly interconnected variety in distinguishable chunks and reduces requirements for those concerned with their cohesion. These strategies to manage complexity are at the core of the VSM and also are sensitive to technological changes. It is apparent that different deployment of technologies may suggest very different chunking of the transformation, underpinning very different structures.

Because variety proliferation is natural in any social situation organizations can be seen as necessary mechanisms to constrain this variety. An effective organization is one that finds ingenious ways to cope with the demands of its environment through innovation (Homer-Dixon 2001). As argued before, organization is a problem-solving device that permits managing a high variety situation with a much lower variety.

Conant and Ashby's theorem that 'every good regulator of a system must be a model of that system' (Conant and Ashby 1970) must be at the core of chunking a desirable transformation; to cope effectively with a complex situation the organization structure must map this fluid and changeable complexity, in other words it must be, from a particular viewpoint, a good model of this complexity. First of all, the situational complexity is *attenuated* by naming a transformation (Chap. 7) and secondly it is further attenuated by chunking it. On the other hand by structurally mapping these chunks people in the organization *amplify* their response capacity in an ongoing process that hopefully constrains with ingenuity the situational complexity. This mapping is a circular learning process that constantly reconfigures resources and relations (see Fig. 8.3). As we explain below, *complexity drivers* help modelling situational complexity and working out structural responses. The Viplan Method uses four complexity drivers for this chunking: technology, customer/ suppliers, geography and time (see Fig. 8.3). Each one allows the chunking of the

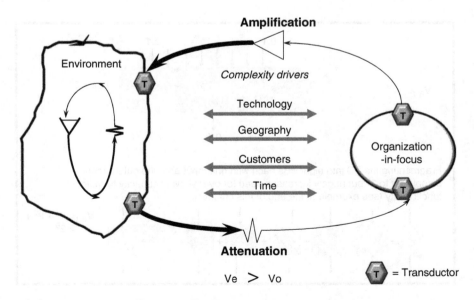

Fig. 8.3 Complexity drivers used to chunk an organization's primary transformation

transformation from different perspectives. How we can build these models and how they can be integrated to show the organization's unfolding of complexity is what we show in the rest of the chapter.

A first driver for chunking is a *technological model*. In the diagnostic mode this model shows the chunks that are used to produce a transformation according to a particular technology in a particular organization. In the design mode this model evolves to possible chunks, perhaps more ingenious and relying on different technologies, to produce the transformation. The design mode is not a map of an ideal chunking but a reconfiguration of resources in response to new technologies and their deployment. Of course different technologies may imply different technological models for the same transformation. In the late nineteenth century, for instance, the main technology of banks was bookkeeping and rudimentary calculators supporting locally the services they offered to their customers. They defined specific roles and implemented particular processes in their offices to take care of their clients' transactions. Nowadays, in the twenty-first century, modern communication technology supports these transactions beyond local boundaries and simple calculations. A completely new chunking of the banking services has been defined and new processes, like e-banking have been set in place. This example, which is further elaborated later in this chapter, shows the flavour of the statement that 'technology drives today's businesses'.

In Fig. 8.4, we show a technological model for Satena, an air services company. Its transformation is offering services for air transport and aircraft maintenance. The first service is chunked into 'passengers', 'mail and cargo', 'charters' and 'aircraft renting'. The clients of the latter are other airline companies.

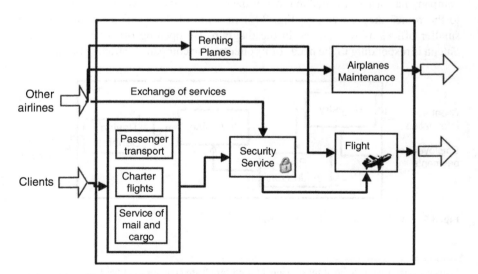

Fig. 8.4 A technological model for Satena

As another example let us take the pension funds company, which is common everywhere. The following is the agreed declaration of identity for AFP that operates in Colombia:

> AFP is a company that administrates pension funds by offering an investment portfolio whose dividends are used both for their clients' future pension and their shareholders.

Figure 8.5 shows a simple technological model for AFP. These chunks were identified from interviews carried out with its main managers.[1] There are four chunks: 'Registry', 'Risk Evaluation', 'Investing' and 'Paying Benefits'.

The third example we would like to show (see Fig. 8.6) is for an aluminium production plant. The agreed declaration of identity for this plant was the following:

> A high volume producer of primary aluminium for international high volume aluminium processors, in a physical form which is suitable for customers' processes, using modern clean smelting technology developed in house, in co-operation with sister companies within the Company.

Here the plant is technology driven and the chunks of its transformation are particular to the company.

But not only technology drives the chunking of an organization's transformation. Its strategies to respond to environmental opportunities and threats provide also complexity drivers. These drivers are the sources of *structural models* in the Viplan Method. Organization may group activities to carry out a particular transformation taking into consideration the localization of customers, suppliers and actors either for economic reasons (mainly regarding cost reductions) or the availability of skilled labour or both. If this is the case, then *geography* could be a complexity driver for chunking the transformation.

Figure 8.7 shows a geographical model for Satena. Here we can see that the company has offices located in most of the cities across the country, mainly related to the routes they cover (see Fig. 8.8). In some of these cities Satena has even smaller offices as we can see in the diagram. By opening offices in these cities Satena is responding to the needs of its clients. The company's strategy points to the

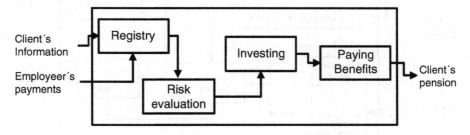

Fig. 8.5 A technological model for the AFP

---

[1]This exercise was developed by students of a postgraduate course run at the Universidad de los Andes in Colombia.

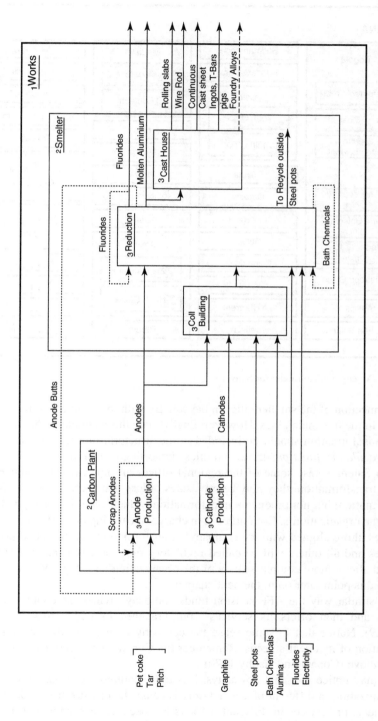

Fig. 8.6 A technological model for aluminium plant

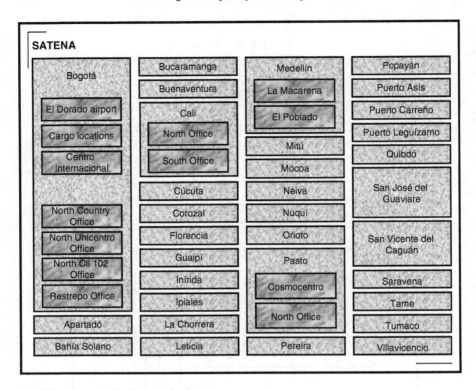

Fig. 8.7 A geographical model for Satena

interconnection of the smaller cities in the country with the main economic centres located in the five main cities. However, finally, only those chunking the organization's transformation should be included in the structural models. In Chap. 6 we called *regulatory functions* those activities supporting or enabling *primary activities*. In Satena's case some of the regional offices are not chunks producing its overall transformation; they may be, say, sales offices that enable a larger office's transformation, but not produce a transformation of their own that is aligned with that of the organization's. Each office is in charge of carrying out different kinds of activities, those aligned with the company's transformation will be called primary activities and all others will be called regulatory functions. But this can only be clarified after a more complete study of the organization's strategy. We will come back to this point later on in the next chapter.

In a similar way the AFP pension funds company divides the country in four regions and then offers its services from branches located across the cities (Fig. 8.9). Notice that in some sense the company is mapping the geographical distribution of its client's needs. Remember the Conant and Ashby theorem mentioned above (Conant and Ashby 1970).

We may notice also that nowadays, it is quite common to group activities of an organization in different places not only because the organization is delivering its products or services to different markets but because of economical, legal or

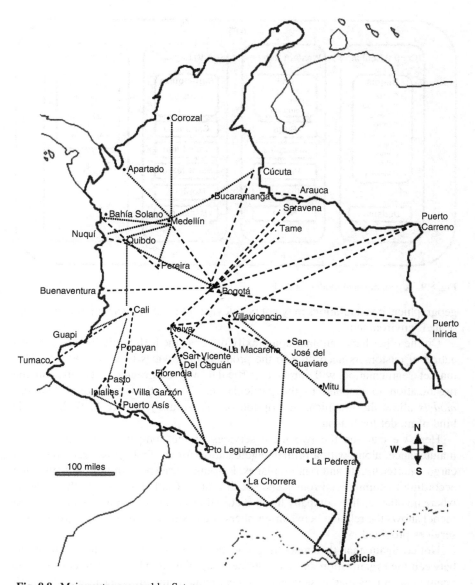

Fig. 8.8 Main routes covered by Satena

political reasons. We have, for instance, companies producing small parts in several countries and yet doing the assembly of those components in another country (e.g., Dell). In all these cases the use of a geographical model helps in visualizing the spatial distribution of the organization's complexity.

Of course it is quite possible that some companies concentrate their main activities in one single site. This is the case of most small local companies. Here

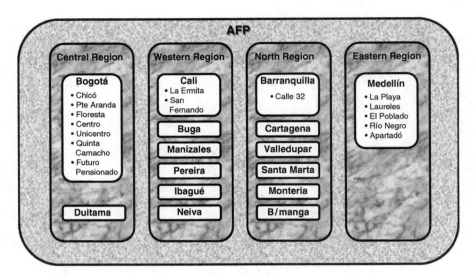

Fig. 8.9 A geographical model for AFP

geographical considerations may not be relevant for the management of complexity of their environment.

On the other hand, another complexity driver is the differentiation and classification of customers according to the products or services that they receive. This market segmentation will imply a particular way of grouping activities in the organization to respond to the particular needs of clients. *Customer-Supplier models* allow the graphical description of this strategy. Figure 8.10 shows this kind of model for Satena.

Here we can see the two main services of the company, air transport and maintenance, along with a further segmentation for the first: passengers, mail and cargo, charter flights and renting planes. Passenger transport, in turn, is segmented according to commercial routes and social routes. The latter refers to those routes where no other airline company flies because they are not profitable. Notice that the model shows the relation between suppliers and customers vis-à-vis the grouping of services provided.

Notice again that this modelling can be used to reflect the actual relations between the organization and its customers/suppliers in Mode I or to consider the opening up of new market segments for a particular company when used in Mode II. The point here is to see that the differentiation of customers could be an important driver for breaking down the organization's primary transformation.

Figure 8.11, in turn, shows this type of modelling for AFP. Here the company offers three main products: statutory pensions, voluntary pensions and off-work subsidies. We can see also that the second product is divided into more specific ones depending on the client's particular needs. The right hand side of the diagram shows this market segmentation; while statutory pensions go to everybody, voluntary pensions go to whoever has the income and willingness to buy them and off-work subsidies got to people previously in employment.

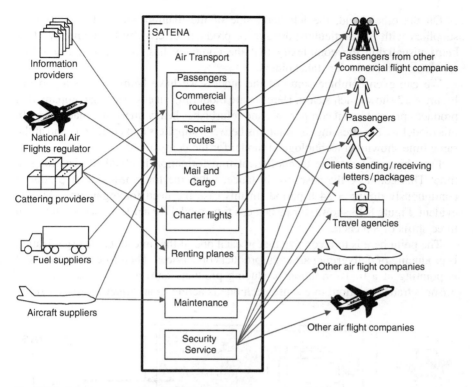

Fig. 8.10 A customer-supplier model for Satena

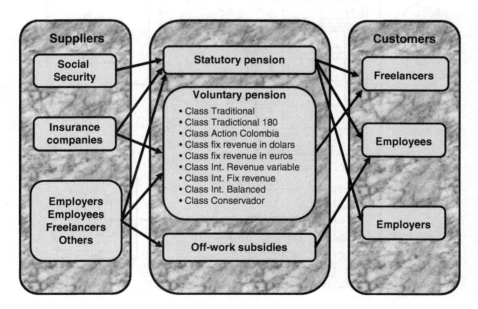

Fig. 8.11 A customer-supplier model for AFP

On the other hand, the left hand side of the diagram shows the relation of suppliers with the particular portfolio of products offered by the company. This helps visualizing the complexity that the company has to face in terms of its relations with particular stakeholders.

We can even combine some of the models we have being discussing so far. Figure 8.12 shows such a case. Here we are modelling an engineering company that produces pressed metal components and refurbishes heavy quarrying machinery. In this model we are stressing the relations between suppliers and customers and at the same time showing a technological model for the company.

Last, but not least, the technological transformation is chunked according to time. This could be the case, for instance, when the transformation is produced continuously during a 24 h period. In this case the need for organizing shifts is evident. Figure 8.13 shows, for instance, a time model for a prison that is running in three shifts of 8 h each.

The point here is to recognize that in each one of the time slots the organization is producing or delivering particular products or services. Therefore, each time slot is pointing at a transformation producing products or services aligned with the prison's transformation. In a sense each one is acting as an organization in itself.

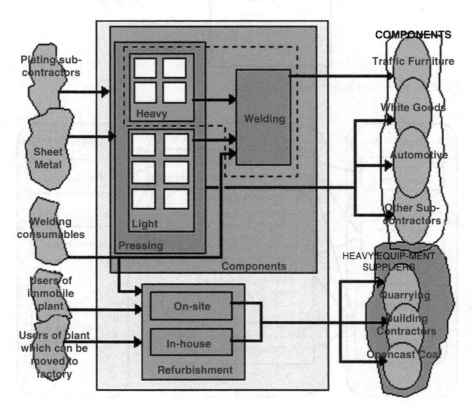

Fig. 8.12 An example of a combined model (Espejo and Bowling 1996)

Fig. 8.13 An example of a time model for a prison with three shifts

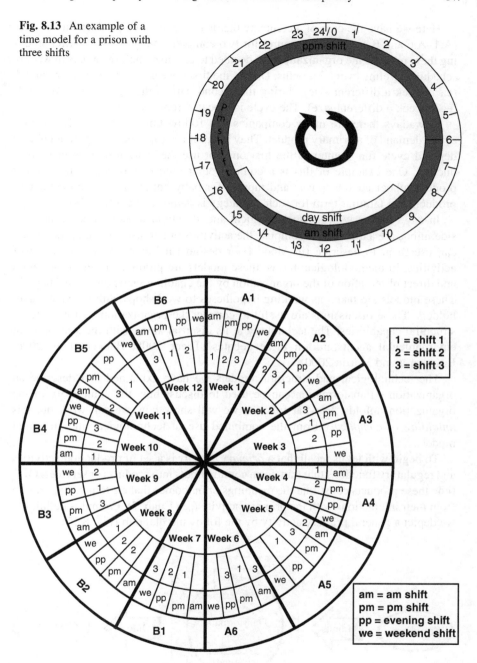

Fig. 8.14 An example of a complex time model

A similar situation may arise if the same technology (i.e., machinery and resources) is used to produce or offer different products or services at different times. In Fig. 8.14, for instance, we can see a complex time model of this sort.

Here we have the case of a company that is producing two products in six sizes (A.1–A.6 and B.1–B.6 in the figure) for two complementary markets. After studying these markets the organization has decided to organize their resources in weekly schedules cycling every 3 months. During the first 6 weeks they produce product A (each week a different size); during the second part of the cycle they produce B (each week a different size). The cycle is repeated four times a year.

Nowadays there are many companies that follow this strategy to deal with a cyclic demand of a primary product. They look for a complementary product whose demand cycle run counter to the first one but use the same resources in its production. One example of this is a company that used to produce as its primary product rubber contraceptives and nipples for baby bottles as its complementary product. The familiar term for such a strategy is *hedging* (Ackoff 1978).

In any case, as with the technological and structural models, when time considerations are a driver to decompose the activities of a transformation process, we can use them to describe (in Mode I) or design (in Mode II) this chunking of activities. In methodological terms, these models are produced using information and direct observation of the organization by the enabling viewpoint (see Chap. 7). These models are taken as working hypotheses to workshops with relevant stakeholders. These discussions are useful to connect the organization's strategy to its structural capabilities. The technology at its disposal along with the stretching of environmental agents inform these debates (Teece 2008; Banker et al. 2006; Eisenhardt and Martin 2000).

The technological and structural models we have explained that describe an organization's transformation can be used to discuss how the complexity of the organization unfolds. In what follows, we will show how we can work out this *unfolding of complexity* from the combined use of technological and structural models.

To begin with let us recall that a *primary activity* is a set of production activities and regulatory functions that transform certain inputs into products or services. Over time these products constitute the meanings or outcomes that customers experience from their interactions with the primary activity (see Chap. 7). From this definition, we depict a general primary activity by the following diagram (Fig. 8.15).

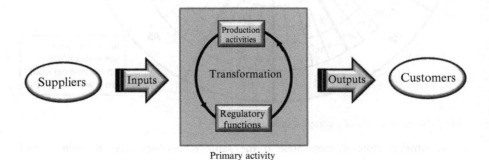

Primary activity

Fig. 8.15 A general representation of a primary activity

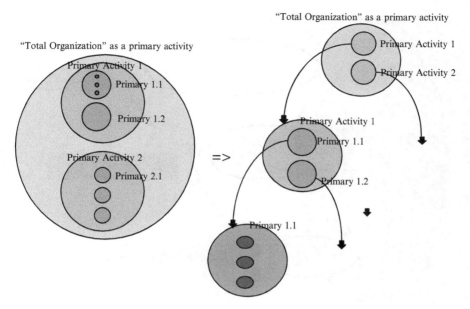

Fig. 8.16 A general unfolding of complexity

From what we have said above, it should be clear that an organization as a whole is a primary activity in its own right. In general, each primary activity contains primary activities. Notice that each one of these primary activities is *contained* within a larger primary one. This process of embedding could go on and on for several levels. The resulting diagram represents the *unfolding of complexity* of the organization in focus (see Chap. 6). Figure 8.16 illustrates this.

We call the diagram on the left hand side of this figure *embedded unfolding* and the diagram in the right hand side the *unfolding of complexity*. These two diagrams are equivalent in showing how an organization groups its activities in chunks of complexity in order to carry out its transformation.

But there is still another way to describe this unfolding of activities if we take into consideration the medium in which the organization exists. We have said that any organization is a primary activity that embodies a particular transformation, as Fig. 8.15 shows. Therefore, we can work out the relevant medium (i.e., environment) to which this organization is structurally coupled (remember what we said about the *participants* of a transformation in Chap. 7 and, in particular, Fig. 7.8). But we can do exactly the same to each one of the (sub) primary activities in which the organization unfolds. In other words, each (sub) primary activity is also structurally coupled to a particular medium that, in turn, is embedded in the medium of the embedding primary activity. Figure 8.17 shows this representation that we called *cascading unfolding*. Notice that, in general, as the reader may have noticed in these diagrams, a primary activity is embedded within (one or more) primary activities and contains more than one primary activity.

Medium

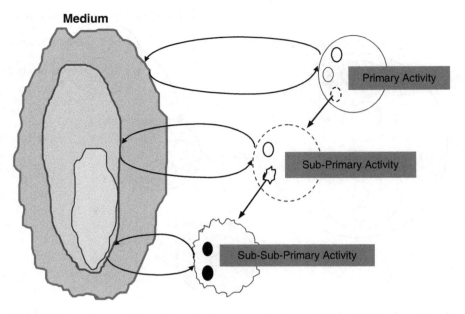

Fig. 8.17 Cascading unfolding of complexity

In all these cases it is important to notice that the relation between a primary activity and its embedded (sub) primary activities is not that of a managerial hierarchy; it is a *relation of inclusion* and constitution of autonomous systems. For instance, Fig. 8.18 shows an unfolding of complexity of a public utility company in a South American country.[2] Here we can see that the transformation of this company is constituted by six primary activities: electricity generation, energy distribution, telecommunication services, water supply, sewerage services, and consultancy in public services. Each one of these is, in turn, subdivided into others (sub) primary activities. For instance, energy distribution is decomposed into electricity supply and gas supply; whereas telecommunication services are carried out through seven (sub) primary activities: local calls, long distance calls, public phones services, special services (such as teleconferencing), dedicated data transmission, cable television and Internet provider. All of these (sub) primary activities are autonomous units of an organization that is constituted, in this particular case, by different services and their natural differentiation.

This last comment suggests that there is a direct connection between the technological and structural models explained above and the unfolding of complexity we are explaining now. In fact, in methodological terms, we work out relevant technological and structural models for the organization in focus before we attempt

---

[2]This unfolding of complexity was worked out by managers of this company during a master course on organizational cybernetics undertaken by them at the Universidad de los Andes in Colombia.

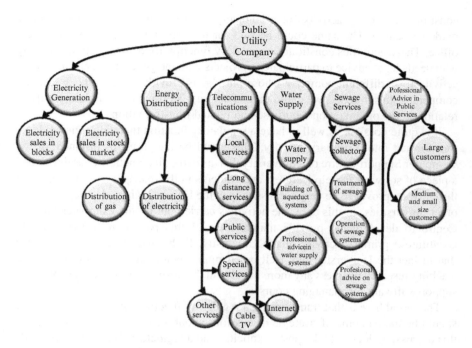

Fig. 8.18 An unfolding of complexity for a public utility company

to draw its unfolding of complexity. But prior to illustrate how we make this connection, it is essential to stress upon the difference between a primary activity and a regulatory function.

We have said that whereas a primary activity produces the total (since the organization is a primary activity in focus) or a part of the transformation of an organization, a regulatory function supports one or more primary activities; in fact, it is participating in the creation and/or regulation of (one or more) primary activities. It is important to strengthen the view that a particular activity *is not* primary or regulatory in itself; it depends on the role it is playing in the transformation process of the organization in focus. Let us clarify this point with some particular examples.

Suppose that one of the purposes of a university is to deliver undergraduate courses in different topics. It follows that the teaching activities are primary activities for this organization. On the other hand, library services and market research to develop new courses are not primary activities vis-à-vis its named transformation; they are supporting (i.e., regulatory) functions for the university.

Let us be clear about this, regulatory functions are not 'underrated' activities; they are as necessary and as important as the primary activities to produce the organization's identity. However, they belong to a different logical category. In the next chapter we will make explicit the relations between regulatory functions and primary activities by means of a tool called the Recursion/Functions Table.

But the difference between the two can be sometimes very subtle. For instance, the same market research activities mentioned in the example of the university will constitute a primary activity for a company whose business is, precisely, doing market research. The same could be said for the activities carried out by a legal office. These activities constitute a regulatory function for a construction company who needs legal advice to participate in projects with the government and a primary activity for a different company whose purpose is providing legal advice to other companies. In summary, we claim that an activity is primary or regulatory only in relation to the organization's purpose and related transformation.

It is quite possible as well to have a regulatory function that with time could be transformed into a primary activity. This could be the case, for instance, of the Computer Support Centre of a university that, as part of its functions, has developed a piece of software to help lecturers and students in the management of courses. If the software proves to be very successful then the University may decide to sell it to other universities. In this case, the activities carried out by the Computer Support Centre to develop and provide maintenance of this particular software would constitute a primary activity of the University. If this happens, however, notice that in fact the University may well be changing its identity; it is not only in the teaching/research business any more but also in the business of producing computer support software for managing courses.

The moral here is that transforming a regulatory function into a primary activity should be the outcome of strategic discussions about the organization's identity. If this discussion does not take place explicitly and a regulatory function becomes de facto a primary activity, the chances are that the structure becomes dysfunctional. We will expand on this point with more detail in Chap. 11 when we discuss the use of Viplan to work out diagnostic points for an organization-in-focus. But for now let us end our excursus into primary and regulatory activities by stating some useful criteria for their study.

We claim that primary activities must develop autonomy; that is, they should have the capacity to create, regulate and produce their transformation process; they are a fundamental strategy to amplify the organization's variety. Regulatory functions, on the other hand, must integrate their resources within the primary activities and not develop autonomy by themselves, as we mentioned in passing in the last paragraph. This autonomy principle regarding primary and regulatory activities may guide strategic discussions on how an organization may deploy its resources to realize its identity. In other words, as we mentioned at the beginning of this chapter, the unfolding of complexity can be used to link strategy to structure in an organizational context. We will come back again to this point towards the end of the chapter. But before that a crucial question remains unanswered: how can we build up this unfolding of complexity for a particular organization in focus? Remember that we said before that there is a direct connection between the technological and structural modelling and the unfolding of complexity. Let us explore this relation now.

A possible unfolding of complexity for Satena is shown in Fig. 8.19. Here we can see that the company groups their primary activities according to a geographical criterion and then, in each city, offers its services. However, the same services are not on offer in every city. In Cali, for instance, they do not rent planes to other

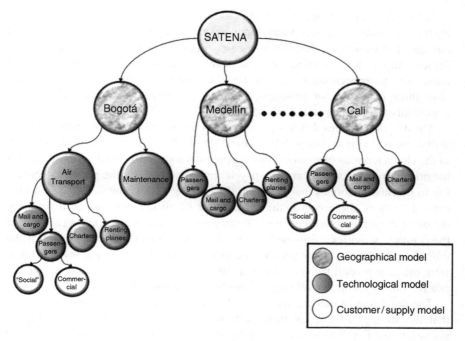

Fig. 8.19 An unfolding of complexity for Satena

companies. In a similar way, only in Bogotá they offer maintenance of planes as a service to other companies. Several of the local offices were only offering regulatory services related to the larger offices; as suggested earlier in the chapter they do not appear in the unfolding of complexity.

The distinction between social and commercial routes came from the discussion about particular needs of customers in some cities where no other companies usually fly. This was made apparent in the customer/supplier model of Fig. 8.10.

It is interesting to see in this particular example that *security service* was debated as a possible technological chunk in the technological model for Satena. This option would have implied Satena offering this service to the air industry, in similar terms to aircraft maintenance. In the end maintenance appeared and security service did not appear in the unfolding of complexity. This last service was subcontracted with a specialized company. In general, we call *secondary activities* those *technological chunks* that can be implied by the named transformation but eventually are outsourced and are not part of the unfolding of complexity.

Let us illustrate now the use of a time model along with other criteria to build up an unfolding of complexity. Let's take again the example of the prison we used in the last chapter. Suppose that the governor of the prison has produced the following name:

> This prison is an organization that provides psychological service, medical care and training to people who have been convicted by a criminal court, in order to help them to join a productive life in society after they accomplish their punishment.

Notice that in this case the primary activities of the prison are naturally grouped in shifts (probably 8 hrs long) and organized according to the characteristics of the inmates. Let us assume that this particular prison has a time model like the one depicted in Fig. 8.13 and that the inmates are categorised according to the type of crime they have been convicted for. For the sake of simplicity, let's say that we have three categories of prisoners. Figure 8.20 shows a suitable unfolding of complexity that corresponds to these criteria.

The diagram implies that this prison carries out activities of basic education and skills training in the morning shift (from 6:00 to 14:00) that are organized according to the characteristics of inmates. During the afternoon shift (from 14:00 to 22:00), the prison provides social care and psychological service for the prisoners according to its classification. Finally, during the evening shift (from 22:00 to 6:00) the main activity of the prison is the surveillance of all inmates. Notice that during the other shifts this activity of surveillance could be seen as a supporting activity of the primary activities mentioned. In the diagram we can see which parts of the unfolding have been taken from which models. The first structural level is taken from the time model; the second structural level comes from the customer model; and the third structural level comes from the technological model.

The unfolding of complexity for AFP is shown in Fig. 8.21. There we can see that the strategy of the company rests in the intersection of its technological activities (see Fig. 8.5) with the geographical and market (i.e., customer/supplier) criteria (see Figs. 8.9 and 8.11 respectively). While AFP registers and pays benefits

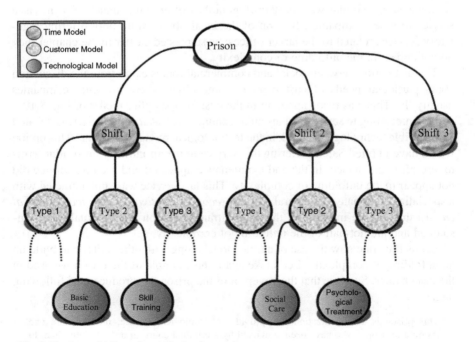

Fig. 8.20 An unfolding of complexity for a prison

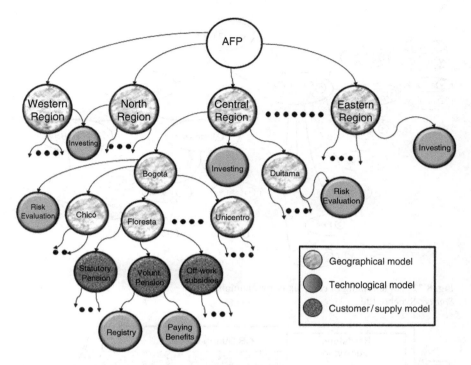

Fig. 8.21 An unfolding of complexity for AFP

to its clients for each product in every office, they do risk evaluation grouping all the information they have at each city. On the other hand, they do the investment in financial portfolios grouped by region. Changes in this strategy may, of course, imply an adjustment of this unfolding of complexity. In a practical situation this should be the outcome of discussions via workshops with relevant viewpoints of the organization-in-focus.

Figure 8.22, in turn, shows the unfolding of complexity for the aluminium plant. In contrast with the previous example, in this case technology is what mainly drives breaking down its primary transformation.

To end this discussion of complexity unfolding in Mode I (diagnostic mode) we would like to illustrate a step by step construction of an unfolding of complexity carried out for a quarrying company in Britain, part of a British construction company.[3] A declaration of identity for this company, that we shall call here GB Quarry, was stated in the following way:

> GB Quarry Company, Ltd. is a European quarry based division of GB Construction plc, producing quarried products within the framework of the Mines and Quarries Act and the Factories Act as relevant, on an ecologically responsible basis, supplying in-house and external customers with dry and coated stone and concrete, in order to ensure a return for GB Construction's shareholders.

---

[3]This is an elaboration of an example in Espejo and Bowling (1996).

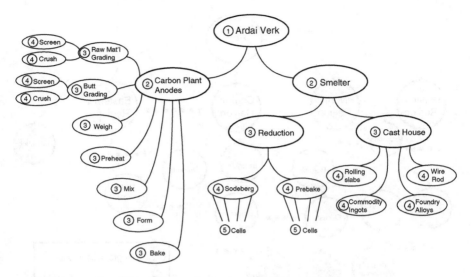

Fig. 8.22 An unfolding of complexity for aluminium plant
Source: Syncho, Ltd

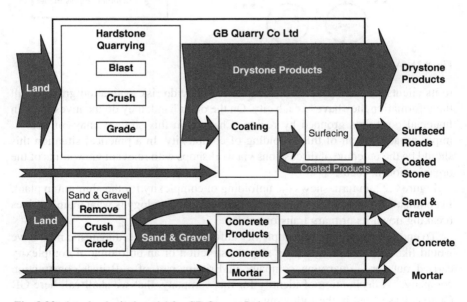

Fig. 8.23 A technological model for GB Quarry, Ltd

In Fig. 8.23 we can appreciate a detailed technological model for the process being carried out for the company to produce quarried and concrete products.

From the name given to the company we can work out its main customers, in this case large and small users of quarried products and concrete. Figure 8.24 shows a more detailed classification of these customers (i.e., road builders, surfacing contractors, brick builders and other small users; all within the construction industry).

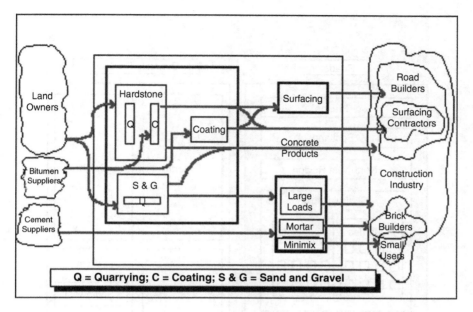

Fig. 8.24 A customer-Supplier model for GB Quarry, Ltd

This Customer-Supplier model also illustrates the relation between landowners, bitumen suppliers and cement suppliers with the company by providing the raw materials needed to produce its products.

On the other hand, the activities carried out by the company are geographically distributed in several regions. Regarding *roadstone* we can identify six regions (i.e., France, Scotland, Northwest Region, Central Region, Southern Region and Eastern Region). The focus of the study was the Central Region where local quarries are identified. Regarding *concrete products* there are four regions (i.e., North, South, East and West) with the Western region divided into three sub-regions (i.e., Southwest, South and Central).

With this information it is possible to build up a detailed geographical model for the activities of the company. Figure 8.25 illustrates this modelling.

Finally, it was clear that customers of GB Quarry were very dependent on the weather (i.e., construction takes place mainly in the open); therefore they needed to have their raw materials delivered on site quickly, in hours. It was found out also that two product categories (i.e., coated materials and concrete) have a very short shelf life. This means that these products had to be delivered in the shortest time possible after being produced.

The above considerations regarding time were also used in the elaboration of the unfolding of complexity for the company.

With all the information gathered from the company and organized in the structural models explained above, it was possible to produce, in Mode I, the unfolding of complexity that is shown in Fig. 8.26.

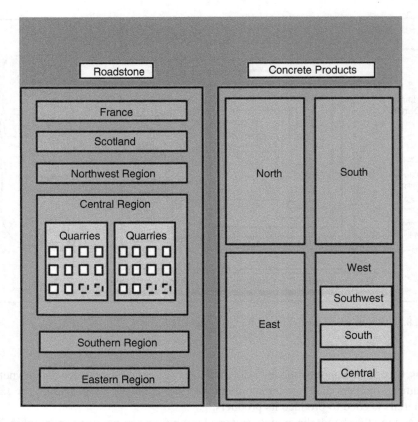

Fig. 8.25 A geographical model for GB Quarry, Ltd. (Espejo and Bowling 1996)

In this unfolding we can appreciate six structural levels. The first one is mainly driven by the technological model. Although Concrete and Roadstone often share the same customers, the technology used in their production is quite different. The second structural level is driven by geographical considerations, so Roadstone and Concrete unfold into geographical regions; six regions correspond to the former and four to the latter.

If we take the Central Region for Roadstone where quarries are identified, then the next structural level is driven by technological and geographical considerations. The technologies used to produce on the one hand sand, gravel and hard materials and on the other surfacing and coating are different. So activities are naturally grouped following these differences. On the other hand, notice that because the location of the identified quarries is grouped into two physically differentiated areas (see Fig. 8.25), the production of hard materials is divided into Hard East and Hard West.

If we now look at the next structural level (i.e., level six) we can see that the production of sand and gravel and hard material, (East and West) is now driven, at this level, by the different customers (see Fig. 8.24). Surface, in turn, needs a further

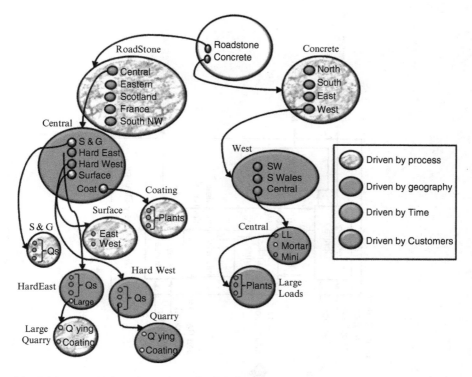

Fig. 8.26 An unfolding of complexity for GB Quarry, Ltd

geographical unfolding in order to take into account the location of the quarries (i.e., East and West).

Coating, on the other hand, needs a closer look. Because the outcome of this process is the production of black material for roads (i.e., coated stones) and it uses bitumen and stone produced by quarrying and has the road surfacing as one of its customers, then the time of delivery plays an important role here. In fact, the plants must be close enough to the customers needing these products; otherwise they will not arrive in good condition to be used. Therefore, coating is unfolded in the next structural level by time considerations.

Now we turn to an example of managing complexity in the design mode (Mode II). Here we explain work that Syncho, Ltd. did in collaboration with the National Westminster Bank (NatWest) and the University of Lancaster (Bowling and Espejo 2000; Espejo 2000). This project (SYCOMT) took place in the mid 1990s at the time NatWest was changing from traditional high street branches, each with their own counter services, lending services and back offices into a New Delivery Strategy, which centralised lending and several back office activities supported by call centres and other information and communication technologies (ICTs). This evolution meant reducing the capacity of branches to customer services and transferring most lending decisions to centres common to several branches in one area (see Fig. 8.27). The structural implications of this change were more sophisticated

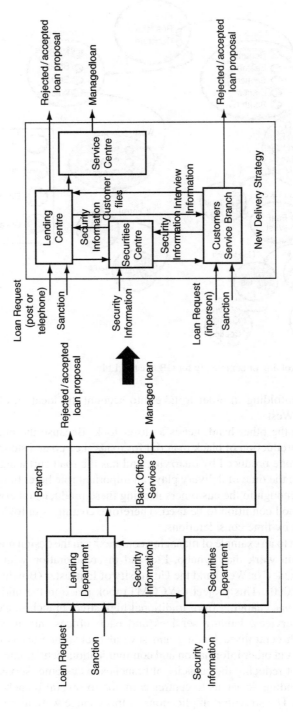

Fig. 8.27 Technological model for loans: change from old branches to new delivery strategy

areas with autonomous functional units taking out from branches some of their traditional competencies (see Fig. 8.28). A thrust of the new delivery strategy was supporting lending activities with high level specialised centres avoiding repetition of operations in each branch. From the perspective of a complexity management strategy this change meant to move from many relatively small primary activities (see Fig. 8.2) to a more aggregated structure (see Fig. 8.1); however those supporting this organizational transformation did not take into account that lending activities were highly interconnected and therefore that the new delivery strategy was fragmenting what previously had been integrated in branches, albeit with lower levels of expertise. The SYCOMT project developed a pilot in the Chester and Wirral Area of the Merseyside Region in the UK to integrate these function using ICTs. They were advised to create a virtual area (see Fig. 8.29) to integrate the fragmented functions. This was supported by an innovative use of ICTs spearheaded by the University of Lancaster; the outcome after 6 months of operations was a virtual area outperforming similar areas by about 25% (Espejo 2000).

In summary, the above examples illustrate the kind of studies regarding technology, time, geography and customer-supplier relations that are needed in order to produce a suitable unfolding of complexity for an organization. But these examples highlight another important point that we would like to stress in this chapter: the difference between the unfolding of complexity and the well-known organization chart. First of all, it should be immediately apparent for the reader that the two diagrams are focused on very different types of relationships. While the organization chart shows hierarchical relations based on power (as we stressed in Chap. 5), the unfolding of complexity shows operational relations based on the autonomy of embedded primary activities as were discussed in Chap. 6. Secondly, whereas building an organization chart is usually determined by functional differentiation of activities, building an unfolding of complexity is determined by 'chunking' the complexity of the organization's transformation according to a set of drivers like technology, geography, time and customers. And thirdly, in an organization chart every box usually has a clear embodiment in a physical space (the office of the CEO, the office of the production manager, etc.) with its corresponding role, whereas every circle in an unfolding of complexity refers to activities done by people in the organization that may have different functions and locations as the example of the bank illustrates.

By now, it should be apparent that producing an unfolding of complexity is not a straightforward matter that can be done right away by looking at the organization chart of the organization in focus. Instead, it is a process that starts by naming systems, working with them as organizational hypotheses by the stakeholders, as mentioned at the end of the last chapter. Remember, these names were the outcome of identity workshops facilitated by the *enabling viewpoint*. Now we use workshops for complexity unfolding.

The second and third stages of Viplan, as explained in this Chapter, consist of analysing the structural implications of these names (in Mode I) or designing new structures (in Mode II). By gathering information from interviews, direct observation, data and reports the enabling viewpoint may produce an initial hypothesis for

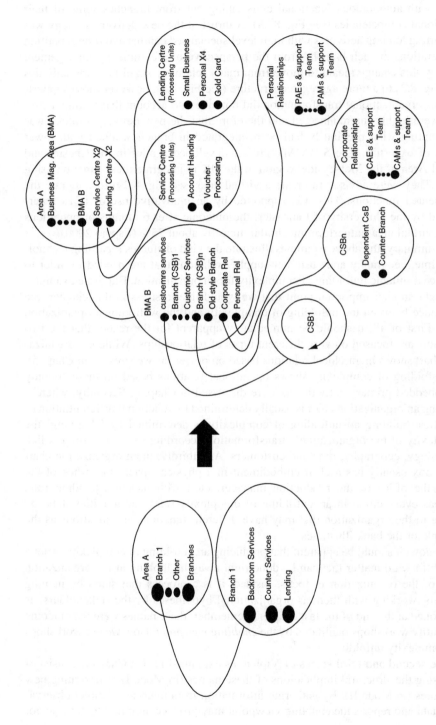

Fig. 8.28 Unfolding of complexity: change from traditional retail banking to new delivery strategy

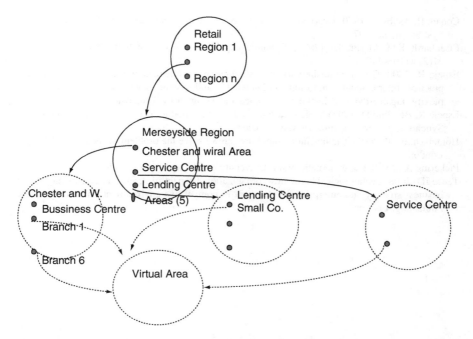

Fig. 8.29 Countering fragmentation with ICTs: design of lending virtual area for Chester and Wirral

an unfolding of complexity. This hypothesis will be used for running one or more *complexity unfolding workshops* to work out its structural implications. All we have said about producing technological and structural models according to relevant complexity drivers, as well as the distinction between primary, secondary and regulatory activities, and the implications of the autonomy criterion for primary activities, are issues to be considered during these workshops.

The outcome of this process, when it reaches a form of closure, is one or two possible unfoldings of complexity for the organization in focus. These are taken again as working hypotheses for the next stage of the method in which the relation between regulatory activities and primary activities is studied to find out a suitable *distribution of discretion*. But this is the aim of the next chapter.

References

Ackoff R (1978) The art of problem solving. Wiley, Chichester

Banker RD, Bardhan IR, Chang H, Lin S (2006) Plant information systems, manufacturing capabilities and plant performance. MIS Quart 30(2):225–246

Beer S (1979) The heart of enterprise. Wiley, Chichester

Bowling D, Espejo R (2000) Exploring computer supported cooperative work in a retail bank'. In: Allen J, Wilby J (eds) ISSS 2000 Intenational Society for the Systems Sciences. ISSS, Toronto

Conant R, Ashby R (1970) Every good regulator of a system must be a model of that system. Int J Syst Sci 1(2):89–97

Eisenhardt KM, Martin JA (2000) Dynamic capabilities: what are they? Strateg Manage J 21(21):1105–1122

Espejo R (2000) Giving requisite variety to strategic and implementation processes: theory and practice. International symposium on knowledge and systems sciences: challenges to complexity. Japan Advanced Institute of Science and Technology, Ishikawa, pp 34–42

Espejo R, Bowling D (1996) Viplan learning system: a method to learn the viable system model. Syncho, Ltd., Birmingham, www.syncho.com

Homer-Dixon T (2001) The ingenuity gap: how can we solve the problem of the future. Vintage, London

Pickering A (2010) The cybernetic brain. University of Chicago Press, London

Teece JD (2008) Technological know-how, organizational capabilities, and strategic management: business strategy and enterprise development in competitive environments. World Scientific Publishing, London

Chapter 9
Distributing Discretion and Designing Structural Mechanisms

Abstract The previous chapter showed how the unfolding of complexity is a useful tool to describe and design the way an organization groups (or should structure) its primary activities. In this chapter the unfolding of complexity is used to discuss the *distribution of resources and discretion* from the organization's global level to the local level of the most basic primary activities. For this purpose it uses the Recursion/Functions Table. This is a tool to discuss the centralization and decentralization of organizational resources and decision-making. Some resources may be centralized but at the same time may be functionally decentralized. Supported by multiple examples of particular transformation processes we discuss in this chapter criteria to decentralize or otherwise the organization's resources. The Table is used to give systemic meaning to business functions; are these functions regulating the inside and now of the organization or are they providing capacity to deal with the outside and then? For a primary activity to be autonomous, and viable in its own right, it needs resources and discretion to make decisions and develop its own identity. In the end this chapter offers a model for the distribution of resources, relations and information throughout the organization to support the design of its structural mechanisms. As such it is a powerful tool to map its complexity.

This chapter explains the last two steps of the Viplan Method; distributing discretion and designing structural mechanisms. In particular it offers a detailed approach to study the distribution of resources in an organization and the design of the cohesion mechanism for viability (see Chap. 6). The last chapter showed how the unfolding of complexity is a useful tool to diagnose (Mode I) and design (Mode II) the way an organization groups (or should structure) its primary activities. This is done by taking into account four perspectives from which it is possible to describe the operation of the organization-in-focus. The tools used were technological, geographical, market segmentation and time models (see Chap. 8).

The unfolding of complexity yields a diagram that enables relevant viewpoints to discuss the distribution of resources and decision-making capacity to carry out the organization's transformation. In this sense it is also a tool that helps to realize the

R. Espejo and A. Reyes, *Organizational Systems*,
DOI 10.1007/978-3-642-19109-1_9, © Springer-Verlag Berlin Heidelberg 2011

connection between the strategy of the organization – as stated in its mission – and its structure – in terms of defining primary activities at different structural levels.

But, in order to define with more precision the structure of an organization, it is necessary to determine the distribution of the roles and resources needed to produce its primary activities. This is the problem examined in this chapter and it is related to the common discussion between organizational centralization and decentralization (Castells 2001; Galbraith 2002; Goold and Campbell 2002; Malone 2004; Nault 1998; Seddon 2008).

It is usual to approach this discussion assuming that these terms constitute a dualism, that is, two opposite poles difficult to reconcile. As a consequence, the organization fluctuates between one pole and the other depending on which is the majority position at the time. It could be said that, in some sense, this issue is posed either as an ideological problem or as a management fad (Beer 1979, 1985).

This chapter shows an alternative position in which the issue is approached as an organizational design problem. But what exactly is the problem that is under examination?

It is clear that an inadequate centralization generates several problems like 'bottlenecks' and 'bureaucracy' in the sense of roles that do not add value to the organization. Excessive centralization is also responsible for people making decisions distant from the local action itself. This increases the chances of poor decisions.

But, on the other hand, an inadequate decentralization can produce serious problems as well. Most of them are derived from a lack of coordination among people who have the responsibility of taking local (decentralized) decisions.

In order to approach the apparent dichotomy between centralization and decentralization, we will introduce the concept of discretion.

Discretion is defined, in this context, as the (explicit or tacit) organizational agreement that managing and using particular resources is the responsibility of particular roles. In other words, a person (or group) has functional discretion if there is agreement that they control the use of the related resources. Discharging this responsibility requires the availability of resources and the competence to make use of them. Therefore, the simple agreement of where responsibility lies is not enough for a role to have discretion.

Notice that it is quite possible to agree a role's discretion in some functions or in aspects of particular functions. For example, it is possible that a manager, who has discretion to select the people working under his/her supervision, does not have the discretion to carry out the necessary staff induction, which will probably be a centralized function of the organization's human resources department.

In these terms, the problem of choosing between functional centralization and decentralization can be restated as a problem of distributing discretion over the organization's resources. This is precisely the organizational design problem that we would like to address in this chapter.

Distributing discretion helps to establish the degree of centralization/decentralization of functions in an organization. In order to do so, it is necessary to remember the difference between primary activities and regulatory/support functions that was established in earlier chapters. While the former are the organizational units producing the products or services of the organization, the latter are the functions creating and regulating these primary activities. These are the functions deciding, managing and reconfiguring resources to achieve the organization's policies. In Chap. 8 we related primary activities with processes producing the organization's transformation and regulatory functions with processes developing, servicing and managing this transformation, that is, with *organizational processes.*

It is clear that we require resources of some kind (people, technology, infrastructure, etc.) to carry out a regulatory function. This, in turn, puts a natural question: Who should be accountable for their use? Two alternatives are possible:

1. The resources needed to fulfil the regulatory function *are not discretionary to the production process* using them but to an embedding primary activity one or more levels above it, with responsibility for their use. For instance an enterprise's accounting resources may be centralized at its corporate level at the same time that costing is necessary for all local production activities. Accounting resources, in this example, are managed centrally but *shared* by several embedded primary activities. This corresponds to a centralized framework. Similarly, in a centralized scheme, every time the information systems of the regional branches of a bank fail, they may need to request help from the Technology Support Office that is located in the headquarters of the bank.
2. The resources needed to fulfil the regulatory function *are discretionary to the primary activity itself.* This corresponds to a decentralized framework, for example, when the regional branches of the bank have their own IT specialists that support their information systems.

But, given that a regulatory function is needed to support several primary activities, which criteria can be used as guide to select the first or the second alternative? The main point is to understand the significance of the regulatory function under consideration to the primary activities that it supports. This significance can be characterized according to the following criteria:

1. The regulatory function is a *critical success factor* (Rockart 1979) for the primary activity
2. The application of the regulatory function has characteristics that are particular to the primary activity that it supports (this aspect will be illustrated with an example later on)
3. The demand for the regulatory function within the primary activity it supports is high (according to a predefined criterion such as being part of its work flow)
4. Necessary financial and specialised resources to carry out this function are available within the primary activity (i.e., are not scarce within the overall organization)
5. The resources necessary to execute the regulatory function are distributable

If these five conditions are met for a regulatory function in relation to a primary activity, then it is highly probable that the second alternative will be the best choice (that is, decentralization). In other words, discretion will be agreed for the primary activity in order to carry out the regulatory function. Conversely, if at least one of these conditions is not fulfilled, it is quite possible that a centralized framework will be the best option. In this case, probably the resources of the regulatory function will be shared with other primary activities. For instance, in a hospital, very expensive diagnostic equipment that is critical to several or all embedded operational departments, at the same time of being particular and in high demand by all of them, may not be distributable.

The following example illustrates the use of these criteria. Let us consider two primary activities of a national institution that offers services to higher education in a country. The first activity is the *national examinations service* (NES) that is in charge of running national exams in education. The second activity is concerned with *monitoring quality services* (MQS) of universities.[1] Let us assume that the regulatory function that is being analyzed is the maintenance of information systems. With this information we have four alternatives regarding the centralization or decentralization of this function (see Fig. 9.1):

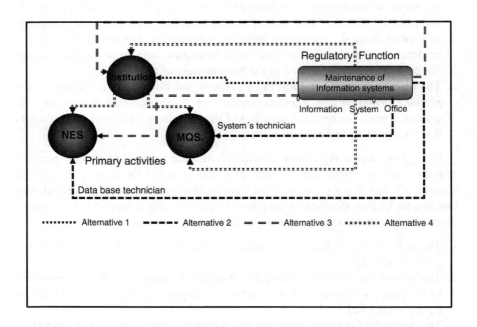

NES = National Examination Services   MQS = Monitoring the quality of services

Fig. 9.1 Distribution of discretion of a regulatory function (four alternatives)

---

[1]Notice that in the larger context of the Educational System, the role of this national institution corresponds to a regulatory function. Therefore, monitoring the quality services of universities will not be a primary activity vis-à-vis this larger system-in-focus. We often call them *missionary activities* but for the sake of simplicity in this discussion we will continue to call them primary activities.

1. The regulatory function is completely centralized, that is, the Information System Office of the institution is responsible for providing the maintenance service to both primary activities
2. The regulatory function is completely decentralized, that is, both primary activities have their own resources to carry out the maintenance of their information systems
3. The regulatory function is centralized for MQS but it is decentralized for the NES. In other words, while the NES has the resources for carrying out the maintenance of their information systems, the other primary activity depends on the services provided by the Information System Office
4. The regulatory function is centralized for the NES and decentralized for MQS

Let us assume that a detailed analysis of the data gathered from the institution provided the following points:

1. The activities carried out in the NES depend fundamentally on its information systems (recording, processing, analyzing and publishing data from national tests)
2. MQS people use basic technology (personal computers, text editors and spread sheets)
3. The technological problems of the NES are mainly related to their information systems
4. The technological problems of the MQS are usually related to a partial damage of a personal computer or a misconfiguration of the word processor or the spreadsheet
5. If a failure in the information systems of the NES is not dealt with promptly the negative impact on its performance is too high, due to the time commitment to deliver the results of the national tests
6. The Information System Office gives support to every department of the institution and not only to the two operational departments carrying out the primary activities mentioned in the example
7. Historically, MQS has had many technological problems (e.g., once per week)
8. Historically, NES has had many technological problems (e.g., once per week)
9. MQS and NES are not sharing a highly specialised resource

It is easy to see that points 1 and 5 are closely related to the first criterion mentioned above, that is, are critical success factors. Similarly, point 3 is related to the second, point 8 to the third and point 9 to the fourth and fifth criteria. Therefore, it makes sense to decentralize the maintenance of information systems for the NES. In other words, the department responsible for carrying out the NES should have enough resources, such as specialised technicians, to take care of the problems arising in their information systems.

On the other hand, and regarding the relation between the regulatory function and the MQS, point 7 relates to the third criterion above but otherwise the evidence would suggest that, in this case, it is convenient to centralize this function. In other words, each time a problem occurs in the MQS primary activity, the Information System Office will assign directly one of its technicians to take care of the problem. Notice

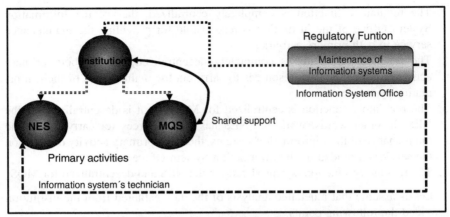

This kind of analysis allows a precise definition of the distribution of
resources (humans, technological, inputs, etc.) for regulatory activities in
all primary activities.

Fig. 9.2 Distribution of discretion of a regulatory function (a proposal)

that, in this case, delays in this service provided by this office do not generate a
significant negative impact on the performance of this primary activity (see Fig. 9.2).

It is important to highlight that having their own resources to deal with its
technical problems not only allows NES to recover faster from unexpected breakdowns but also facilitates the chances of a learning process. Indeed, technicians
may become specialized in solving the particular failures of these information
systems and, therefore, develop preventive practices.

Notice, as well, that discretion to carry out a regulatory function does not
necessarily imply increasing the staff of the primary activity. It is quite possible,
for instance, that a single person be in charge of performing several regulatory
functions in a primary activity. We will go back to this point later on.

The recursion/functions table is an appropriate tool to do an analysis of discretion as the one described in the previous example. The table is used to cross an
organization's primary activities with its regulatory functions. In the table primary
activities are grouped according to the *organization's unfolding of complexity,* as
seen in the previous chapter. Figure 9.3 illustrates the unfolding of complexity for
the airline Satena (see Chap. 8).

The regulatory functions, on the other hand, methodologically can be identified
through interviews of organizational roles recognised with the support of process
maps or even organization charts (as are often available in organizations). The
primary activities are written in the first column of the recursion/functions table
preserving their structure in the unfolding of complexity. We will go back to this
point later on. The regulatory functions, in turn, are written in the columns of the
table (see Fig. 9.4).

A mark (e.g., a dot) in the cell where a regulatory function (a column) crosses
with a primary activity (a row) indicates that this primary activity has discretion to

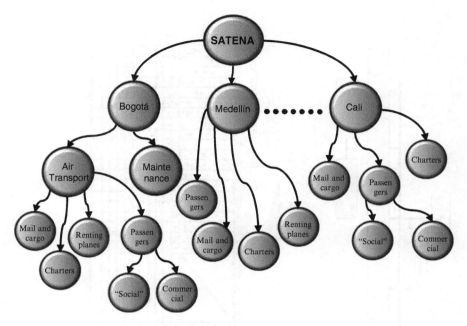

Fig. 9.3 Satena's unfolding of complexity

carry out this regulatory function. For example, in Fig. 9.5 the black dot in the cell where the *personnel* function crosses with the row called Company (i.e., the first recursion level), indicates that discretion for this regulatory function is at the organization's highest structural level. In other words, personnel management is completely centralized in this company.

On the other hand, the dots in the *training* column indicate that the resources for carrying out this function are spread throughout the company. This shows that each of the three primary activities of this organization has its own resources for training the people working in it (Fig. 9.5).

Regarding the distribution of discretion, an overview of this table indicates the following:

1. The functions of personnel management, production scheduling, process development and logistics are centralized and integrated at the company level. This fact can be expressed in three other equivalent ways:
   (a) Every one of these regulatory functions is carried out at the company's highest structural level.
   (b) There is no discretion to perform these regulatory functions in any of the three embedded primary activities.
   (c) The resources required for performing these regulatory functions are shared by the three primary activities.[2]

---

[2]There is an exception to this interpretation that will be explained later on.

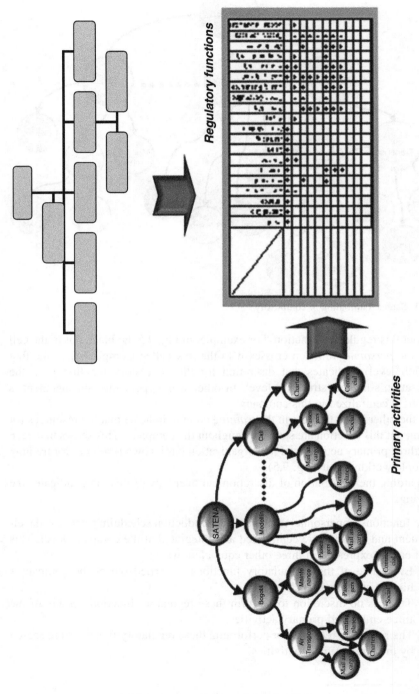

Fig. 9.4 Basic structure of the recursion/functions table

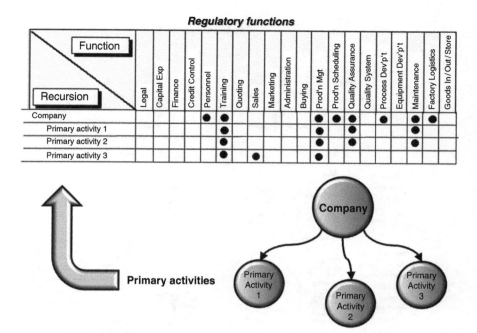

Fig. 9.5 An example of a recursion/functions table

2. Training, production management, quality control and maintenance are all decentralized functions in this organization. This can also be expressed in the following equivalent statements:
   (a) These regulatory functions are carried out at all structural levels of the organization.
   (b) The three embedded primary activities have discretion to carry out these regulatory functions.
   (c) The resources required for performing these regulatory functions are distributed throughout the primary activities.

In order to show how to use the recursion/functions table as a tool to describe an organization's distribution of discretion, we will take Satena as an example. Figure 9.6 is the organization chart of this company and Fig. 9.3, as mentioned, shows its unfolding of complexity.

Figure 9.7 shows the recursion/functions table for Satena. The following points come from analysing this table:

- Human resources management, training, fees setting, bookings, acquisitions and planning and systems are all centralized functions.
- The company branches in Bogotá and Medellin have discretion to manage their own budget. On the other hand, the budget is consolidated and distributed in the central level of the company.

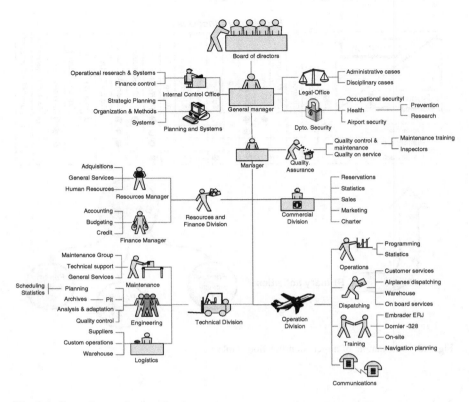

Fig. 9.6 Satena's organization chart

- Different levels in the company have discretion regarding the sales function. The primary activities with this discretion are: Satena itself; branches in Bogotá and Medellin; passengers, mail and cargo; charter flights; renting planes.
- The marketing and advertising function is executed, discretionally, in all of the company's structural levels with the exception of the following primary activities: commercial and social routes, mail and cargo, renting flights and maintenance services.
- The marketing and advertising of the commercial and social routes are carried out by the level in charge of passenger transportation.
- The level in charge of air transport is responsible for doing the marketing and advertising of mail and cargo and renting planes services as well.
- Marketing and advertising of the maintenance service is carried out directly from Bogotá.
- General services, operation control and security are functions that are distributed among the central level and the branches in Bogotá and Medellin.
- All structural levels in the company have discretion to carry out their own internal control function.

Primary activities \ Regulatory functions	Human resource managt	Budget	Training	Fees setting	Bookings	Sales	Marketing and advertising	General services	Acquisitions	Operations control	Internal control	Planning & systems	Security
Satena	•	•	•	•	•	•	•	•	•	•	•	•	•
Bogotá		•				•	•	•		•	•		•
Air transport							•				•		
Passenger transportation						•	•				•		
Commercial routes											•		
"Social" routes											•		
Mail and cargo						•					•		
Charters						•	•				•		
Renting planes						•					•		
Maintenance											•		
Medellín		•				•	•	•		•	•		•

Fig. 9.7 Recursion/functions table for Satena

Notice that the points mentioned above come from reading the table's columns. If reading the same table is focused on the rows, it is possible to describe the *functional capacity* of each primary activity of the company. The following points are inferred by analysis from Fig. 9.7.

- The Bogotá and Medellín[3] branches have capacity and resources necessary to manage the budget, sales, marketing and advertising, general services, operations control, internal control and the security of their own jurisdictions.
- The level in charge of air transport services has the competence (discretion) to handle marketing, advertising, and the internal control of its activities.
- The primary activities doing passenger transport and charter flights include resources to carry out the functions of sales, marketing, advertising and internal control.
- Mail and Cargo along with the renting of planes include their own sales and internal control functions.

---

[3]Note that everything said for Bogotá and Medellín is equally applicable for all the company's branches which appear in its unfolding of complexity (see Fig. 9.3).

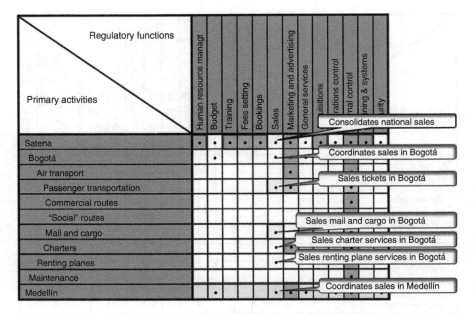

Fig. 9.8 Scope of the sales function at each recursion level that has discretion

It is very important to clarify that when a regulatory function is distributed at several structural levels, it does not mean that the same activity is being done in each one of these levels. Figure 9.8 illustrates this point for Satena's sales function.

The scope of sales differs at each of the structural levels where it is performed. Indeed, while the central level *consolidates* national sales, the company's branches *coordinate* sales at the regional level. On the other hand, passenger transport in Bogotá includes ticket sales. Similarly, Sales supports Mail and Cargo, Charters and Renting Planes in each branch. Later on, we will make a special emphasis on the proper use of verbs to delimit with precision the scope of the regulatory functions when these are distributed among several structural levels in an organization.

On the other hand, notice that from the perspective of complexity regulatory functions can be *decomposed* in a similar way to that of primary activities, except that in this case we talk about *levels of resolution* and not of recursion. For instance, human resources management can be decomposed into selection, hiring, training and evaluation. In a similar way, the information systems management function can be decomposed into design, development, maintenance and training. Figure 9.9 illustrates the decomposition of regulatory functions taking as an example a small university.

Of course, each sub-function, depending on its complexity, could be decomposed even further. When do we stop? The decomposition of a regulatory function stops when the distribution of discretion implies (sub-) functions that overlap exactly the primary activities they serve. Once this is the case, these sub-functions could be grouped under a single name (or function) and allocated to the primary

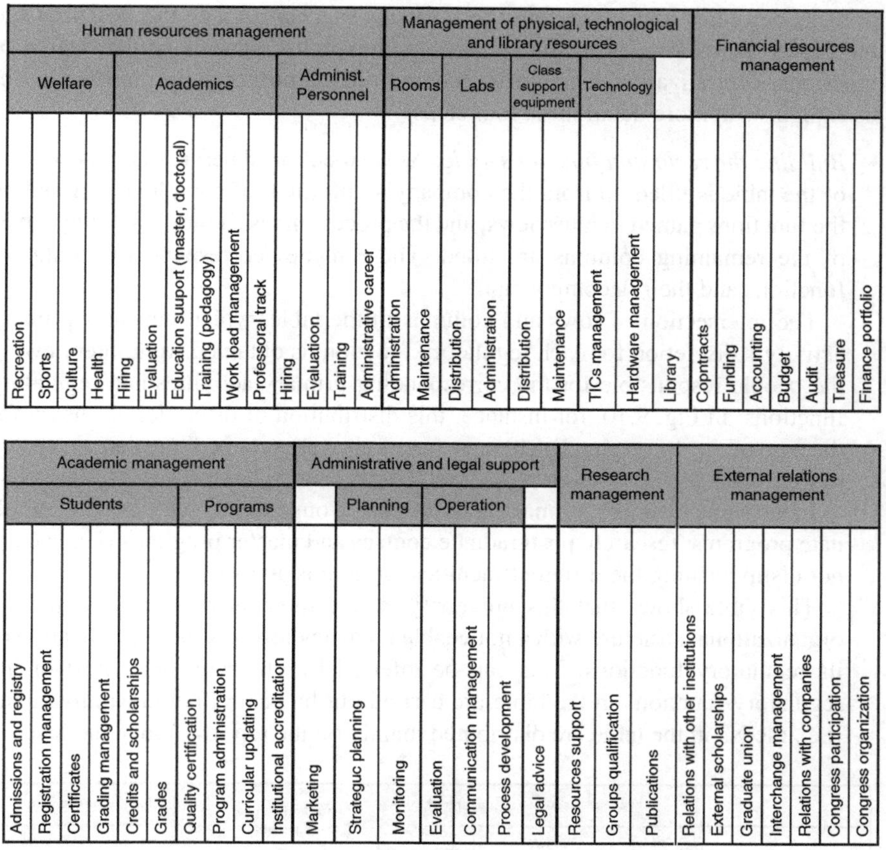

Human resources management			Management of physical, technological and library resources					Financial resources management
Welfare	Academics	Administ. Personnel	Rooms	Labs	Class support equipment	Technology		

Human resources management — Welfare: Recreation, Sports, Culture, Health. Academics: Hiring, Evaluation, Education support (master, doctoral), Training (pedagogy), Work load management, Professoral track. Administ. Personnel: Hiring, Evaluatioon, Training, Administrative career.

Management of physical, technological and library resources — Rooms: Administration, Maintenance. Labs: Distribution, Administration. Class support equipment: Distribution, Maintenance. Technology: TICs management, Hardware management. (unlabeled): Library.

Financial resources management: Copntracts, Funding, Accounting, Budget, Audit, Treasure, Finance portfolio.

Academic management		Administrative and legal support			Research management	External relations management
Students	Programs		Planning	Operation		

Academic management — Students: Admissions and registry, Registration management, Certificates, Grading management, Credits and scholarships, Grades. Programs: Quality certification, Program administration, Curricular updating, Institutional accreditation.

Administrative and legal support — (unlabeled): Marketing. Planning: Strateguc planning, Monitoring, Evaluation. Operation: Communication management, Process development, Legal advice.

Research management: Resources support, Groups qualification, Publications.

External relations management: Relations with other institutions, External scholarships, Graduate union, Interchange management, Relations with companies, Congress participation, Congress organization.

Fig. 9.9 An example of the decomposition of regulatory functions in a small university

activities with which they overlap. Visually, in the recursion/functions table this is evident when the distribution of dots in the columns corresponding to these sub-functions crosses only individual primary activities.

Before explaining a method to build the recursion/functions table, it is important to mention that nowadays it is possible to centralize highly specialized resources and, simultaneously, decentralize the support they give. Modern ICTs (Information and Communication Technology) allow the development of these mechanisms. Call centres are a concrete example when they are used as an internal support of the company's primary activities. For example, specialized maintenance of software packages could be done via on-line communication through the company's intranet. In this case, the specialized resources (i.e., engineers) could be centralized while their accountability is decentralized to primary activities. The response speed and the capacity of the communication channel make this possible.

There are four steps to study discretion: (1) building the recursion/functions table; (2) study centralized regulatory functions; (3) estimate the functional capacity of primary activities and (4) design the *cohesion mechanisms* of the decentralized regulatory functions. The result of this study is first diagnosis of the degree of functional centralization/decentralization and second proposals to improve it. Let us explain with more detail these four steps.

- *Building the recursion/functions table*: As we mentioned before, the first column of the table is filled up from the company's unfolding of complexity. Based on the functions named in interviews, and the process maps (if they exist) the names of the remaining columns are filled. These names correspond to regulatory functions and their decomposition.

  The intersection of rows and columns in the table, which indicates primary activity's discretion for each regulatory function, is obtained from interviewing the people responsible for the corresponding primary activities and regulatory functions. In Fig. 9.10, for instance, this distribution of discretion is shown for the case of the university. Regulatory functions were grouped together according to Fig. 9.9.[4]

  In the same example, primary activities are grouped into faculties, undergraduate programs, research, postgraduate courses and master programs (i.e., we are not distinguishing the different faculties, programs and so forth).

  This table shows that this university, at the moment of the study, had an organizational structure with a noticeable tendency towards the centralization of its regulatory functions. This can be inferred by observing that most of the regulatory functions in the table are carried out by central administrative units (i.e., the Xs in the table are distributed mainly on the top row above the level of

| | Human resources management | | | | | | | | | | | | | | Financial resources management | | | | | | | Academic management | | | | | | | | | |
| | Welfare | | | | Academics | | | | | | Administ. Personnel | | | | | | | | | | | Students | | | | | | Programs | | | |
	Recreation	Sports	Culture	Health	Hiring	Evaluation	Education support (master, doctoral)	Training (pedagogy)	Work load management	Professoral track	Hiring	Evaluatioon	Training	Administrative career	Contracts	Funding	Accounting	Budget	Audit	Treasure	Finance portfolio	Admissions and registry	Registration management	Certificates	Grading management	Credits and scholarships	Grades	Quality certification	Program administration	Curricular updating	Institutional accreditation
UNIVERSITY	x	x	x	x	x	x	x	x	x	x	x	x	x	x	x	x	x	x	x	x	x	x		x		x	x	x	x	x	x
FACULTIES					x	x	x	x	x	x				x								x							x	x	
Programs																															
Research																															
Postgraduate courses																															
Master programs																															

Fig. 9.10 Distribution of discretion of a university

---

[4]For the sake of simplicity we only show the distribution of discretion for three regulatory functions: human resource management, financial resources management and academic management.

faculties). On the other hand, faculties have little discretion (that is, there are fewer Xs related to faculties and none at the bottom of the table).

- *Analyzing centralized functions*: the next step identifies all the centralized regulatory functions and checks out for "bottlenecks" or similar problems (see Fig. 9.11). This perception arises from the interviews previously done. For each of these functions it is necessary to study if it is feasible to delegate them, keeping in mind the five criteria mentioned above.

In order to specify the appropriate level of discretion for a particular regulatory function it is important to involve in the discussion, in one or several workshops, the viewpoints relevant to this function. The purpose of these workshops is agreeing the level of responsibility that each primary activity is willing to have in performing the regulatory function under consideration, considering other related functions and available technology. For instance, the table in Fig. 9.12 shows the distribution of responsibility for hiring lecturers in the university. Notice that there are four central administrative units and four other units that perform aspects of this function at other levels of recursion. The degree of discretion at each level is described with the precise use of verbs. It is important that each verb delimits precisely the responsibility of carrying out the function at each level. We avoid using verbs such as *to accompany*, *to help*, *to support*, *to stimulate* or similar. It helps using verbs which recognise the accomplished function (see Fig. 9.12).

Primary activities \ Regulatory functions	Human resource managt	Budget	Training	Fees setting	Bookings	Sales	Marketing and advertising	General services	Acquisitions	Operations control	Internal control	Planning & systems	Security
Satena	•	•	•	•	•	•	•	•	•	•	•	•	•
Bogotá		•					•	•	•		•	•	•
Air transport							•						
Passenger transportation						•	•					•	
Commercial routes												•	
"Social" routes												•	
Mail and cargo						•						•	
Charters						•	•					•	
Renting planes						•						•	
Maintenance												•	
Medellín		•				•	•	•		•	•		•

Fig. 9.11 Identifying centralized regulatory functions (Satena's case study)

Roles .vs. Functions		Human Resources management / Academics / Hiring
University		
President´s Office		
Academic Vice-President	•	Proposal of hiring policies
Registry		
Finance and Administrative Direction	•	Approves budget for hiring
Human Resources Department	•	Manages hiring process
Academic Council		
University´s Council	•	Decides hiring policies
Auditing Committee		
Dean´s Office	•	Approval of candidate
Programme Committee	•	Advertise position
Programme Direction		
Director of Special Studies	•	Short listing applicants
Director of Post Graduate Studies	•	Making offers

Fig. 9.12 A proposal for distributing discretion to hire lecturers in a faculty

	Human resources management														Financial resources management							Academic management									
	Welfare				Academics						Administ. Personnel											Students						Programs			
	Recreation	Sports	Culture	Health	Hiring	Evaluation	Education suuport (master, doctoral)	Training (pedagogy)	Work load management	Professorial track	Hiring	Evaluatioon	Training	Administrative career	Contracts	Funding	Accounting	Budget	Audit	Treasure	Finance portfolio	Admissions and registry	Registration management	Certificates	Grading management	Credits and scholarships	Grades	Quality certification	Program administration	Curricular updating	Institutional accreditation
UNIVERSITY	•	•	•	•	•	•	•	•	•	•	•	•	•	•	•	•	•	•	•	•	•	•	•	•	•	•	•	•	•	•	•
FACULTIES					•	•	•	•	•		•	•						•				•	•		•	•			•	•	•
Programs					•	•	•	•	•	•	•	•	•					•				•	•		•				•	•	•
Research																															
Postgraduate courses					•	•		•	•									•				•								•	•
Master programs					•	•		•	•													•								•	

Fig. 9.13 Design of a new distribution of discretion for a small regional university

By running these workshops it is possible to agree the decentralization of functional discretion. Let us notice that on the left side of each verb in Fig. 9.12 there is a dot. These dots are used as a visual synthesis of the outcome of all workshops to build up a new recursion/functions table, which shows the new distribution of discretion that is desired for the organization. Figure 9.13 illustrates the outcome of this exercise to adjust the centralized structure of the small university that we are using as an example.

In this particular case we can see a new communication structure in which faculties and programs have a greater responsibility in performing different functions than before. It will be in those primary activities that the execution of most of these regulatory functions will be accomplished. Remember that each dot in this table is associated with one or several verbs specifying the scope in the execution of the corresponding regulatory function.

A row-by-row analysis in this table allows agreeing the functional capacity necessary at each structural level. This analysis is the following step of the method.

- *Estimating the functional capacity of primary activities*: rows in the recursion/functions table show the primary activities' structural levels. Each row, as it was mentioned at the beginning of the chapter, corresponds to one of the circles of the unfolding of complexity. If we look at one of these rows, for instance, the one corresponding to the faculties in a university (Fig. 9.13), it is possible to identify the regulatory functions with discretion at this level. Indeed, by observing each of the dots from this row it can be concluded that faculties will have discretion performing the following functions: hiring, evaluation, education and training of lecturers; workload administration; academic career administration; hiring, evaluation, education and training of the faculty's administrative staff; budgeting; aspects of admission and registry processes; reception of new students; graduation; scholarships and loans administration; management and updating the curricula; and accreditation of the faculty's academic programs.

  Remember that the scope of each of these functions has been defined precisely by the verbs used to delimit responsibilities (Fig. 9.12). Comparing this proposed design with the current situation, as reflected by the recursion/functions table in Fig. 9.10, allows the participants in the design determining the profile of the roles required to assume these new responsibilities. Manuals describing these functions could also be updated based on the information derived from this table.

  Finally, the number of people required for each structural level, for instance the staff supporting the faculty in the example of the university, could be calculated in terms of the complexity of each regulatory function. This complexity is related to the demand for each function and the required resources to respond to this demand. Notice, therefore, that each dot in the table, as mentioned before, does not correspond to a single person but to a functional capacity within a process. A single person, for instance, could be in charge of performing more than one function. The outcome of this detailed analysis will be an estimation of the functional capacity required for the adjustment in the distribution of discretion in the organization.

- *Designing cohesion mechanism accounting for decentralized regulatory functions*: The need for cohesion arises when together with the organization's complexity unfolding, regulatory functions are decentralized to various primary activities. In other words, discretion and empowerment require establishing a mechanism that guarantees the cohesion between the different primary activities when performing these regulatory functions. The following story exemplifies this problem.

Cohesion is necessary for each primary activity. This implies that together with the organization's complexity unfolding, there is a need to integrate their regulatory functions in the context of their primary activity. An implication is that when functional discretion is allocated to embedded primary activities it is necessary to establish a mechanism that guarantees the cohesion between them as they perform locally these regulatory functions. An old but illustrative story exemplifies this problem.

In the mid 1980s a nationwide organization in a South American country decided to systematize all its processes. For this purpose its strategy was to decentralize Information Systems that, up to that moment, had been concentrated in a big office in the country's capital. The general office decided to create a system's office in each 1 of the 32 regional divisions of the organization; the function was delegated to the regional directors. In other words, and using the terminology presented before, the regional branches had discretion to systematize the processes that concerned them. Each office received a budget with a goal of implementing the information systems they require within the following 2 years.

Two years later, every regional branch had implemented an information system. However, when the national head office requested consolidated reports, these were almost impossible to produce; the different regional systems were incompatible. Each branch, through a bidding mechanism, had hired the most cost-effective systematization of *their* processes. Even though each regional director behaved in an honest and diligent manner, the lack of a cohesion mechanism generated the described mishap.

The cohesion mechanism has four closely related components: (see Chap. 6 and Fig. 9.14): three of them constitute the cohesion function and one the coordination function. The three constituting the cohesion function are the *resource bargaining bi-directional channel*; the *monitoring channel* and a channel issuing centralized *intervention rules*. The cohesion and coordination functions together constitute the cohesion mechanism. Each one of these will be examined next:

The channel issuing centralized rules allows the definition and divulgence of guidelines and general conditions or restrictions that are considered non-negotiable, because they are beyond the competence of the organization. For instance, an example in personnel management is minimum wages for workers. In fact, these are policies reflecting the ethos, principles and values of the organization or society and, therefore, they are non-negotiable. Other examples are: internal quality standards; gender equality when hiring new personnel; policies on environmental protection; industrial security regulations; restrictions on the use of illegal software; policies regarding the use of communication platforms, etc.

Discretion means delegation plus action capability. This implies that when an organization goes for decentralization of functions, it has to allocate the necessary resources for the proper execution of the functions. Now, because resources in an organization are always limited, a communication channel to facilitate resources bargaining becomes fundamental. But, at the same time,

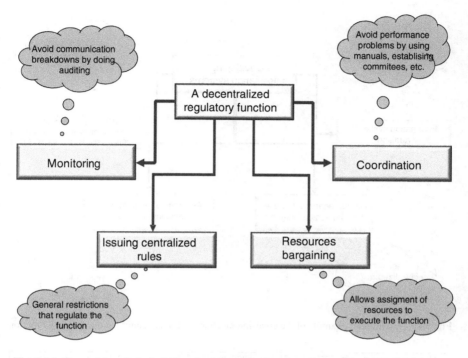

Fig. 9.14 General description of the cohesion mechanism for a decentralized function

those who undertake the responsibility to perform a decentralized function commit themselves to comply with a set of outcomes. This is part of the negotiation process.

Coordination on the other hand, has the purpose of enabling the autonomy of primary activities and also avoiding (or anticipating) any performance problems during the execution of the decentralized function. The creation of committees that gather periodically to deal with atypical cases; producing and distributing manuals, standards and formats; designing and using information systems and doing training courses are all examples of this systemic function that helps coordinate decentralized regulatory functions.

But even with coordinated activities breakdowns are relatively common in the daily execution of business functions. These breakdowns often happen because of failures in communication processes and poor alignment of interests and meanings. Another possibility is, of course, the outcome of deceitful acts. No matter the case, it is important to have a monitoring channel that ensures stability of commitments and agreements for the regulatory function under consideration. Auditing is a particular instance of this monitoring.

Coordination and the other channels must be designed and implemented for each regulatory function in which discretion has been granted. Figure 9.15 shows an example of a *cohesion mechanism* for the decentralization of information systems in the story of the public organization mentioned above.

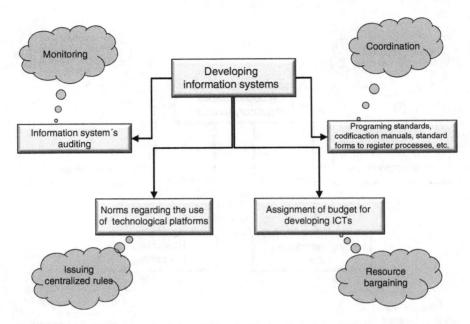

Fig. 9.15 A particular example of the cohesion mechanism for a decentralised regulatory function

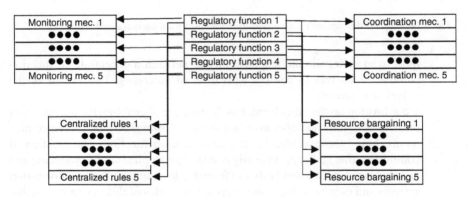

Fig. 9.16 A generic cohesion mechanism

The generic mechanism can be seen on Fig. 9.16 for all centralised and decentralised regulatory functions. By now the reader should be aware that this mechanism was explained in Chap. 6 when we presented the viable system model. Indeed, it is possible to build up the VSM for a given organization by using as a guide the recursion/functions table. Showing this, however, goes beyond the scope of this book.[5]

---

[5]The interested reader could visit the page www.syncho.org to get the Viplan software where a step-by-step construction is shown.

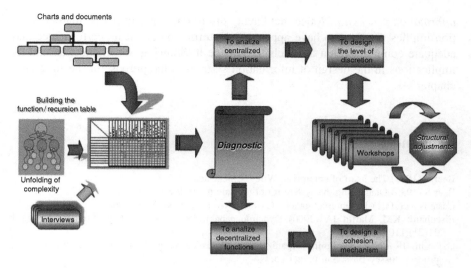

Fig. 9.17 A method to study the distribution of discretion

The outcomes of the method described in this chapter are first of all, a diagnosis of the degree of centralization/decentralization of functions in an organization, and secondly a proposal for a more effective distribution of discretion of regulatory functions. This design can help eliminating bottlenecks, speeding up the work flow of primary activities and promoting the balance between organizational autonomy and cohesion. Figure 9.17 illustrates the method.

A similar approach can be used to design an organization's adaptation mechanism. It should be kept in mind that each primary activity needs functional capacity to adapt to its surroundings and to make things happen. Conceptually this implies that we would expect that each primary activity, from the organization as a whole to the most local, will have resources embodying the five systemic functions, that is, policy, intelligence, cohesion, coordination and implementation. In practice organizations find it difficult to devolve autonomy; however this is an issue of relationships that goes beyond the scope of this chapter (see Chap. 6).

We can add that the discussions of this chapter are particularly relevant to reconfiguring an organization's resources and therefore to the development of its dynamic capabilities. New technologies – in particular ICTs – are making possible more imaginative forms of co-evolution of an organization with its environment, while more effective forms of centralization and decentralization are also a possibility (Eisenhardt and Martin 2000; Teece 2008).

Indeed, the recursion/functions table is also useful to make a connection between strategy, structure and communications in an organization. In order to show this connection it is important to add an additional distinction to the processes. So far we have distinguished between primary processes (e.g., business processes) and organizational processes (e.g., cohesion processes). The former are responsible for the value chain, the latter for its regulation. Now we need to bring forth the concept of *information processes*. Notice that having discretion to perform a regulatory function implies the need to have appropriate information about its performance and adequate communication channels to manage it. Showing this connection and its implications in the design of information systems is the purpose of the following chapter.

References

Beer S (1979) The heart of enterprise. Wiley, Chichester
Beer S (1985) Diagnosing the system for organizations. Wiley, Chichester
Castells M (2001) The internet galaxy. Oxford University Press, New York
Eisenhardt KM, Martin JA (2000) Dynamic capabilities: what are they? Strateg Manage J 21(21):1105–1122
Galbraith JR (2002) Designing organizations, An executive guide to strategy, structure and process. Jossey-Bass, San Francisco, CA
Goold M, Campbell A (2002) Designing effective organizations. Jossey-Bass, San Francisco, CA
Malone T (2004) The future of work: how the new order of business will shape your organization, your management style, and your life. Harvard Business School Press, Boston, MA
Nault B (1998) Information technology and organizational design. Manage Sci 44(10):1322–1335
Rockart JF (1979) Chief executives define their own data needs. Harv Bus Rev (March–April):81–93
Seddon J (2008) Systems thinking in the public sector. Triarchy Press, Axminster, UK
Teece JD (2008) Technological know-how, organizational capabilities, and strategic management: business strategy and enterprise development in competitive environments. World Scientific Publishing, London

Chapter 10
Business, Organizational and Information Processes

Abstract This chapter offers a method to carry out variety engineering throughout an organization. Is the current design of implementation activities effective? Does the structural distribution of regulatory functions offer a good strategy to manage the complexity implied by the organization's purposes? The method first offers a diagnosis of the current complexity management strategies and then helps to design better strategies. This chapter illustrates the alignment of *business processes* with *organizational* and *information processes*. It uses the Viplan Method and the Soft Systems Methodology to study information processes. The argument evolves a particular business process in an enterprise. This process provides the platform to work out information requirements and structural alignments. It explains in some detail the alignment of information, business and organizational processes.

This chapter elaborates in further detail resources and discretion centralization and decentralization with a focus on variety engineering. We have said that an organization emerges when the recurrent interactions of a group of people *create, regulate* and *produce* collective meanings. However, for effective performance a balance should be achieved between actions *producing* the intended collective purposes and actions *enabling* this production. In the extreme, if all actions went into production there would be neither capacity to support connectivity and cohesion nor capacity to adapt to a changing environment. We have called the actions producing the products implied by collective purposes *primary activities,* and those enabling them *regulatory/support activities.* Viable systems emerge from the connectivity (i.e., communications and interactions) among its primary and regulatory/support activities. A purpose of this chapter is offering a method to engineer the variety of implementation and development processes with the support of information and communication processes. This method should also help with studying the configuration of resources with the idea of developing the organization's capabilities.

Key distinctions we make in this chapter are those of business, organizational and informational processes. Under the generic name of *business processes* we include *implementation and development processes,* which are different to the already discussed cohesion and adaptation organizational processes (see Chap. 6). Business processes are completely focused on 'activities' regardless of their

R. Espejo and A. Reyes, *Organizational Systems,*
DOI 10.1007/978-3-642-19109-1_10, © Springer-Verlag Berlin Heidelberg 2011

organizational embodiment; these activities may be subcontracted to third parties or performed by other primary activities within the same organization, on the other hand organizational processes are completely embodied in the organizational system (cf. the cohesion and adaptation mechanisms of the VSM). The connectivity of resources, whether internal or external to the organizational system, requires *information processes* that are enabled by information and communication technologies (ICTs). We understand implementation processes as a set of interrelated activities producing the products or services that the organization delivers to its customers. On the other hand a set of interrelated activities such as marketing, finance and research and development aiming at creating a viable new product is an instance of a development process. This chapter gives methodological support to explore the interdependence of business, organizational and information processes. To make simpler our presentation we will focus on implementation processes, which often are related to the supply chain producing the organization's products and services (Porter 1985).

The idea of primary activities suggest that beyond managing the value chain, those producing products and services at the local level need to have flexibility to define their own policies. This hugely amplifies local variety to respond to local needs and avoids the imposition of hierarchical, insensitive, global policies. On the other hand, distributing the activities of an implementation process at different structural levels, beyond the flexible response of autonomous local teams, increases the chances of reducing them to post boxes distributing to other groups the responsibilities to deal with customers' requirements. As they do this, local teams lose contact with the very people that they are supposed to service.

There is no doubt that structurally, it is desirable to have relatively small teams responsible for the value chain of an implementation process in an organization; they can operate from inputs to outputs through a transformation process that is theirs. These teams absorb most of the customers' variety locally; customers can see the 'faces' of those responsible for the products and services they consume. For instance citizens in need of housing services would be able to interact with the unit responsible for assessing their needs as well as for delivering the services. This avoids fragmenting service delivery; proximity allows for the right hand to know what the left is doing. However, the increasing complexity of people's demands, the extraordinary pace of technological developments as well as the constraints imposed by culture and resources tend to force some degree of centralization as organizations look for synergies and economies of scale.

Most significantly, local teams may benefit from global information to effectively close local loops. Among others, policy priorities may be decided globally, specialised knowledge and resources may be pooled together beyond local teams and the economies of scale offered by available technologies may tempt centralization. But, centralization increases the chances of functionalism at the expense of holism. Implementation teams risk becoming customer service units with limited appreciation of, and responsibility for, the total service they offer (Seddon 2008).

In this effort for holism the cost of communications is changing the balance between centralization and decentralization. Today's decreasing cost of communications makes possible creating virtual teams that facilitate decentralization (see Chap. 8). Members of centralized groups with specialised knowledge can be effective contributors for the creation and implementation of local policies. People responsible for the use of expensive centralized resources can be made (virtually) part of local teams and thus accountable to the team. These are cases of resource centralization and functional decentralization (see Chaps. 9 and 12). Equally, those working in these groups, with local knowledge of stakeholders in general and customers in particular, can influence more effectively global policies by communicating to policy-makers local responses to existing policies.

From the perspective of organizational design the challenge is fostering a cascading of self-contained product and service teams which make possible the progressive integration of functions into larger self-contained groups that match customers' needs at different performance requirements. For instance, for housing services, local teams focused on providing particular types of services can be embedded in regional units with functional capacity for the deployment of building and maintenance resources according to local needs. What is particular to this proposition is that building and maintenance resources provide a more global performance requirement, namely building and maintenance capabilities, at the same time that they are contributors and accountable to local teams for local services. *As the cost of communications is reduced the allocation of resources can be reconfigured transforming the organization's capabilities.* Constituting effective local teams and coordinating these multiple teams in a global context becomes increasingly challenging but also, with the support of new information and communication technologies, manageable and potentially more effective.

Performing a complex implementation process, such as air transportation, at its most detailed level may require hundreds or even thousands of interrelated activities. Structurally, we would like that implementation processes correspond to primary activities all the way to the last level of the unfolding of complexity. However, this proposition needs some qualifications that we clarify in this chapter. Our purpose in modelling implementation processes is improving the organization's management of its complexity; this requires variety engineering. It makes sense that those activities that are highly interconnected are managed together in one organizational unit (see Chaps. 5 and 8). In simple terms, if highly interrelated implementation activities correspond to different primary activities their coordination becomes more difficult, as a consequence of perhaps a badly organised workflow. Equally we would expect that the chunking of the organization's transformation be done in chunks of similar complexity. In general it makes no sense to manage at the same structural level high and low complexity primary activities. A principle of variety engineering, as clarified in Chap. 8, tells us that interrelated implementation activities should belong to one primary activity rather than being distributed among two or more. As the structural recursion of an implementation process is increased the same principle applies. This implies that for as long as practically possible implementation processes should be contained within nested primary activities all the way to the lowest structural level. However, whenever the workflow requires the contribution of activities not embedded in the primary activity owner of the implementation process the organization should be prepared to increase regulatory resources to maintain an effective flow of activities. This is indeed the idea of a cohesive organization.

However, to proceed systematically with the argument we will assume that all the activities of each of the implementation processes correspond with a primary activity from the global to the most local structural level. At the end of the chapter we will discuss how to remove this restriction and accept that activities such as procurement, dispatching and so forth, at the same time of constituting local implementation processes, may be resources at the discretion of more global primary activities.[1] Therefore from the perspective of distribution of resources we are talking about functional decentralization and resource centralization.

Is the current design of implementation effective? Does the structural distribution of regulatory/support functions offer a good strategy to manage the complexity implied by the organization's purposes? This extension of the Viplan Method starts from a diagnosis of the current complexity management strategies and then helps to design better strategies. It illustrates the *alignment of business, organizational and information processes* with the support of Brian Wilson's application of Soft Systems Methodology (Checkland 1981) to information processes (Wilson 1984). We start with the illustration of implementation processes in an enterprise. These processes provide the platform to work out regulatory and information requirements for their management.

Let's take for instance the airline company of Chap. 8. Figure 10.1 shows its unfolding of complexity. We recognise five implementation processes in which the company is involved: passenger transportation, mail and cargo service, chartering planes, renting planes to other companies and offering maintenance services to other airline companies. These five implementation (business) processes are marked in the figure at the bottom of the unfolding of complexity.

Notice that Satena encapsulates these business processes in higher levels of recursion according to the regional segmentation of its activities. In general, implementation processes are *vertically integrated* according to structural complexity drivers such as geography, time and market segmentation (see Chap. 8). Implementation processes show, in addition to the chunks of complexity necessary to produce a transformation, the other activities necessary to get supplies and deliver products and services. Figure 10.2, for instance, shows Satena's aggregated implementation business processes.

Information is necessary to carry out implementation processes. To sell an airplane ticket we need information from the client but also information about flight schedules. We also need price information, seats available, hotel reservations, car rentals and so on in order to meet clients' expectations. Of course we also need to process information internally for accounting, financial and monitoring purposes.

---

[1]Implementation activities can also be subcontracted to external organizations but we will not consider this case here to simplify the argument.

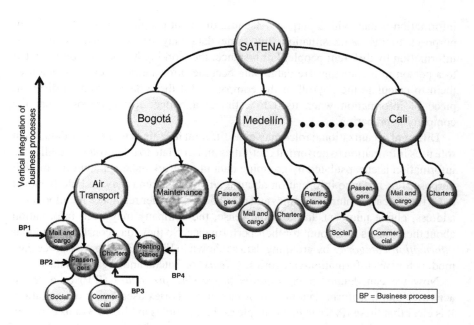

Fig. 10.1 Satena's business processes

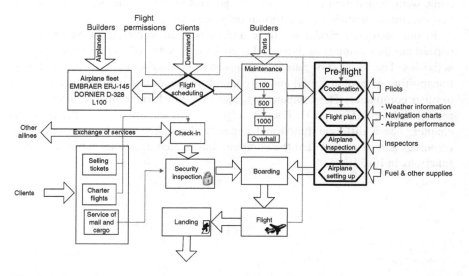

Fig. 10.2 Satena's simplified implementation business processes

But before going any further in showing the structural relation between implementation and information processes, let us define the latter with more rigour.

Bateson (1972) defined information as the difference that makes a difference. In this definition he was implicitly making a distinction between data and information;

information is data with a purpose. Because different people may ascribe different purposes to the same situation, the same data may be construed as different information by different people. For instance, the working hours per month related to a person in a company are data. Data become information when someone uses them to calculate the payroll of the company. But these data become a different piece of information when used to estimate a budget for a proposal that the company is preparing.

Different organizational roles may give different meanings to the same data. Each role uses information to perform its activities and to relate to other roles. Usually this information is encapsulated by grouping data in order to make apparent its implicit purpose. For instance information about a *client* for Satena may include personal data (identification number, name) and data about his or her residence location (city, address, phone number). In the same sense, the company may need information about their planes to account for their performance. So they may construe particular *information-categories* by grouping data as shown in Fig. 10.3. Here we can see data models for two information-categories: *Clients* for Satena and flight *statistics*.

Now we can define an *information processing procedure* (IPP) as a set of activities that transform data into information categories used by an organization. It is clear that these IPPs can be as simple as the examples in Fig. 10.3 or as complex as interpersonal information management procedures. The former are associated with components of information systems and the latter with communication systems. With these definitions in mind, let's go back to show some structural relations between implementation and information processes.

In our restricted model we have agreed that an implementation process is carried out by a primary activity and is enabled by some of its regulatory/support activities. The mission of Satena, for instance, is offering services to its clients: transporting passengers, mail and cargo, renting planes and maintenance services to other companies. The company organizes its transformations enabling several recursion levels (Fig. 10.1). Each recursion level, as explained in the previous chapter, has a different functional capacity depending on the distribution of resources and discretion that the company has agreed upon (see table recursion/ functions in Fig. 10.4).

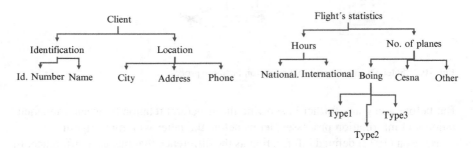

Fig. 10.3 Data models of two information-categories for an airplane company

Regulatory functions → Primary activities ↓	Human resource managt	Budget	Training	Fees setting	Bookings	Sales	Marketing and advertising	General services	Acquisitions	Operations control	Internal control	Planning & systems	Security
Satena	•	•	•	•	•	•	•	•	•	•	•	•	•
Bogotá		•				•	•	•		•	•		•
Air transport								•			•		
Passenger transportation						•	•				•		
Commercial routes											•		
"Social" routes											•		
Mail and cargo						•					•		
Charters						•	•				•		
Renting planes						•					•		
Maintenance											•		
Medellín		•				•	•	•		•	•		•

Fig. 10.4 Distribution of discretion for Satena

Remember that each dot in this table delimits the scope to perform that particular regulatory function in a particular level of recursion. This can be established by using one or more verbs to describe this function as we showed in Fig. 9.8 (previous chapter). Regarding the sales function, at the corporate level they *consolidate* national sales whereas in the office located in Bogotá they *coordinate* sales in the city. On the other hand, in the primary activity called passenger transportation, they actually *sell* the tickets and so on (Fig. 10.4).

Having said this, it should be clear that in order to perform the transformation of each primary activity the information necessary to carry out each of the regulatory functions at each level must be available. Remember that each dot in the table represents the level of responsibility for carrying out a particular function (a column) in a given primary activity (a row). This level of responsibility can be expressed by one or more specific verbs. In order to perform these tasks in a proper way, people in the organization need updated information that should also be aggregated at the right level. This level of aggregation, again, can be derived from the levels of recursion at which a particular function has been distributed in the recursion/function table.

If a local manager, for instance, has discretion to define and execute the publicity campaign for local products, it makes sense for him or her to have updated and detailed information about product sales over time. It will be of little use to have only aggregated sales numbers. On the other hand, to give regularly too detailed information of particular local products to the company's sales managers will easily overload them and take them away from the sales managing loop of the global company.

In other words, we need information processing procedures and information-categories that provide the necessary information to each regulatory function at each particular level of recursion. This information should be coherent with the verbs describing the corresponding function it supports. In the case of Satena, at the corporate level we need information regarding the aggregation of sales at the national level; in Bogotá we need access to information regarding sales in the city; and in the unit in charge of passenger transportation, we need information to close the sale of a ticket.

Information processing procedures allow the connection between regulatory functions and primary activities and, in doing these links they support the execution of the company's implementation processes. From the point of view of design, notice that once we have built a recursion/function table (such as Fig. 10.4) for a particular organization, it can be used to specify the information systems needed to define the information provisions across the organization's structure. This is the reason we refer to the recursion/functions table as the organization's conceptual information system.

We have examined so far the close relation among primary activities, implementation processes and regulatory functions. We also have illustrated how information processing procedures (via information systems) are important for establishing and maintaining this relation. We would like to develop now, with more precision, the notion of organizational processes and its relation to information processing procedures.

In general terms, as explained in Chap. 6, organizational processes are constituted by the mechanisms for adaptation and cohesion. Figure 10.5 shows the mechanism for adaptation. Once a relevant issue for the adaptation of the organization is selected, the debates between the people concerned with the 'outside and then' (intelligence function) and the people concerned with the 'inside and now' (cohesion function) should be enabled and monitored. For policies to be effective we need IPPs supporting this mechanism in at least four ways, as shown in Fig. 10.5.

In the first place the people constituting the intelligence function need to be in permanent interaction with agents in the organization's problematic environment. Gathering relevant information is vital in order to define new products and services, find new markets, learn about the competition, find new suppliers, learn about new regulations that may affect the organization and so forth. We need IPPs that permanently support these activities (IPP1 in Fig. 10.5). Nowadays there are several information systems available to fit this purpose such us: innovation trend analysis (Vibert 2000), patent busting, technology scanning,[2] business intelligence (Turban et al. 2010) and scientometric analysis (Vinkler 2009).

---

[2]See for instance: http://www.pathnet.org/sp.asp?id=15636

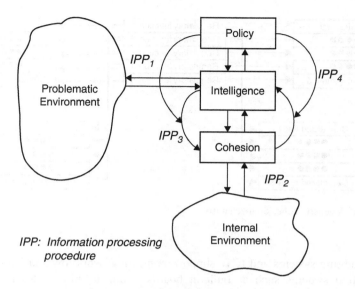

Fig. 10.5 Information processing procedures supporting the mechanism for adaptation

On the other hand, people related to the cohesion mechanism should develop a deep understanding of the 'inside and now'. Multiple IPPs support the cohesion function. For instance, knowledge management systems that enable organizational learning are part of information processes at this level (IPP2) (Espejo et al. 1996). These IPPs, considering our attention to implementation (business) processes are the focus of our discussions below.

The adaptation mechanism requires that people in intelligence and cohesion are highly interconnected (see Chap. 6). Information and communication processes can be set in order to support this relationship (IPP3). Microsites developed in the internal web and the use of virtual communication technology such as videoconference and video-presence are only a few examples at this level. In addition to these there are other technologies that offer a good way to orchestrate the relation between intelligence and cohesion. Stafford Beer's Syntegration is a very good example (Beer 1994).

Finally, people related to the policy function need to be aware of the quality of relations between intelligence and cohesion. In the early development of the VSM this kind of technology was associated with Project Cybersyn's 'operations room' (Beer 1975, 1981). More recently similar environments, based on more advanced technologies, support this task (Holtham et al. 2003).

In a similar way an organization needs to develop IPPs to support the effective operation of the cohesion mechanism. Figure 10.6 shows this generic mechanism for all regulatory functions that are the discretion of the organization in focus (see Chap. 9).

From the discussion of the cohesion mechanism in the previous chapter, it should be clear that information technology enables its operation. Among other

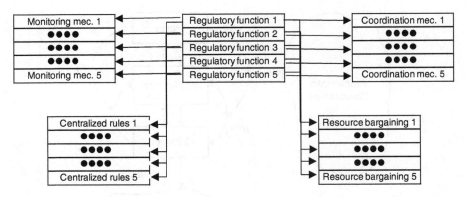

Fig. 10.6 A generic cohesion mechanism

IPPs, auditing systems and ICTs support monitoring; workflow and internal communication systems such as bulletin boards, intranets, micro-sites and similar systems support coordination; budgeting systems support resource bargaining and internal communication systems support issuing centralized rules.

To summarize: organizational processes constitute the two mechanisms for viability – adaptation and cohesion. We have illustrated IPPs and ICTs enabling their operation. This discussion provides a structural context for the development and use of these technologies.

Now we are ready to explore more in depth the relations between implementation, organizational and informational processes; this exploration at this stage is simplified by our initial assumption that an implementation process is fully contained by a primary activity. Here the tool we will use to connect primary activities, IPPs and information categories is an adaptation of Wilson's Maltese Cross (Wilson 1984).

Figure 10.7 shows the general structure of our Maltese Cross. In the central column, at the top (N or North axis), we have all primary activities of the organization according to its unfolding of complexity. In the same column, but at the bottom (S or South axis), we have all the IPPs used by the organization. The main row (W or West axis and E or East axis), on the other hand, contains the information-categories that underpin the information flows along the organization. Before explaining the use of this tool, let us see how it is completed.

Every primary activity can be modelled, by a transformation process of inputs into goods or services (see Fig. 7.7). Information is necessary in order to carry out this transformation. For instance, as mentioned before, to sell a flight ticket the company needs information about the client, flight schedules, prices, number of passengers per plane and so on. As a result of the transformation, this information is modified. In the previous example, after selling a ticket the information about the number of passengers in the plane is changed and also we have to update information regarding sales, statistics and so on. In other words, any transformation process of a primary activity has associated multiple IPPs.

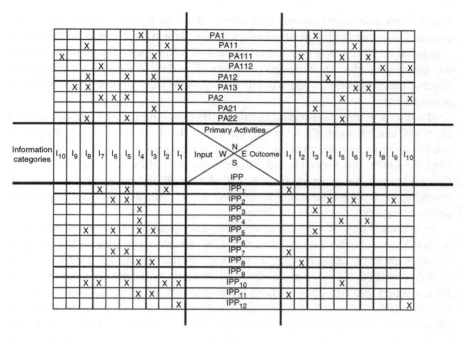

Fig. 10.7 The Maltese Cross

Having said this, a close examination of the transformation processes of all primary activities allows the construction of the relevant information-categories for the organization's implementation business processes (see as an example, Fig. 10.3). These information-categories form the main row of the Maltese Cross. Notice that the East axis is mirrored in West axis of the main row.

To fill in the north part of the Maltese Cross, we take primary activities one by one and select all the information-categories needed to carry out their transformations. We mark this relation with an X in the north-west part of the Cross. Then we find out what information-categories are modified as a result of the transformation. We mark them with an X in the north-east part of the Cross. By doing this for each primary activity we fill in the Xs of the North part of the Maltese Cross.

In order to fill the south part of the Maltese Cross, we need to identify IPPs in the organization. They are often computer based and manual information systems; however, they can also be communication IPPs, such as meetings and operational setups. They form the bottom part of the main column of the Cross. By examining which information-categories are used as an input for each IPP and which ones are modified, we fill out the south part of the Cross.

Having explained how the Maltese Cross is constructed, let us see how it can be used as a variety engineering tool to align implementation, organizational and information processes in an organization.

Organizations are continually improving their information procedures in response to technological developments and new stakeholders' expectations.

Usually this continuous process is neither carried out by the same personnel nor uses the same methodological approaches. So, with time, there is a vertiginous expansion of IPPs which may not be aligned with previous developments or with the adjustments of implementation processes. The Maltese Cross is a useful tool to observe these problems. Here we will show four of them in order to illustrate its potential use.

If we look at the south-west quadrant of the Cross in Fig. 10.7, we can see that every column has more than one X. This means that each information-category is used as an input by more than one IPP. Take for instance the information-category I3 in this figure. It is needed in order to carry out three IPPs [IPP5, IPP8, IPP11]. If these information-categories are not part of a single database, there is a risk of managing inconsistent information. In other words, this analysis may be useful to define a strategy to integrate databases.

In a similar way, if we look at the south-east quadrant and find columns with several Xs, we may have a case of unnecessary redundancy in IPPs. In Fig. 10.7, for instance, the information-category I3 has two Xs which means that it is the outcome of IPP3 and IPP5. Now, if we see which information-categories are inputs for these IPPs, we find that all inputs for IPP3 are also inputs for IPP5. In other words, we have two IPPs that modify the same information-category and the input of one is a subset of the other. This is precisely the case of an unnecessary redundancy we mentioned above. In other words, probably with a few adjustments in IPP5 we can eliminate IPP3 without losing any functional capacity.

If we examine now the south-east quadrant and look for a column that does not have Xs, it indicates an information-category that is not produced as an outcome of the operation of any of the existing IPPs. This is the case of I8 in Fig. 10.7. However, as we can see in the same figure, I8 is one of the inputs needed for several primary activities (PA11, PA12, PA13 and PA22). This suggests the importance to incorporate the generation of I8 as part of any of the existent IPPs or to build up a new IPP to take care of its production. In any case, this particular analysis can be used as a guide to improve the scope of actual IPPs in the organization.

Finally, if we look at the columns in the quadrant north-east and find an information-category with several Xs, that means that this information is the outcome of various primary activities. This is the case of I3 in Fig. 10.7. But looking at the quadrant south-east, we can see that I3 is produced by two IPPs (IPP2 and IPP5). This implies that the primary activities that modify I3 should coordinate themselves in the use of either IPP2 or IPP5 in order to avoid managing inconsistent information.

The above discussion illustrates four ways of using the Maltese Cross as a diagnostic tool in order to keep a certain degree of cohesion among business processes and information processing procedures in an organization.

So far we have introduced a tool to relate primary activities, which we have assumed match implementation processes, to information processing procedures. However, it should be apparent that Fig. 10.7 is a short hand for the full information system of an organization. The south axis, unless we restrict its scope, includes all of the organization's information processing procedures since the north axis includes all the organization's primary activities. For the same reason the west-east axis would include all imaginable information categories. This would be an extremely high variety, unmanageable, Maltese Cross. The challenge is restricting this variety to make this tool useful. An alignment of organization and information processes suggests two major types of information systems, namely, cohesion and adaptation information systems. The cohesion information system, as implied earlier in this chapter (see Fig. 10.6), is constituted by the resources bargaining and coordination information systems. The resources bargaining information system is restricted to working out Critical Success Factors, essential variables and performance indices for each of the organization's primary activities (Espejo 1992; Reyes 2007). This was the variety engineering of the Cyberstride information system designed by Stafford Beer for the Chilean economy in the early 1970s. Our discussion of the IPPs shown in Fig. 10.5 related this information system to the other communication and information systems of Project Cybersyn as developed in Chile (Beer 1981; Espejo 1980, 2009). But perhaps from the perspective of variety engineering the most challenging information processing procedures are those supporting the coordination of process activities, such as implementation. These IPPs are discussed below.

Summarizing, so far we have matched primary activities' transformations and implementation processes at different levels of recursion. In a primary activity, implementation processes transform inputs into higher value outputs and for this, in addition to the transformations of its embedded primary activities, it requires *support functions* such as procurement, distribution, transportation and many other logistic activities, and also it requires *regulatory functions* such as finance, marketing and personnel to manage them. The challenge is grouping these support/ regulatory functions together in the necessary organizational processes for the primary activity's viability and the viability of the total organizational system. Information processing procedures allow the necessary information flows to connect primary and support/regulatory activities. So far we have shown how the unfolding of complexity, the recursion/function table and the Maltese Cross can be used to relate implementation, organizational and information processes in an idealized situation (see Fig. 10.8). We now want to remove this restriction.

An important assumption of all the above discussion was that primary activities matched implementation processes, or, in other words, that their complexities are contained within individual primary activities, however, a common situation is that activities constituting the implementation process not only are the discretion of other primary activities as is the case of centralized functions supporting several business processes, but are sub-contracted elsewhere. We need additional methodological support to deal with implementation processes that are not contained in one primary activity, as is, for example, the procurement of raw materials and the dispatch of products when they are centralized beyond this primary activity to support several of them.

The following extension of the method presented so far removes the restriction we imposed at the beginning of implementation processes mapping one-to-one primary activities. It uses the Maltese Cross and the recursion/function table to

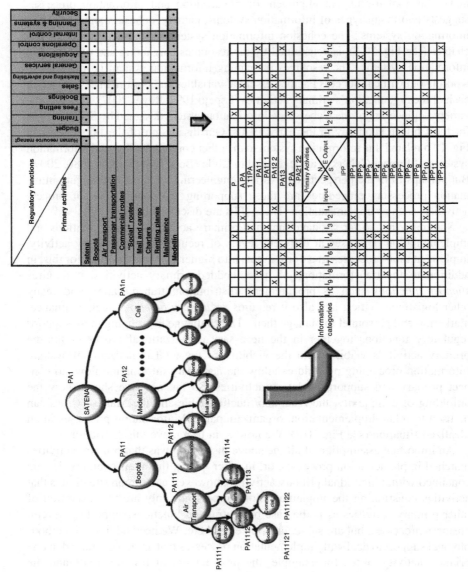

Fig. 10.8 The use of unfolding of complexity, the recursion/functions table and the Maltese Cross to align business, organizational and information processes

discuss the effective interrelation of implementation processes, organizational processes and information processes. We will discuss this methodological extension for one business process; however, the recursiveness of the VSM implies that the same method applies to all business processes.

The methodological tools used in this extension are interdependent and their application is not linear. This is a reflection of the fact that implementation, information and organization processes are co-evolving together in loops of mutual influence. Our focus is on one implementation process – Information-acquisition of a simulated enterprise: COMLIS,[3] and the aim is showing the interdependence of all these processes and their use to work out alternative structures for implementation processes. For instance, the use of this tool may make apparent that a centralized resource can be effectively integrated as an activity of an implementation process at a lower structural level. The general method is as follows:

1. *Naming the organization-in-focus.* The general tool is naming systems (see Chap. 7). The following is the name for COMLIS:

   A commercial provider of business and technical information, transmitted by any media or source to the subscribing organizations, in order to satisfy their information needs in a timely, efficient and cost-effective way

   The corresponding TASCOI for this name is the following:

   T = available information in the market into information provided
   A = people working for COMLIS
   S = publishers, information services, other libraries
   C = subscribing organizations
   O = COMLIS corporate management
   I = shareholders, competitors, professional bodies, regulatory bodies

2. *Structural underpinning of COMLIS.* Figure 10.9 shows a technological model of COMLIS and in Fig. 10.10 we see the unfolding of complexity.

3. *Naming an implementation process of interest.* Information-acquisition is an implementation (business) process for COMLIS closely related to *collection acquisition, information services* and *data capture*. The process was named as follows:

   Information-acquisition is a COMLIS business process to satisfy customers' information requirements with information available, inside and outside the enterprise, up to customers' expectations of a reliable and timely service

4. *Producing a descriptive model of current implementation process.* The aim is to clarify its value chain, that is, the activities linking sources-suppliers-transformation-outputs-receivers. Figure 10.11 offers a simplified descriptive process mapping for information-acquisition.

---

[3]This case study was developed by Raul Espejo and Robert Gilmore of Syncho Ltd., to support consultancy and training programmes. Its purpose is communicating the method rather than showing its full-fledged and conceptually complete application to a 'real world situation'.

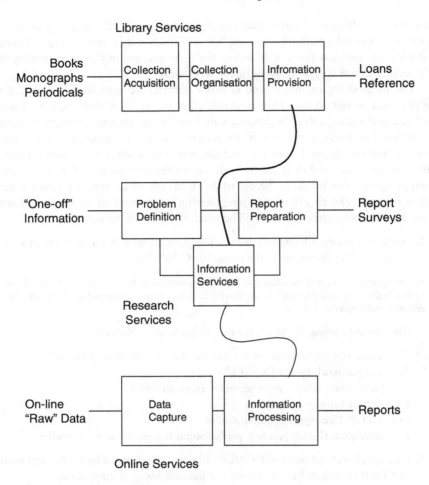

Fig. 10.9 A technological model for COMLIS

5. *Determining information requirements and provisions for the existing process.*
   Figure 10.12 is a Maltese Cross for information requirements and provisions.
6. *Working out the organization's recursion/function table.* Figure 10.13 shows a
   recursion/function table for COMLIS.
7. *Systemic purposes and recursion levels of the implementation (business) process activities.* The systemic purpose of some of the activities is producing
   products (implementation) and of others these purposes are resources bargaining and monitoring and coordination activities. Figure 10.14 is a Maltese
   Cross that links recursion levels, *business functions* as they are named in the
   company (e.g., systems support, assessment of information requirements, intelligence on sources and so forth), systemic functions (i.e., the systemic purposes
   of the business functions) and implementation business process activities.

   A first key aspect of this step is distinguishing the systemic purposes of
   the activities; is their purpose implementing or supporting/regulating the

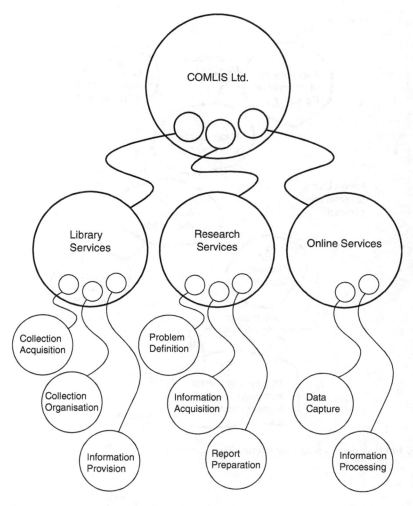

Fig. 10.10 Unfolding of complexity for COMLIS Ltd

transformation implied by the organization's purposes? If it is implementing they are parts of the organization's primary transformation; if it is anything else, they are regulatory/support components of the business process. This clarification helps mapping the business process activities onto the distinction primary activities and regulatory functions.

A second aspect is establishing the levels of recursion involved in this business process. If an organization has no recursion (i.e., does not have primary activities) and therefore has only one implementation business process, the situation is that described in the first part of this chapter. For the general situation of an organization with complexity unfolding, the recursion/function table separates implementation and regulatory activities at several

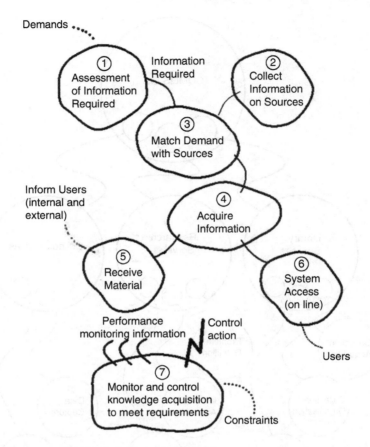

Fig. 10.11 A process model for information-acquisition

levels of recursion. Mapping the table of Fig. 10.13 onto the SE quadrant of Fig. 10.14 is the starting point of this step of the method.

The second is the mapping of business functions onto their systemic functions as is done in the SW quadrant of Fig. 10.14. Notice that in this case the implementation column is empty because all functions in column S are regulatory. The third is the mapping of business process activities onto systemic functions as can be seen in the NW quadrant. In the case of COMLIS Ltd, the first four are the implementation business process activities for Information-acquisition, whereas Receive Material, System Access and Control are regulatory/support activities for this business process. Finally, the NE quadrant of the Maltese Cross maps business process activities onto recursion levels.

The overall purpose of this step is descriptive; diagnosis and design are the concern of the next steps.

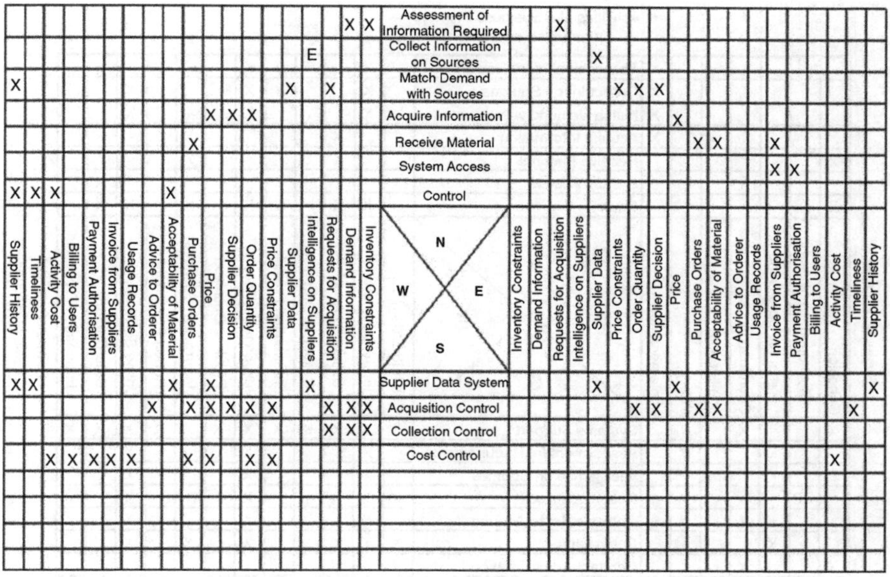
Assessment of Information Required
Collect Information on Sources
Match Demand with Sources
Acquire Information
Receive Material
System Access
Control
N
W
E
S
Supplier History
Timeliness
Activity Cost
Billing to Users
Payment Authorisation
Invoice from Suppliers
Usage Records
Advice to Orderer
Acceptability of Material
Purchase Orders
Price
Supplier Decision
Order Quantity
Price Constraints
Supplier Data
Intelligence on Suppliers
Requests for Acquisition
Demand Information
Inventory Constraints
Supplier Data System
Acquisition Control
Collection Control
Cost Control

Fig. 10.12 A maltese cross for information-acquisition in COMLIS

FUNCTION / RECURSION			Systems Support	Assessment of Information Requirements	Intelligence on Sources	Resoures Audit	Choice of Information to Acquire	Purchasing	Contract Administration	Response to Enquiries	Sales and Marketing	Liaison With Other Bodies	Pricing	Staff Training	Recruitment	Personnel	Financial Reporting	Capital Expenditure	Budgetary Control	Cost Control	Research & Development
COMLIS Ltd.			●			●		●	●		●	●	●	●	●	●	●	●	●	●	●
	Library Services		●	●	●	●	●	●				●							●	●	●
		Collection Acqisition	●					●													
		Collection Organisation	●																		
		Information Provision	●							●											
	Research Services		●	●	●	●	●	●				●							●	●	●
		Problem Definition	●							●											
		Information Services	●					●													
		Report Preparation	●																		
	Online Services		●	●	●	●	●	●				●							●	●	●
		Data Capture	●					●		●											
		Information Processing	●							●											

Fig. 10.13 Recursion/function table for COMLIS

Activities of a Business Process (Information acquisition)

Cohesion	Monitoring	Resource bargaining	Coordination	Intelligence	Policy	Implementation	Activity	COMLIS Ltd	Library Services	Collection Acquisition	Collection Organisation	Information Provision	Research Services	Problem Definition	Information Services	Report Preparation	Online Services	Data Capture	Information Processing	Primary Activities	Levels of Recursion
						X	Assessment of Inf Required		X				X			X					
						X	Collect Inf on Sources		X				X			X					
						X	Match Demand with Sources		X				X			X					
						X	Acquire Information					X			X			X			
X							Receive Material					X			X						
		X					System Access													X	
X							Control	X	X			X			X		X	X			

Centre diagram (diamond with axes):
N (top), W (left), E (right), S (bottom).

Regulatory Functions

Cohesion	Monitoring	Resource bargaining	Coordination	Intelligence	Policy	Implementation	Activity	COMLIS Ltd	Library Services	Collection Acquisition	Collection Organisation	Information Provision	Research Services	Problem Definition	Information Services	Report Preparation	Online Services	Data Capture	Information Processing	Primary Activities	Levels of Recursion
X		X					Systems Support	X	X	X	X	X	X	X	X	X	X	X	X		
						X	Assessment Inf Requirements		X				X			X					
			X				Intelligence on Sources		X				X			X					
	X						Resources Audit	X	X				X			X					
			X				Choice of Inf to Acquire		X				X			X					
		X					Purchasing	X	X	X			X			X		X	X		
X					X		Contract Administration	X													
					X		Response to Enquiries							X		X			X	X	
			X	X			Sales and Marketing	X													
					X		Liason with Other Bodies	X	X				X				X				
		X	X				Pricing	X													
					X		Staff Training	X													
					X		Recruitment	X													
X					X		Personnel	X													
X					X		Financial Reporting	X													
X							Capital Expenditure	X													
	X						Budgetary Control	X	X				X			X					
	X						Cost Control	X	X				X			X					
						X	Research & Development	X	X				X			X					

Fig. 10.14 Diagnosis of the alignment of business and organizational processes

Remember, the axes of this table contain the following:

N = business process activities

W = systemic purpose of regulatory functions (Cohesion; resources bargaining and monitoring; Coordination, Intelligence, Policy and Implementation)

S = organization's regulatory functions

E = organization's primary activities

Therefore each of the quadrants reflects the following relations:

SE = is the recursion/function table for COMLIS

SW = helps to clarify the systemic purpose of regulatory functions of COMLIS

NW = makes the distinction between primary and regulatory purposes for activities of the business process

NE = clarifies the recursion level at which business process activities take place

8. *Focus on implementation activities.* Clarifying which are the implementation business process activities allows us to work out a strategy to achieve the primary activity's transformation or, at the more global level, the organization's transformation. Some of the implementation activities may be right for the primary activity-in-focus, others may need reallocation to other primary activities, others may be sub-contracted with external suppliers and so forth. This clarification allows the focusing of the implementation business process activities on one recursion level. Does it make sense to keep a low complexity activity at the same level of high complexity activities, or is it better to embed it in one of the more complex process activities? The outcome of this step is a reallocation of the implementation activities of the business process.

9. *Focus on regulatory activities.* The information produced by the NE quadrant of step 7 allows us to study the cohesion mechanism relevant to the business process (cf. Fig. 10.6); it is now possible to detect gaps and possible communication problems in its regulation. This step brings together organizational and business processes and may imply either new regulatory activities to fill the gaps detected from the information provided by step 7 or reallocating discretion in the allocation of resources throughout the organization's recursive structure. Considering the available resources, technologies, in particular ICTs and best practices, is it better to centralize or decentralize the resources of a regulatory activity of the value chain?

10. *Designing total business process.* As outcomes of step 8 the implementation business process activities are aligned with the transformation of a primary activity and as an outcome of step 9, the regulatory business process activities are aligned with business functions and regulatory mechanisms at one or more recursion levels.

    The same Maltese Cross as described in Fig. 10.14 is now used in a design mode. Figure 10.15 shows this design mode; changes are shown in the cells marked in grey. The North axis shows the activities of the value chain in full, which include the necessary regulatory and implementation business process activities as emerging from steps 8 and 9.

    The West axis makes explicit the systemic purposes of these activities. The South axis shows the list of revised business functions; most likely this list will be very similar to the equivalent of Fig. 10.14, occasionally adding or subtracting one or more new business functions. In this case Purchasing has been renamed as Negotiation with Information Suppliers.

    The East axis is the list of recursion levels and the SE quadrant maps business functions onto recursive levels; this quadrant is the revised recursion/function table. In the NE quadrant we expect to see all the implementation business process activities aligned in single columns, producing the transformation of the respective primary activity, and the regulatory business process activities possible at several recursion levels (see Fig. 10.15).

11. *Aligning organizational processes with the designed business process.* This alignment depends on the distribution of discretion accepted for this business process in the organization as displayed in the NE quadrant of Fig. 10.15. Mapping regulatory activities of the designed business process onto the

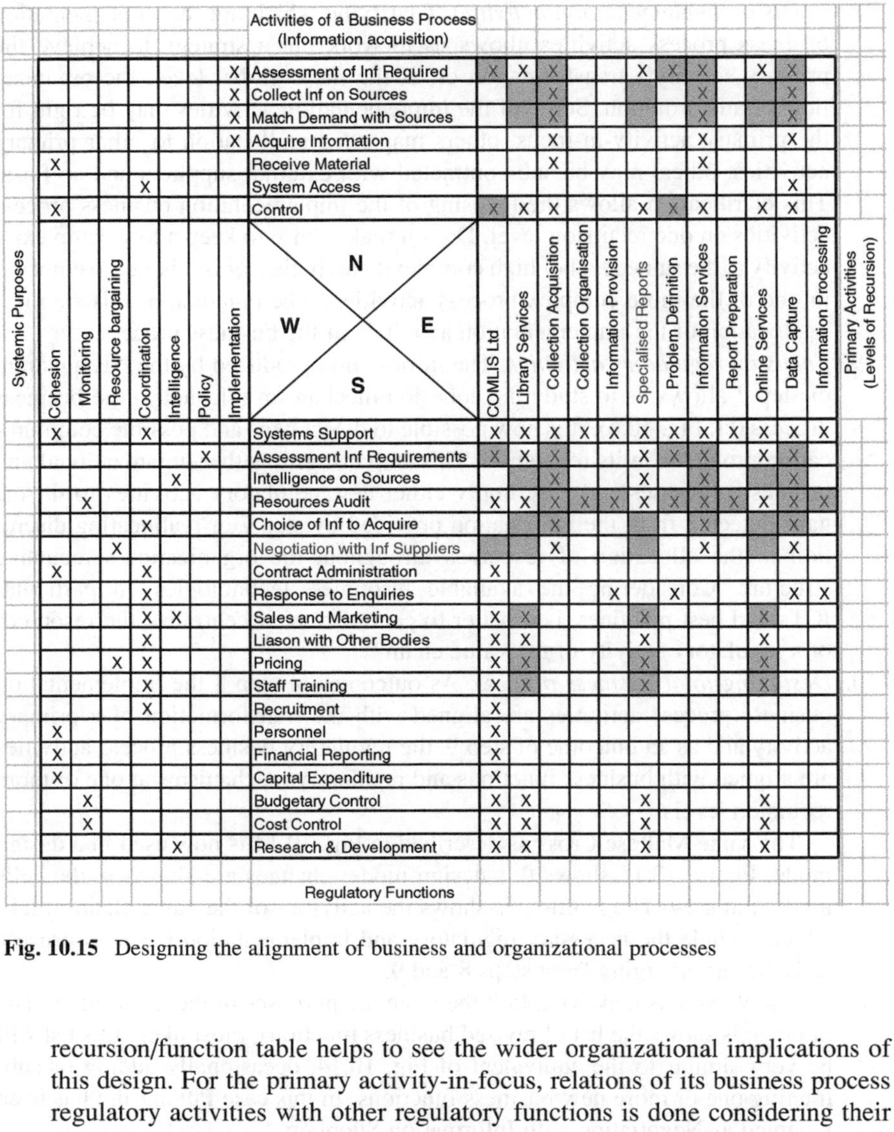

Activities of a Business Process (Information acquisition) / Systemic Purposes (left) / Primary Activities (Levels of Recursion) (right)

Cohesion	Monitoring	Resource bargaining	Coordination	Intelligence	Policy	Implementation	Activity	COMLIS Ltd	Library Services	Collection Acquisition	Collection Organisation	Information Provision	Specialised Reports	Problem Definition	Information Services	Report Preparation	Online Services	Data Capture	Information Processing
						X	Assessment of Inf Required	X	X	X			X	X	X		X	X	
						X	Collect Inf on Sources			X					X			X	
						X	Match Demand with Sources			X					X			X	
						X	Acquire Information			X					X			X	
X							Receive Material			X					X				
			X				System Access											X	
X							Control	X	X	X			X	X	X		X	X	

Center compass: N / W – E / S

Cohesion	Monitoring	Resource bargaining	Coordination	Intelligence	Policy	Implementation	Regulatory Functions	COMLIS Ltd	Library Services	Collection Acquisition	Collection Organisation	Information Provision	Specialised Reports	Problem Definition	Information Services	Report Preparation	Online Services	Data Capture	Information Processing
X		X					Systems Support	X	X	X	X	X	X	X	X	X	X	X	X
						X	Assessment Inf Requirements	X	X	X			X	X	X		X	X	
				X			Intelligence on Sources			X			X		X			X	
	X						Resources Audit	X	X	X	X	X	X	X	X	X	X	X	X
			X				Choice of Inf to Acquire			X					X			X	
		X					Negotiation with Inf Suppliers			X					X			X	
X		X					Contract Administration	X											
		X					Response to Enquiries							X		X		X	X
			X	X			Sales and Marketing	X	X				X				X		
		X					Liason with Other Bodies	X	X				X				X		
		X	X				Pricing	X	X				X				X		
		X					Staff Training	X	X				X				X		
		X					Recruitment	X											
X							Personnel	X											
X							Financial Reporting	X											
X							Capital Expenditure	X											
	X						Budgetary Control	X	X				X				X		
	X						Cost Control	X	X				X				X		
					X		Research & Development	X	X				X				X		

Regulatory Functions

Fig. 10.15 Designing the alignment of business and organizational processes

recursion/function table helps to see the wider organizational implications of this design. For the primary activity-in-focus, relations of its business process regulatory activities with other regulatory functions is done considering their contribution to the wider organizational processes of which they are part, that is, the processes maintaining its cohesion with 'sister' primary activities. The outcome may be a revision of the recursion/function table (Fig. 10.16).

12. *Aligning business, organizational and information processes.* Once the design of organizational processes is stable, it is necessary determining information provisions and requirements for the re-designed business process activities using the same approach as the one used for the existing process in Fig. 10.12.

With the description of this general method, we are advancing ideas about how to align implementation business processes with organizational and information

RECURSION \ FUNCTION			Systems Support	Assessment of Information Requirements	Intelligence on Sources	Rescures Audit	Choice of Information to Acquire	Negotiation with Information Suppliers	Contract Administration	Response to Enquiries	Sales and Marketing	Liaison With Other Bodies	Pricing	Staff Training	Recruitment	Personnel	Financial Reporting	Capital Expenditure	Budgetary Control	Cost Control	Research & Development
COMLIS Ltd.			•	•		•			•	•	•	•	•	•	•	•	•	•	•	•	•
	Library Services		•	•		•				•	•	•	•						•	•	•
		Collection Acquisition	•	•	•	•	•	•													
		Collection Organisation	•			•															
		Information Provision	•			•				•											
	Specialised Reports		•	•	•	•				•	•	•	•						•	•	•
		Problem Definition	•	•		•				•											
		Information Services	•	•	•	•	•	•													
		Report Preparation	•			•															
	Online Services		•	•		•				•	•	•	•						•	•	•
		Data Capture	•	•	•	•	•	•		•											
		Information Processing	•			•				•											

Fig. 10.16 Proposed distribution of discretion for COMLIS

processes at the same time of providing a method to manage their variety in an organizational context. As the reader may have noticed, most of the methodological tools described throughout the book have being used in this section.

We now proceed to the final part of the book, which is focused on a problem solving methodology and systemic thinking.

References

Bateson G (1972) Steps to an ecology of mind. Ballantine, New York
Beer S (1975) Platform for change. Wiley, Chichester
Beer S (1981) Brain of the firm, 2nd edition. Wiley, Chichester
Beer S (1994) Beyond dispute: the invention of team syntegrity. Wiley, Chichester
Checkland P (1981) Systems thinking, systems practice. Wiley, Chichester
Espejo R (1980) Cybernetic praxis in government: the management of industry in Chile 1970–1973. Cybern Syst Int J 11:325–338
Espejo R (1992) Cyberfilter: a management support system. In: Holtham C (ed) Executive information systems and decision support. Chapman & Hall, London, pp 145–169
Espejo R (2009) Performance management, the nature of regulation and the Cybersyn project. Kybernetes 38(1/2):65–82
Espejo R, Schuhmann W, Schwaninger M, Bilello U (1996) Organizational transformation and learning. Wiley, Chichester

Holtham C, Lampel J, Brady C, Rich M (2003) How far can business war-rooms provide an effective environment for management learning? Educational innovation in economics and business (EDINEB 2003), Salzburg

Porter M (1985) Competitive advantage. The Free Press, New York

Reyes A (2007) A practical method to distribute a management control system in an organization. Inf Resour Manage J 20(2):122–137

Seddon J (2008) Systems thinking in the public sector. Triarchy Press, Axminster, UK

Turban E, Sharda R, Delen D (2010) Decision support and business intelligence systems. Prentice-Hall, Boston, MA

Vibert C (2000) Web-based analysis for competitive intelligence. Quorum Books, London

Vinkler P (2009) The evaluation of research by scientometric indicators. Chandos Publishing, Oxford

Wilson B (1984) Systems: concepts, methodologies and applications. Wiley, Chichester

Part III
Methodology and Systemic Thinking

Part II was about method. Its concern was how to model an organization using the Viable System Model. Part III is about methodology and systemic thinking. Its concern is about problematic situations, going from those that make necessary the design of an organization, to all kind of relational situations that require an appreciation of the whole in which they are experienced. We have argued that organizations emerge to deal with the problems we tacitly or explicitly construct. Organizations can be ingenious responses to challenging situations, whether opportunities or threats. They are complexity management strategies that permit managing large complexity with a much smaller complexity.

However, most of our time is not focused on designing new organizations but on making sense of situations that challenge us. Attempts to improve these situations are often carried out without an appreciation of their systemic embedding. We deal with them as if they had a cause, ignoring the non-linearity of events in the world we operate. Linearity in thinking and action is a strategy that fragments complexity in ways that possibly sever strong natural connectivity and increase the chances of undesirable consequences. Overcoming linearity requires systemic thinking that goes beyond building complex interrelations in the informational domain of a situation; it requires an appreciation of these interrelations in the operational domain of organizations. Not recognising the embodiment of interrelations in complex networks, with adaptive capacity, increases the chances of visualising what may be necessary to do but not doing what is necessary to do.

This part of the book offers embodied systems thinking. Chapter 11 develops the Viplan Methodology. This methodology had its origins in the 1980s (Espejo 1988) and is still evolving today. It braids the problem situations that people construct in their conversations with the organizational systems in which these constructions happen. The structuring of problematic situations is done taking into account their systemic contexts. Improving the structure of these contexts is sometimes enough to dissolve them, however, in any case, it is more likely that with this methodology 'problem solvers' will have a better chance to assess the consequences of possible courses of action, taking into account their systemic ramifications. For this to be the case 'problem solvers' need skills *to observe* organizational systems. This is the focus of the book's final chapter.

Chapter 12 develops a graphic language to observe organizational systems and uses this language to diagnose identity and structural shortcomings. These short-comings tend to be recurrent and can be hypothesised as identity and structural archetypes underpinning problematic situations. A first version of these archetypes was developed for the National Audit Office of Colombia in the 1990s (Espejo 1997).

References

Espejo R (1988) A cybernetic methodology to study and design human activities, PhD Thesis, Management centre. University of Aston, Birmingham

Espejo R (1997) Structural archetypes: internal document for the Contraloria General de la Republica de Colombia. Syncho, Ltd., Birmingham, UK

Chapter 11
On Methodology: Context and Content

Abstract This chapter gives methodological guidance to support transformational processes rather than occasional problem solving exercises. It offers guidance to manage change in situations where organizations absorb problematic challenges. The methodology is grounded in an appreciation of issues of communication and complexity. It highlights structural shortcomings hindering the implementation of change. The Viplan Methodology puts the emphasis on the distinction between systems as 'epistemological' devices and systems as unities emerging from human communications with closure. Systems are always languaged by observers, but as epistemological devices they are ideas to think about the world; as emergent unities they are constructs to diagnose and improve human communications. Therefore systems are not only bounding ideas but also the 'real world' communicative processes that underpin the quality of the ideas created and produced by a collective. For diagnosing and improving organization structures the methodology uses the Viplan Method. Diagnosis can help seeing the necessary structural changes to improve communications of stakeholders in change processes. This is a methodology to understand both systemic shortcomings and to work out desirable improvements.

This chapter explores a methodology for problem solving grounded in the Viable System Model. The VSM is a powerful construct that helps our thinking about organizations; however its use is often in response to problematic situations. In our practice it is not modelling the organization for its own sake that triggers its use but the fact that we are constantly confronting transformational situations. The value of the VSM is that it helps seeing these situations in holistic terms as part of learning processes.

Beer's following words summarize what we want to overcome with the Viplan Methodology (VM):

> We are the inheritors of categorized knowledge; therefore we inherit also a world-view that consists of parts strung together, rather than of wholes regarded through different sets of filters. Historically, synthesis seems to have been too much for the human mind – where practical affairs were concerned. The descent of the synthetic method from Plato through Augustine took men's perception into literature, art and mysticism. The modern world of

R. Espejo and A. Reyes, *Organizational Systems*,
DOI 10.1007/978-3-642-19109-1_11, © Springer-Verlag Berlin Heidelberg 2011

science and technology is bred from Aristotle and Aquinas by analysis. The categorization that took hold of medieval scholasticism has really lasted it out. We may see with hindsight that the historic revolts against the scholastics did not shake free from the shackles of their reductionism. (Beer 1980)

The VM is a response to our entrenched reductionism. Fragmenting complexity is often easier and more manageable than bringing parts together; however reductionism in social situations is more likely to produce undesirable consequences and inadequate performance. In this chapter we use the VM as a joining up instrument to deal with the multiple transformational challenges that we confront today in all kinds of enterprises, large and small.

Mapping an institution or a set of institutional parts onto the model is a starting point but not enough to get the best out of it. Once the mapping is done, often the question is: and now what? Equally, broad diagnostic points may be insightful at a first glance but they seldom help to uncover deep systemic failures. The VSM contributes with systemic insights to effective organizational learning processes (Espejo et al. 1996).

Diagnostic points such as asserting that a company has inadequate intelligence and policy functions or that the policy function has collapsed onto the cohesion function are fine but the model can offer less obvious insights than finding out that management is short sighted and inward looking and that the organization lacks vision. Seldom relevant situations are as clear cut as suggested by these examples; it is in the assessment of relationships that the most insightful diagnostic points are found. For instance, to find out that an organization is being weakly challenged by environmental agents and that as a result of this its intelligence function is not developing a deep grasp of the 'outside and then' and therefore that this function is not challenging effectively those trying to grab resources for the organization's 'inside and now' gives us a deeper insight about the shortcomings of an organization's policies. In this example people experiencing the situation may be aware that the enterprise is missing market opportunities or that managers are recurrently unaware of environmental challenges that have the potential to influence the company's performance. These are the common ways managers experience and express their difficulties; it is the systems thinker that needs structuring the situation to help seeing the situation in relational terms. This kind of thinking is what we want to support with the Viplan Methodology (VM).

We all experience problematic situations and express them in our idiosyncratic terms. As we plod ahead with conversations new evidence helps structuring situations in one form or the other. This is a process of situational clarification that may lead to corrective actions. If the situation recurs, further enquiries may follow coupled to more action in an effort to learn from the situation. These are common learning loops triggered by a variety of symptoms. Our view here is that this learning can benefit from systemic thinking grounded in organizational cybernetics. This is the methodological challenge that we discuss in this chapter.

In this chapter we discuss first some of the philosophical underpinnings of the methodology. Secondly, we clarify how the VSM helps contextualising the symptoms that people experience as they try to make sense of problematic situations.

We argue that the learning triggered by problematic situations is enhanced if it happens in an organizational context that enables distributed performance. Thirdly, the methodology is presented as the embedding of situational learning loops in cybernetic organizational loops. It is necessary to make the organizational context of a problematic situation more effective; these loops are at the core of the Viplan Methodology. Finally, to make this methodology more accessible we offer its full application to nuclear waste management in Sweden.

System thinkers ask questions about resources and their relations. These are questions that people encounter and answer one way or the other as they operate in any organization. If the situation is an implementation failure then questions about the implementers' competencies may be necessary but certainly not sufficient. Among many, questions about relations and resources as well as about related organizations are necessary. These are necessary to make meaningful implementation shortcomings. It is this systemic context that needs clarification. The VSM gives us a wide range of questions to test whether the complexity management strategies of implementers have been adequate or not. Furthermore the VSM gives us heuristics to improve the situation. Though improving problematic situations can be achieved in the short term by treating symptoms, in systemic terms improving the structures underpinning them gives a much stronger and durable improvement. It is the interplay between people's experiences and the structural context of these experiences that concerns the Viplan Methodology. This interplay between content and context happens in both directions; on the one hand problematic symptoms may well be signals of yet unseen structural deficiencies, on the other glaring structural weaknesses may underpin classes of problematic situations.

Our discussions of complexity in Chaps. 3 and 4 made apparent that organizational actors are confronted by an unknowable variety and often an unmanageable complexity. They use models that trigger many distinctions that give them the impression that they are controlling the situation, however unless these distinctions are matched by effective actions they will be lost. And, the need for this matching makes apparent that distributed performative learning processes are necessary. Actors have to increase the effectiveness of their complexity management strategies. New distinctions emerging from a situation may require more ingenuity to deal with them. It is the collective evolution of shared models and distributed performance that may make situations more transparent. To make situations more transparent problem owners depend on communications among themselves and with a wide range of stakeholders. Actors require negotiating meanings among them and together finding effective means for action (i.e., learning). *The cybernetic point here is that these communications are often restricted by the structures in which actors operate.* Who are the relevant participants in these communications? This is critical to establish the strategies for managing complexity in problematic situations. Indeed it is not the analytical skills of a few people creating sophisticated models that will ground these meanings in the organization and improve its performance. Even the analytical skills of many actors may not be enough for this purpose if they are not the *right ones*. These are important epistemological and methodological issues. Who are the right participants in a situation?

What are the relevant communications that need attention? How do we know who should be involved in the relevant communications?

Actors construct problem situations in their conversations (Maturana 1988; Glasersfeld 1995); this is a relational approach where actors develop their appreciation of the situational complexity as they experience new challenges for which they need to find new responses. Their existing response complexity may not be enough to handle these situations. They need to relate distinctions to response capacity in loops of circular causality. This is an ingenuity challenge (Homer-Dixon 2001). Different participants articulate differently these problems; they have different experiences. In a methodological sense they are *naming different systems*. The challenge is making explicit these systems to support their communications. These communications are at the core of making sense of situations. Through them actors make explicit their tacit conceptual models and as they negotiate these models possibly they agree actions to influence the situation. Learning happens if these *learning loops* trigger effective action in the shared action domain. For this purpose the key issue is to have the right participants in these communications. Without the right participants necessary inputs to appreciate better the situational complexity may not be available, nor may resources reach those who can produce effective action. This is where the VSM plays an important role. Problem situations don't happen in a vacuum; they are embedded in organizations of one kind or another. Just as *naming organizations* was offered as a methodological tool to find out about structures (see Chap. 7), naming systems for performative situations is suggested as a methodological tool to focus attention on these situations. This is a variation of Checkland's issue based root definitions (Checkland 1981, 2000).

Organizational names provide a platform to diagnose the structure of relevant organizations (as discussed in Part II). As these structures are improved, necessary actors are involved and resources reconfigured and deployed. The participation of the right actors, for the shared purposes, improves the quality of conversations, which in its turn improves the recognition of relevant actors and resources, thus increasing the collective appreciation and management of problem situations. This is the *cybernetic loop* to deal with problem situations. It is apparent that there is an interplay between the learning and cybernetic loops. The VM aims at clarifying further this interplay.

> The heuristic for problem solving of the Viplan Methodology is involving the relevant participants in situational conversations and creating effective communication mechanisms between them to deal with the problematic situations to the best of the organization's available resources.

While the idea of naming systems comes from Checkland's Soft System Methodology (SSM), our understanding of systems is significantly different; the Viplan Methodology (VM) has evolved within a constructivist rather than phenomenological framework. The philosophical position of the phenomenological stance gives primacy to the mental processes of observers rather than to the external world (Checkland 1981, p. 305), while the constructivist stance gives primacy to the communications producing coordinated action, thus constituting the life-world.

This clarification is necessary since we share with SSM its emphasis on purpose, learning and appreciation but the VM emphasises that *human communications produce systems in the life-world* rather than *human activity systems* helping to think about the world. The emphasis of the VM is managing complexity to enable learning in related change processes.

Maturana's statement that 'everything said is said by an observer to another observer that could be him or herself' (Maturana 1988, p. 27) is of significance. Whatever view we might have about a reality independent of ourselves, it is apparent that that *reality* is construed by observers. As already said we emphasise the distinction between systems as *epistemological* devices (Checkland 1981) and systems as human communications with closure (cf. Chap. 1). Systems are mental constructs, because in the end they are always languaged by observers, however in the first case they are constructs of ideas for thinking about the world and in the second they are constructs of people's relationships (with closure) in the world. Systems are not only bounding ideas to make sense of the life-world, but are bounding communications. The related communicative processes are critical to the construction of *reality*. It is this last aspect that makes of communications and complexity such important concepts in the Viplan Methodology.

Communications constitute the operational domain of participants in an action domain where they communicate and coordinate their actions (see Chaps. 3 and 4). In contrast, the informational domain is the domain where people reflect upon their relevant worlds. In this epistemology the models in-use (that is, the operational models as opposed to the models in the informational domain) are not representations but constructions emerging from networks of communications. The valuable aspect of this distinction is that anyone can think and reflect about an organization, something that, if the opportunity is seized, may give to the organization a huge potential for innovation and creativity, however if in the end these reflections are not geared with the organization's processes, these reflections remain as irrelevant in the organization's informational domain. Problem formulation may be in the operational domain of a think tank; their domain of action is problem structuring. But, to be in a particular organization's operational domain this structuring has to be the outcome of processes producing this organization. However, if problem structuring is weakly articulated with the organization's implementation processes these reflections will not be embodied in that organization's structure.

The organization's performance in its environment is constituted by the myriad communications among actors and between them and external agents. In this context disembodied problems remain as constructs shared by strategists but not by the organization. The other way around is also interesting; if the communications of actors produce high organizational performance in the environment, which has not been explicitly reflected by them, it would appear that they are implementing a very successful tacit *strategy* (see the example of a car manufacturer in Chap. 5). What is important to reinforce is that the complexity of the organization is in its operational domain and though conversations in the informational domain could be extremely useful to speeding up learning processes if they are not structurally coupled within the organization, they may remain as valuable ideas but not more than that. However, in organizations it is natural to expect that over time multiple informational domains will transfer to their operational domains.

As for the epistemological grounding of naming systems the Viplan Methodology understands them as constructs of life-world transformations. Furthermore we can say that while the phenomenological stance gives priority to the informational domain the constructivist stance gives priority to integrating the creation and production of meanings in the operational domain. What is significant is that the emphasis of the Viplan Methodology is *creating and producing meanings* through the effective communications between the *right actors*. It is clear that unless an effort is made in this direction reflections will remain outside the organization's boundaries.

The VM aims at increasing the chances of creating meanings that are aligned both with the collective's purposes and its operational capabilities. How do we increase the chances for the *right participants* to trigger these new meanings and how do we increase the chances for these new meanings to trigger effective action? For transformative situations it is important to clarify the context in which meaning creation and production take place. Often this context is not a particular institution or enterprise; it can be a number of groups, people, institutions and/or institutional parts. The challenge is to understand their systemic contribution; are they contributing to the policy, intelligence, cohesion, coordination or implementation functions of what organization? And how are meaning creation and meaning production intertwined? This intertwining is complex and happens at multiple structural levels. These are methodological issues for the VM.

Transformative situations are appreciated differently by the participants. These appreciations are grounded in culture and more specifically in the distinctions that these participants make about the situation. We have already argued that a transformative situation makes necessary new distinctions and also makes necessary new practices to improve performance; in other words the participants have to recognise and develop new complexity about the situation (as explained in Chap. 3). Developing complexity requires creativity. This is the purpose of a wide range of possible modelling techniques, starting from simple conceptual models (Checkland 1981) going to sophisticated complex adaptive models (Arthur et al. 1997). But more than modelling and new distinctions it is necessary performative responses in the life-world. These responses, using the language of this book, are amplifiers of the variety created by those contributing to modelling the situation. These responses are resource enabled communications, leading to the coordination of actions among organizational actors and between these and environmental agents. These communications are intended as complexity management strategies. These are structural couplings where participants make sense of their communications and hopefully steer them in directions that are aligned with the organizational shared purposes.

In summary, the Viplan Methodology is a methodology to increase the chances of coordinated actions in an organization, with the purpose of aligning participants' actions with the requirements for organizational viability. This organization is not necessarily a well defined institution or enterprise; working it out is in itself a methodological challenge. We have said that however relevant might be distinctions and practices in a domain different to this organization's action domain they will remain in its informational domain. Distinctions and practices need to be incorporated in the organization's operational (action) domain. This incorporation, when it happens, may lead to developing transformative complexity to deal with break experiences (Fig. 3.5 explains these learning processes).

We now explain more in depth the Viplan Methodology and its use. Two loops are necessary to explain the VM; the *(situational) learning loop* and the *cybernetic (organizational) loop* (see Fig. 11.1).

The *learning loop* depicts the situation from the perspective of observer participants. These observers may or may not all be actors of the performative situation; however together they create new insights from within and/or outside the situation. This loop's purpose is supporting situational appreciation. Actors naturally experience, over time, breaks that trigger performative situations; problems or possibilities. They experience these breaks as changes that trigger the need to language new distinctions and incorporate new practices; both as individuals or organizations they are learning along the way. The learning loop is no more than the well known 'observe-analyse-design-implement' loop (Kim 1993). Here the loop is discussed from a methodological stance.

Learning loops relate to all kinds of performative situations from public participation in policy processes, educational failures, innovation breakthroughs, introduction of best practices in an industry, absorbing significant climatic changes, or dealing with structural weaknesses. Observations increase participant's sensitivity

**Viplan Methodology
to Manage Change Processes**

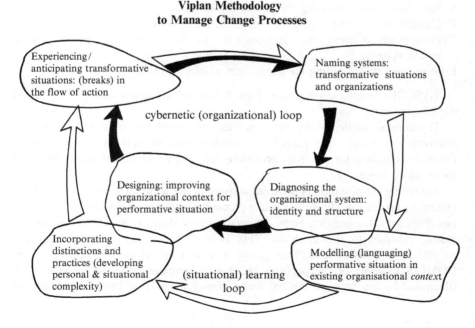

Fig. 11.1 The viplan methodology to manage change processes

to breaks of all kinds. Methodologically enhancing and improving participants' observational capabilities is a major issue and we don't delve in it (see Zeeuw 2004).

However, participants construe situations differently; they may share the same inputs (or signals) but construe them differently; they are structure determined. Individuals or groups express their *viewpoints* as they construe situations. This construing happens naturally as people converse with each other and share their appreciations of the situations at hand. From our methodological perspective the concern is making explicit these constructs emerging from human communication systems.

Our emphasis, as already said, is on human communication systems, which emerge from the closure of people's communications. It is this closure that makes them distinguishable to observers, who name systems from their particular viewpoint. It is clear that several if not many meanings can emerge from the actors' interactions. However, in the VM a primary concern is working out the meanings *created* by participants and stakeholders about performative situations. Different viewpoints assess the situation differently and name, tacitly or explicitly, different systems. Some of these names may lack insight others may be insightful but all are relevant if produced by relevant actors. In all cases the systems we are interested in are those focused on real world transformations. We use the mnemonic TASCOI to clarify the participants (see Chap. 7):

T: Transformation (what inputs are transformed into what outputs)
A: Actors (those producing the transformation)
S: Suppliers (those providing the inputs to this system)
C: Customers (those receiving the outputs of the system)
O: Owners (those responsible – accountable – for the values and the resources used by the system)
I: Interveners (those setting the parameters within which the system operates)

TASCOI, as explained in Chaps. 7 and 8, is a tool to name meaningful chunks of complexity in the world.[1]

This concise naming of observations is the second activity of the VM. Names are platforms to enhance the participants' appreciation of performative situations. Often these names for the transformations relevant to the situation are produced by *enabling viewpoints*.

Modelling the situation is the third activity of the learning loop; this modelling underpins languaging the situation in a process similar to that illustrated in Chap. 3 (see Fig. 3.5). Languaging helps articulating new distinctions, so far not appreciated, relevant to the situation. This is a conversational process supported by different forms of modelling; going from conceptual models as used in the COMLIS example of the previous chapter to communicative action models as illustrated by the Swedish nuclear waste management issue below. Any form of

---

[1]See note 8 in Chap. 7.

modelling can be used to increase the participants' appreciation of a shared situation. Modelling is a means to make distinctions that are relevant to the problem situation. Methodologically this modelling at early stages is likely to happen in the informational domain of the relevant organization; however the idea is to involve over time the *right actors* in this process. The aim of this modelling is to increase the participants' understanding of the shared situation in the organization's operational domain. The purpose of naming systems and modelling activities is to use them as catalysts of relevant situational conversations in the methodology's fourth activity (i.e., incorporating distinctions and practices).

Incorporating the distinctions made in the informational domain is the fourth activity of the learning (outer) loop in our methodology. For this the *right people* need to be involved in the situational conversations. The cybernetic loop will come, as is explained next, to our rescue for this purpose. The related issues of appreciation and implementation are of particular significance in this activity. As it is the case for Checkland's methodology, Vickers' idea of appreciative systems (Vicker 1970) is relevant to this methodology. It is apparent that through time, in healthy learning processes, with the right participants and communications, participants develop a more sophisticated view of situations. Their individual and situational complexities develop. Relevant conversations enrich their situational constructs, which help them to adjust their judgments of facts (what is the case?) and values (is this good or bad, acceptable or unacceptable?), developing in the process desirable relationships. The participants' actions keep appreciative processes evolving; they make decisions and implement desirable transformations. Though the incorporation of new distinctions may produce personal learning, methodologically we are interested in organizational learning, that is, in the development and incorporation of organizational practices (Espejo et al. 1996, Chap. 7). Participants need involvement in collective change. This is action in the situation's operational domain, which closes the loop by triggering new observations about the situation.

How good is the quality of the learning process? To what extent are actors appreciating the consequences of their actions? Key to these assessments is the organizational system giving context to the problem situation. We have made clear that organizational systems are different to formal institutions (see Chap. 5); through self-organization resources come together to produce organizational systems with different boundaries to those of the most obvious formal institutions related to the situation. The Swedish example below will illustrate this idea of organizational system. Performative situations may or may not be contained in particular institutions; often they are shared by several institutions and/or institutional parts. However, one way or the other, we postulate that they have a systemic embedding. The situation may emerge from relation within the system or from relation with environmental agents; in all cases we identify an organizational system, which provides the context to the situation. Working out which is this system and diagnosing the quality of its relationships is the concern of the cybernetic (organizational) loop of the methodology. Discussions in the previous four chapters have illustrated methodological aspects relevant to observing organizations. Here we want to highlight the significance of naming organizational systems relevant to particular performative situations. These are the systems where relevant change processes are expected to happen. These are the systems that focus the study of complexity management and support systemic thinking. These names help us to work out the stakeholders relevant to the situation.

From interviews, workshops and related observations it is possible to hypothesise the organizational system relevant to the named situation. We *name* this organizational system. Weaknesses in some of its relationships may be the root of the performative situation. Equally, effective structures may open new possibilities; perhaps additional resources and new relations may be necessary to enable the reconfiguring of resources to overcome currents constraints. The purpose is producing effective complexity management strategies.

Organizational learning is triggered by current breaks or by symptoms anticipating possible breaks in the organizational system. We name these systems and model their strategies to manage complexity using the VSM and the Viplan Method; these models identify relevant systemic roles and their relation. All this may happen in the informational domain, however, methodologically, if possible, it makes sense to involve the relevant actors. Methodologically we are naming the relevant organizational systems to the situation; we are naming the system and working out participants with the support of TASCOI. In fact each named system is a working hypothesis (see Swedish illustration). We diagnose the organization's structure and design improvements using the Viplan Method. Reconfiguring the resources and relations directly related to the problem situation is the main purpose for this diagnosis and design. This reconfiguring may be led by experts. However, the fourth activity of the cybernetic loop – concerned with producing necessary structural changes (i.e., reconfiguring the use of resources and their relations) – happens in the operational domain; participants stretch each other using all their political and communicative practices. This is a transformational process in the operational domain which is dealing with the context of the problem situation.

Anticipating possible changes, by improving the organization's structure, is an important aspect of the Viplan Methodology. This is the cybernetics of anticipation. Capacity to anticipate breaks is not forecasting specific events but building structural capacity to deal with the unforeseeable. In the next chapter we argue that by observing particular symptoms it is possible to diagnose structural and identity problems, we call them archetypes, which may hinder the anticipation of possible breaks. This is systemic thinking in practice. Equally, experiencing breaks as opportunities for higher organizational performance is of particular interest to us in this methodology. This relates to reconfiguring resources and developing new capabilities (Teece 2008).

From a processual perspective the *enabling viewpoint* is improving the *cybernetics of the situation*, that is, improving the complexity management of the situational context. This is the point of *intersection of the cybernetic and learning loops*; we can now answer questions about who should be the situational participants. These are the roles that should ground the learning loop's modelling work in conversations between the right stakeholders.

The Viplan Methodology (VM) guides change processes in the relevant organization. As such, in general, it is used as a heuristic for learning rather than as a contrived, formal framework for problem solving. The activities of the learning and cybernetic loops are pointers for thinking over time rather than activities that need to be followed in sequence. Iterations between them are natural and may take place over relatively long periods of time. In the end the methodology is fundamentally heuristic. No doubt the cybernetic loop requires studying the identity and structure of relevant organizations and for this the Viplan Method is used, however flexibility in its application is paramount. What is necessary is having good catalysts or enabling viewpoints, with a critical perspective, of change processes. Actors need not know about the methodological tools in use, though in practice they will be aware of their systemic epistemology. The VM facilitates change processes as participants articulate and implement new policies and/or programmes. Often these change processes produce significant breaks and the challenge for actors is absorbing the implications and possible consequences of these changes for their own good and for the good of the affected stakeholders. This is an issue of boundary judgments that is fundamental for ethical changes.

The last part of this chapter illustrates the use of the Viplan Methodology. This methodology has been applied in a wide range of situations, mainly with clients in processes of intervention and also in research (Bowling and Espejo 2000). It has been applied in large manufacturing companies, banks and also in policy studies (Espejo and Gill 1998, p. 4; Andersson et al. 2004, p. 8, 2006). Recently it has also been applied by Harwood in SMEs (Harwood 2010). An application of this methodology over several years was done by the book's first author for the management of nuclear waste in Europe (Andersson et al. 1998, p. 5, 2004, p. 8, 2006); an aspect of this application is illustrated in what follows.

In recent years nuclear energy is receiving a great deal of attention; the use of fossil fuels for energy generation is becoming more restricted as their extraction becomes ever more difficult and their environmental impacts become clearer. For many, even for people who opposed it in the past the option of nuclear energy is becoming more attractive; however a significant problem affecting its development is the long-term impact of its waste. What to do with it? The problem was considered of sufficient significance by countries like Sweden and Germany to decide to set time limits for their nuclear energy programmes. In any case the disposal of existing and future waste needs a solution. A favoured option is its disposal in deep repositories underground. However, beyond technological and geological issues, a key problem is acceptance by the affected communities of repositories in their backyards. At the same time, over the past decades, communities are increasingly aware of their rights and the fact that in democratic societies it is unacceptable for central governments to impose unilateral solutions. In fact, in countries like Sweden, with long democratic traditions, the process of finding a site for this waste is taking decades rather than years. Licensing a proposal for a repository is increasingly more difficult and requires the full participation of the affected communities. They are not prepared to accept solutions already agreed by the experts; they expect participation in the appreciative process from the beginning and this poses difficult challenges to politicians and experts. In particular these communities are concerned with the legitimacy of decision processes and the authenticity and scientific competence of the experts involved in the related studies. It is in this context that the Swedish nuclear regulators (SKI: the Swedish Nuclear Power Inspectorate, and SSI: the Swedish Radiation Protection Institute) asked to energy and cybernetic experts an appraisal of government and private institutions' communications with affected communities.

Interviews with key individuals, workshops with the regulators' representatives and a Team Syntegrity (Beer 1994) meeting with participation of Swedish and British players (Andersson et al. 1998, p. 5) gave to the team responsible for this study a deeper appreciation of nuclear waste management in Sweden. This appreciation of the situation highlighted some of the issues involved in the interactions between experts, policy-makers and external stakeholders in the communities potentially affected by the proposal of a deep repository. What was the meaning of the proposed repository? Was it a 'waste container' as seen by private sector companies or was it a 'safe container' as those with a public concern suggested? These two different identities for the Nuclear Waste Management System appeared at the core of the problem situation.

These two names emerged for the situation: one emerged as a public concern and the other as a private concern. Though safety was *increasingly* paramount for all concerned, there was evidence that *tacitly* resource allocation did not always follow this priority. Eventually, in line with much of the debate that had taken place in Sweden through the early 1990s, the issue was seen as the *transparency of policy decisions*, which was understood not only as an issue of making information available to stakeholders but of building up effective communications among institutions focused on nuclear waste management and between them and the communities. The study of these interactions was the beginning of the application of the Viplan Methodology to the Swedish nuclear waste management programme (Espejo and Gill 1998, p. 4).

From the perspective of the cybernetic loop the problem was defining the organizational system embedding this problem of transparency. Considering the above discussions two hypotheses were advanced for the Swedish Nuclear System;

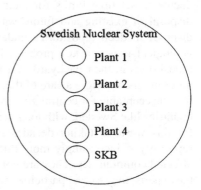

Fig. 11.2 Hypothesis 1 (the Swedish Nuclear System example)

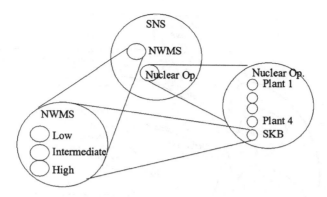

Fig. 11.3 Hypothesis 2 (the Swedish Nuclear System example)

the first (Fig. 11.2) put the emphasis on the Swedish Nuclear Fuel and Waste Management company (SKB) owned by the nuclear plants. Together this waste management company and the nuclear plants constituted a privately-owned Swedish Nuclear System (SNS). In this perspective they were referring to what people saw as a commercially oriented organizational system operating in the regulatory context of the Swedish Ministry for the Environment. The second name put the emphasis on the public responsibility of nuclear waste management (Fig. 11.3). The hypothesis was of a publicly accountable Nuclear Waste Management System (NWMS), which included all the government resources focused on nuclear waste management and the privately owned SKB, which, together with the Nuclear Operations constituted the SNS. This second hypothesis made apparent that the unclear identity of the NWMS, most certainly, had an influence in its transparency. The identity of this system was blurred in the eyes of the people. Was the NWMS identical to SKB as in Hypothesis 1 (a private enterprise) or was it a publicly accountable system as in Hypothesis 2? It was necessary for transparency purposes to clarify the system in focus. While SKB had a good reputation as a private sector organization, the NWMS was more than SKB; it also included a number of other public resources, such as the National Council for Nuclear Waste (KASAM) and parts of the Ministry of the Environment, SKI and SSI. Was the nuclear waste management system an organization driven by the private ethics of commerce or was it driven by the ethics of the public good. This issue dominated discussions with SKB and more generally with stakeholders. In the end it was clear that the system in focus was the public Nuclear Waste Management System and not SKB alone. This agreement made clear the need to study the quality of the communications within the NWMS and between this system and the communities. SKB's organization structure was considered in general good, but it was more difficult to say the same about the NWMS.

A mapping of the NWMS resources onto the VSM is in Fig. 11.4. This mapping was intended as a platform to discuss the communications and systemic roles of different institutions in the SNS and NWMS. In Fig. 11.4 the system in focus is the NWMS, except for the two triangles and box at the top of the figure, which relate to

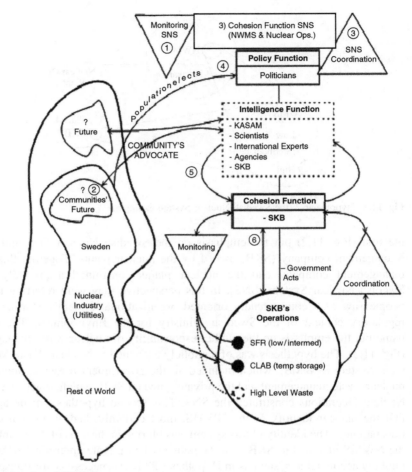

Systemic roles of SKI/SSI

Role 1: as regulators monitoring total industry

Role 2: as stretchers of NWMS Intelligence Function (Community´s advocate)

Role 3: as auditors of operational coordination between NWMS and Nuclear Ops

Role 4: briefing Government Ministers on nuclear matters in addition to KASAM

Role 5: as auditors of balance between the Intelligence & Cohesion functions

Role 6: reviewers of SKB 3 year Plan including R & D; authorise spending of Nuclear Waste Fund

Fig. 11.4 Using the VSM for diagnosing NWMS

the higher level of recursion (i.e., SNS). The systemic points that are made in what follows were offered as discussion points rather than as definitive diagnostic points; in the end the issue of communities *stretching* the NWMS became the most insightful. This issue is discussed below. Much debate happened around the diagnostic points; something that helped to increase the appreciation of the structural context for improving communications between communities and the NWMS. From a structural perspective our key concern was discussing the public sector's auditing of the quality of the multiples communications producing the NWMS; this quality was necessary for transparency (cf. RISCOM Model inWene and Espejo 1999).

The fact that the NWMS, rather than SKB, was the system in focus meant to see the Swedish Nuclear System as a system aligned with the public sector. But this required appreciating the communication consequences of Hypothesis 2; not developing effective communications within this system increased the risk of seeing the NWMS only as SKB, that is, as a private sector enterprise (Hypothesis 1). Of course everyone was aware of the nuclear plants and SKB as private enterprises, however without an awareness of Hypothesis 2 the plants would not be seen as an organizational system in their own right (i.e., Nuclear Operations), constituting the SNS together with the publicly focused NWMS. The fragmentation of a private SNS and public institutions focused on nuclear waste would have made more likely that necessary communications between these institutions, SKB and communities were not considered and developed. And, it also made more likely an overlap of SKI/SSI roles with SKB roles, as it would have required the formers' more detailed regulation of nuclear waste management activities, something that would have been necessary had SKB not been seen as part of the NWMS. These are implications of seeing the SNS as the synergistic interactions of two primary activities: Nuclear Operations and the NWMS. However, are there resources to manage SNS as a whole? This view of the SNS implies that there should be resources focused on the cohesive management of Nuclear Operations and the NWMS. In fact the energy produced by nuclear plants in Sweden has a levy for each distributed kwh, which forms the Nuclear Waste Fund. This fund could be used to develop a mechanism of monitoring-control with a holistic view of Nuclear Operations and the NWMS. This mechanism required in addition to capacity for resources bargaining, the monitoring and coordination of the two primary activities. From this view, which assumed Hypothesis 2, several systemic communications were suggested for the cohesive management of both the SNS (the total system) and the NWMS (one of its primary activities).

In our role of enabling viewpoint and using Fig. 11.4 as a discussion reference we challenged the key situational actors. Questions like: to what extent is there a clear structural difference between monitoring (auditing) the Central Interim Storage for Spent Nuclear Fuel (CLAB) and the Final Disposal Facility for Low and Intermediate-level Waste (SFR) as well as monitoring the NWMS as a whole (systemic Role 1 in Fig. 11.4)? In other words, to what extent is it clear for the regulators the difference between being internal or external auditors to the NWMS? It seems that both SKI/SSI and SKB do the monitoring of CLAB and SFR, albeit in different aspects. What was not clear to us was why should SKI/SSI get involved in monitoring safety indicator limits and not leave that to SKB, keeping for them the responsibility of monitoring whether SKB was doing this job properly? Figure 11.4 shows SKB as the only instance of monitoring its embedded programmes. This is the way it should be in order to avoid possible inefficient overlaps. In a normative sense we were suggesting that SKI/SSI's role should be monitoring the NWMS as a whole (external auditors) and not its programmes (internal auditors). However, the unwitting fragmentation of the public sector regulators and SKB, a consequence of seeing the SNS as in Hypothesis 1, apparently had made necessary, in the view of the relevant actors, to have SKI/SSI as internal auditors. In systemic terms this situation makes less likely that SKI/SSI will stretch SKB, as implied by the Role 2 that is discussed below.

How are the operational oscillations between Nuclear Operations and the NWMS damped? For instance, are there operational systems in place to avoid, over time, a mismatch between waste management capacity and waste production? What anti-oscillatory systems are in place to align the decommissioning of nuclear plants with the nuclear waste management programmes? These are particularly interesting systems to avoid the uncoordinated development and use of resources in the two subsystems. What's the role of SKI/SSI in this task? Do the regulators have adequate resources to audit how is the SNS dealing with these possible oscillations? This is systemic Role 3 for regulators in Fig. 11.4.

The *implementation function* of the system in focus is the activity of the contractors responsible for SFR and CLAB current waste management operations. This last primary activity is evolving towards a Deep Repository for high radioactive waste. That is the reason for the third circle in dotted lines in the Figure; it will not exist until the deep repository is operational and this is likely to take some time.

How efficient is the 'inside and now' management (the *cohesion function* in Fig. 11.4) of these nuclear waste management programmes? This is the management of existing programmes as approved by government on the advice of the Environmental Protection Agency, SKI/SSI, the Environmental Court and others (Licensing process). While it is clear that SKB is responsible for this management, what are the responsibilities of the public sector regulators? The perceptual illusion of Hypothesis 2 has here an effect. It is clear that SKB negotiates waste management programmes with contractors (Role 6) however we may also expect that SKB negotiates resources with those in the public sector managing the nuclear waste fund. Role 6 takes place at two levels, the internal to SKB and the external between the NWMS and the embedding SNS. Are people's views of these contractors' activities in the communities consistent with the activities these contractors negotiate with SKB? Should these views be inconsistent then people in the communities will fail to experience authenticity in the implementers' operations. Indeed this inconsistency can be seen as a lack of transparency.

The *intelligence function* in Fig. 11.4 is concerned with the outside and then of the NWMS. How are relevant resources integrating their contributions? This question relates to SKB's R&D work on the transportation, encapsulation and disposal of nuclear waste in a deep repository. All this research is considered in the context of social concerns about the long-term effects of this waste to local communities and society at large. This suggests the need to consider the dialogue between these communities and the NWMS (Role 2 in Fig. 11.4). In the interest of society it is important to create independent capacity to challenge the views and decisions of this system, perhaps in the form of academic centres supporting communities and environmental NGOs, but also in the form of SKI/SSI's role of *communities' advocates*. This is at the core of transparency. Paradoxically, even if it is not apparent on the surface, there is the risk of conflating the interests of society with those of the nuclear industry. This is likely to be the case if those, like SKI/SSI, responsible for society's interests are also made part of the NWMS, by being too close to SKB, as it appears to be the case today (see discussion of Role 1 above). Their systemic role should be creating relevant issues for the NWMS to respond, rather than operating from within. Since it is necessary to regulate the industry at the same time of challenging it, it may be necessary to consider two types of roles, those focused on auditing (Role 1) and those focused on challenging the NWMS. This role of creating challenging complexity for SKI/SSI is Role 2. If for instance SKI/SSI carry out nuclear waste management R&D and de facto operate from within the NWMS, the chances are that their role as *stretchers* of that system will suffer. They will reinforce the NWMS intelligence work from within and thus produce pre-emptive closure, that is, reinforce internal perspectives, rather than stretch directly or indirectly policy making from the outside.

Finally, from the perspective of the *policy function* there is a need to monitor the quality of debates forming policy (Role 5) and to make policy recommendations to government about licenses for SKB (Role 6). In particular it should be considered the quality of the debates between those doing Environmental Impact Assessments (EIAs) for planned developments and those responsible for agreeing NWMS programmes. Is there an adequate balance between the resources available for those operating under the Natural Resources Act (NRA) and those operating under the Nuclear and Radiation Protection Acts? It would appear that if this balance does not exist, and for instance those making decisions under the Nuclear and Radiation acts are much stronger than those under the Natural Resources Act, then, the long-term of the communities may be compromised to the detriment of society at large. This would be the case if those in the cohesion function, that is, those operating under the nuclear acts, have more resources than those in the intelligence function, that is, those operating under the NRA. The argument is that those operating under the NRA should be creating complexity (i.e., issues of concern) for the nuclear industry to take a more enlightened and robust view of the longer term. In order to increase this robustness it is necessary to increase the challenges of society (Role 2) and also increase the quality of decisions within the nuclear system. This improvement of policy processes is Role 5 in Fig. 11.4.

The above discussions braided the learning and cybernetic loops of our methodology. Without intending to offer a comprehensive study of the cybernetics of the situation, the discussions showed the use of the VSM as a *systemic tool* that helped in the discussion of transparency. The NWMS was hypothesised as a viable system and its boundaries and mechanisms were discussed with a focus on the communications of experts and policy-makers with community groups. Perhaps Role 2 was one of the most insightful for this particular situation; stretching guided the response to nuclear waste management of one of the most affected local authorities. Stretching makes apparent that the system in focus becomes stronger as environmental agents increase their pressure to improve communications within it. This idea of improving communications was seen as essential to making the system more transparent and therefore more trusted by stakeholders.

A good deal of work has followed this initial study making increasingly clear the conditions for a genuine communication between nuclear experts and lay people who know about their local conditions. Communications between those constituting the public sector (e.g., experts and policy-makers) and the private sector (e.g., SKB) and those in the communities (e.g., those communities proposed as possible sites for a deep repository) became the crucial issue. Clarifying the communicative competence of participants in the multiple dialogues in progress became the core of the methodology's learning loop. Indeed, communicative competence is much more than a good organization structure (Habermas 1979). It was more than an issue of experts' scientific competence; it was also about participants' individual authenticity in their interactions as well as actors' legitimacy (see Fig. 11.5). This aspect of communicative competence applied at all levels of meaningful debate, and this was a problem of variety engineering where the recursive model had something to say. It became clear the need to design levels of meaningful dialogue between the local and the global. The design of meetings lacking in requisite variety between senior people in central government and hundreds of community representatives at the same time was replaced by a cascading of dialogues following the recursive structure of the organizational system (see Fig. 11.6). The triangle of communicative competence together with the Viable System Model became the

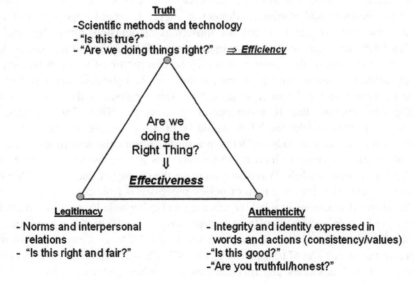

Fig. 11.5 Communicative action: a competent speaker makes three claims that he is willing to redeem
Source: Wene and Espejo 1999

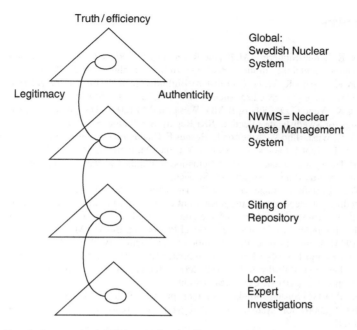

Fig. 11.6 Levels for meaningful dialogue (Source, Wene and Espejo 1999)

cornerstones of the RISCOM Model (Wene and Espejo 1999), which was developed over a number of years. RISCOM has spearheaded significant work for transparency in nuclear waste management in Sweden in the last few years (Andersson et al. 2003, p. 32).

The Viplan Methodology in nuclear waste management was used with all the sophistication of its structuring and modeling requirements. Issues and organizations were named; the structure of the NWMS system was studied and its braiding with the issue of transparency gave significant insights. These were efforts in the informational domain of the institutions involved. However, a number of workshops, including the Team Syntegrity meeting, work of stakeholders in the communities and multiple conversations with policy-makers and experts took the outcomes of this work into the operational domain of the NWMS where it has had significant influence (Andersson et al., 2004, p. 8).

The VM is offered as means of overcoming reductionism in dealing with performative situations. Often this reductionism is the outcome of our inability to deal with the huge complexity of our world. This *recursive methodology* offers a heuristic to counteract fragmentation and to design communications with requisite variety. This is going to be further explored in the next chapter of the book, where structural and identity archetypes of systemic problems are discussed.

References

Andersson K, Drottz-Sjöberg B-M, Espejo R, Fleming PA, Wene C-O (2006) Models of transparency and accountability in the biotech age. Bull Sci Technol Soc 26:46–56

Andersson K, Espejo R, Wene C-O (1998) Building channels for transparent risk assessment, RISCOM pilot study. Swedish Nuclear Power Inspectorate, Stockholm, Sweden, p 5

Andersson K, Wene C-O, Sjöberg B-MD, Westerlind M (2003) Design and evaluation of public hearings for Swedish site selection. SKI Report, Stockholm, Sweden, p 32

Andersson K, Westerlind W, Atherton E, Besnus F, Chataîgnier S, Engström S, Espejo E, Hicks T, Hedberg B, Hunt J, Laciok A, Leskinen A, Lilja CM, Pierlot S, Wene C-O, Vira J, Yearsley R (2004) Transparency and public participation in radioactive waste management. RISCOM II final report. SKI Report, Stockholm, Sweden, p 8

Arthur WB, Durlauf S, Lane DA (1997) The economy as an evolving complex system II: proceedings of the studies in the sciences of complexity. Perseus Books, Reading, MA

Beer S (1980) Prologue to autopoiesis and cognition by Humberto R. Maturana and Francisco J. Varela (*Autopoiesis and Cognition*). Riedel Publishing, Boston, MA

Beer S (1994) Beyond dispute: the invention of team syntegrity. Wiley, Chichester

Bowling D, Espejo R (2000) Exploring computer supported cooperative work in a retail bank. In: J Allen and J Wilby (eds) ISSS 2000 Intenational Society for the systems sciences: accession number 20151. CD-ROM, Toronto

Checkland P (1981) Systems thinking, systems practice. Wiley, Chichester

Checkland P (2000) Soft systems methodology: a thirty year retrospective. Syst Res Behav Sci 17:11–58

de Zeeuw G (2004) Fighting for science. Kybernetes 33(3/4):717–725

Espejo R, Gill T (1998) The systemic roles of SKI and SSI in the Swedish nuclear waste management system. SKI Report 98, Swedish Nuclear Power Inspectorate, Stockholm, p 4

Espejo R, Schuhmann W, Schwaninger M, Bilello U (1996) Organizational transformation and learning. Wiley, Chichester

Habermas J (1979) Communication and the evolution of society. Beacon Press, Boston, MA

Harwood SA (2010) The management of change and the cybernetic methodology in practice. under review (author's personal communication)

Homer-Dixon T (2001) The ingenuity gap: how can we solve the problem of the future. Vintage, London

Kim D (1993) The link between individual and organizational learning. Sloan Manage Rev (Fall):37–50

Maturana H (1988) Reality: the search for objectivity or the quest for a compelling argument. Irish J Psychol 9(1):25–82

Teece JD (2008) Technological know-how, organizational capabilities, and strategic anagement: business strategy and enterprise development in competitive environments. World Scientific Publishing, London

Vicker G (1970) Freedom in a rocking boat. Penguin Books, Harmondsworth, Middlesex, UK

von Glasersfeld E (1995) Radical constructivism: a way of knowing and learning. Falmer Press, London

Wene C-O, Espejo R (1999) A meaning for transparency in decision processes. In: Andersson K (ed) VALDOR; values in decisions on risk, Symposium, Proceedings. Stockholm, Sweden, pp 404–421

Chapter 12
Identity and Structural Archetypes

Abstract This chapter uses the VSM to understand and observe how people in organizations manage their own complexity as they strive to maintain stability in a chaotic environment. The VSM offers strategies to manage complexity at the least cost to people and organizations. People manage organizational complexity intuitively and of course in the process they make more or less costly mistakes. The aim of this chapter is increasing our ability to observe and diagnose shortcomings in this management. It offers practical support to diagnose common communication failures. These failures tend to be archetypical in the sense that they are recurrent observations made in many organizations. The value of archetypes is facilitating the diagnosis of identity and structural problems. From a methodological perspective they highlight the shortcomings of the organizational systems in which people experience performative situations or difficulties in implementing change.

Previous chapters made clear that a challenge for managing effectively the complexity of self-constructed performative situations is *naming and chunking transformations*. Chapters 7 and 8 specified that naming transformations requires ingenuity to deal with occasional intractable problems and chunking them effectively implies distributing complexity throughout the organization's structure in such a way that all participants have the opportunity to develop their competencies and talents and no one is overloaded unnecessarily. Naming and chunking transformations underpin learning processes, that is, performative processes through which organizations are constantly anticipating and adapting their strategies to absorb social, technological and cultural changes. As discussed in Chap. 6 distributed implementation and adaptation are at the core of recursive organizations. Chapters 9 and 10 offered detailed approaches to engineer this distribution of variety in organizations; we discussed the distribution and alignment of resources and decision-making capacity in order to improve constantly the matching of organizational and environmental varieties at acceptable or competitive levels of performance. In this chapter we highlight common relational aspects that make apparent inadequate management of complexity. These aspects are archetypical instances of poor variety management.

R. Espejo and A. Reyes, *Organizational Systems*,
DOI 10.1007/978-3-642-19109-1_12, © Springer-Verlag Berlin Heidelberg 2011

The Viplan Methodology is used to visualise archetypes. This visualisation is done through organizational audits that first of all require appreciating the issues of concern such as communication difficulties, lack of response capacity, counterproductive individual and group behaviours, loss of competitiveness, inadequate performance and so forth; second, naming the organizational system implied by these issues, which can be either existing enterprises or in more general terms self-organizing systems; third, modelling these organizations using the VSM and the Viplan Method; fourth, hypothesising *identity and structural archetypes* that help to explain the systemic meaning of performative issues of concern, fifth, discussing these hypotheses with relevant organizational stakeholders, designing improvements and taking actions where necessary and feasible.

The VSM as a tool for systemic thinking helps observing self-organizing wholes rather than collections of largely independent parts. Overcoming fragmentation requires improving and enabling desirable relationships (see Fig. 12.1).

Each archetype is the outcome of observations revealing identity and structural shortcomings. These are the kind of diagnostic points that experts are expected to make as they observe either enterprises or the resources and relations contributing to a policy or transformation. We offer archetypes to support inquiring processes and not to replace them. Converging too quickly into diagnostic points may stifle debates. On the other hand using archetypes, as hypotheses to support conversations, may make it possible to bring forth a new and insightful understanding about a situation. These archetypes originated in our personal experience with the National Audit Office of Colombia (Espejo 1997). About 30 archetypes emerged from this work. They were offered to auditors as a tool for auditing processes or for *second order auditing* (Espejo et al. 2001; Reyes 2001; Espejo 2008)

The value of thinking with the support of archetypes is that they focus our observational attention on relationships rather than on particular organizational functions and resources. The issue is not so much to use the VSM to model in

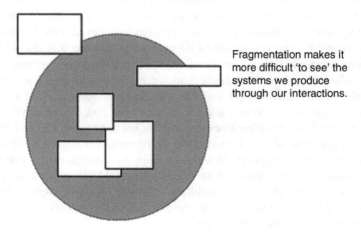

Fragmentation makes it more difficult 'to see' the systems we produce through our interactions.

Fig. 12.1 Fragmentation and organization

full an organization, but to focus attention on the most immediate relations that may help explaining performative shortcomings. Are actors' activities aligned with their collectively declared purposes? Are they developing and deploying the necessary structures to absorb current and anticipated environmental conditions? Does existing relations support aligned primary activities within a cohesive organization? What are the structural implications of their relationships? How effective are their relationships with external stakeholders? Often it is possible to diagnose obvious functional problems, like lack of necessary resources for a particular task, however the emphasis of the archetypes is to highlight systemic weaknesses in organizational processes. They are focused on aspects such as the integration of resources to match better environmental challenges or the enabling of a cohesive organization aligned with its policies.

Identity archetypes reveal organizations with unclear transformations. Discrepancies between discourse and behaviour make it difficult to *recognise* their doing. Also are relevant when observing organizations as black boxes does not yield clear identities. *Structural archetypes* reveal an inadequate deployment of resources and poor regulation of organizational activities. Often these two types of archetypes are intertwined and we find that identity problems have structural implications and vice-versa. The VSM helps us to organize these observations in a limited number of archetypes some of which are related to identity as recognition of what they do, some others to relations as instances of the relationships for viability.

In this chapter we use a generic graphic language to explain and illustrate different archetypes. Its purpose is facilitating their visualisation to provide a context to discuss issues of concern. Organizational systems are shown with three recursive levels: the first is the global organization, the second is the intermediate and the third is the local structural level. Of course the global can be made more global and the local more local however, three levels are enough to illustrate diagnostic issues (see Fig. 12.2). Whenever the circle is dotted the corresponding organizational system has an identity problem. The relationships between the policy, intelligence, cohesion, coordination and implementation functions and between them and environmental agents are presented in Fig. 12.3. Achievement (1), Cohesion (2), Policy-making (3), Stretching (4), Ownership (5) and Citizenship (6) relationships are shown in that figure (Espejo 2008). *Dotted lines for any of*

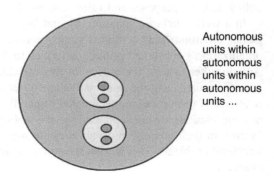

Autonomous units within autonomous units within autonomous units ...

Fig. 12.2 Organizational recursion

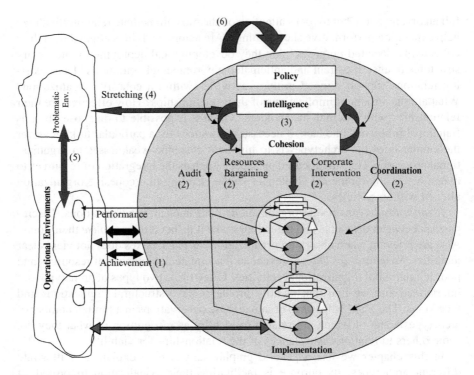

Fig. 12.3 The viable system model: reference model

these relationships, whether internal to a primary activity, in between primary activities or between them and environmental agents reflect structural archetypes. Sometimes we show dotted circles and dotted lines to make apparent that we are identifying identity and structural problems together.

Structural archetypes emerge whenever the relations between people and other resources produce dysfunctional organizational processes, and in particular they emerge from inadequate relations with customers, hierarchical relations within the organization, unbalanced attention to the short and long terms, weak relations with challenging agents in the problematic environment, misaligned stakeholders' and policy-makers' purposes and values and weak contextual belonging.

In a well-structured situation, by and large, global resources should deal with global environmental complexity, appropriate to their level, leaving it to the organization's subsumed primary activities to deal with issues at their own level. Among other factors, the quality of this matching depends on the distribution of scarce resources and the imaginative use of technological options to support their relations. If resources are misdirected or people are over-loaded or under-utilised, or their relations are not supported by an enabling context, or communications lack in trust, or their adaptation capabilities are weak, and so forth, we are recognising structural problems. This is what the structural invariances of the VSM allow us to observe.

Identity archetypes as external recognition of what the organizational system does, relate to its black box description (see Chaps. 1 and 7). Relations as instances of relationships refer to operational descriptions. The former are focused on transformations and stakeholders, the latter on relations between these stakeholders. In Chap. 7 we said that black box descriptions, or identity statements, were a platform to work out the complexity of an organizational system, and operational descriptions – supported by the VSM – helped visualising *relationships and relations*. For instance hierarchical relationships influence all interactions in an organization, from those between colleagues to those between senior managers and shop floor workers, but hierarchical relations between specific managers at different structural levels may inhibit the formation of autonomous primary activities with deep structural implications for the organizational system.

Archetypes related to black box descriptions of the organizational system reflect the way people in the organization see themselves and the way external observers see the organization. What is its purpose? What business is the enterprise in? What transformation is it doing? An inspection of the organization's products and services may make apparent a mismatch between this doing and what people in the organization think they are doing. In the language of Argyris and Schön (1978, 1996) this is the *archetype purpose-in-use is different to espoused purpose*. The extent to which people are conscious or not of this mismatch is not always clear. The situation may be subtle, such as when there is a mismatch in appreciation, such that members of the organization think genuinely they are doing something different to what stakeholders and informed observers see they are doing. In other cases, it may simply be that events are superseding their self-defined image.

For instance this is the case of an enterprise where a *regulatory function starts behaving as a primary activity* and carries profitable business with external clients at the same time as providing internal services (Fig. 12.4). In this case, in our

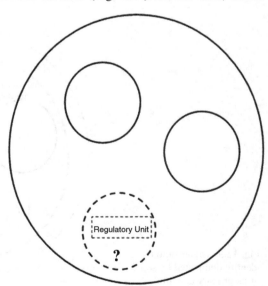

Fig. 12.4 Regulatory function behaving as a primary activity

methodological language, there is a chunk of complexity that is not part of the transformation they have named in their identity statement. This chunk often is an unseen primary activity that is poorly managed. The problem is that this regulatory function becomes increasingly concerned with its own viability at the expense of the organization it should serve. An example is a *manufacturing* company evolving towards *non-manufacturing* businesses, for instance as a result of customers wanting to use its knowledge about suppliers to purchase not only final products from them but also spares and parts. This company's procurement unit (a regulatory function) over time is becoming a business in its own right, however the company continues to see itself as a manufacturing company (Espejo 1989a).

A variation of the above archetype is the case of an enterprise developing a new business that is not recognised explicitly. This is the case of *unseen primary activities* that for the very reason of not being seen are not structured properly as business units. For instance a shoot off of an existing product illustrates this point, as could be the case of a bakery starting to produce fish products using a local pool where they dispose returns of their daily production. This is the case of a new chunk that may or may not be consistent with the organization's transformation but in any case is not immediately seen as a new business.

Another variation of this archetype is *an organization's identity dominated by some of its primary activities at the expense of those left out* (Fig. 12.5).

This is an archetype emerging from a mismatch between the formal and informal structures of an organization. It happens when a set of synergistically related primary activities share with others less related primary activities a global (or intermediate) primary activity. Sometimes the synergistic set develops an embryonic common embedment in the form of an *emergent virtual organization* that dominates the organization's identity. At the same time the unrelated ones are left out on their own. However, the mechanism providing cohesion to the emergent

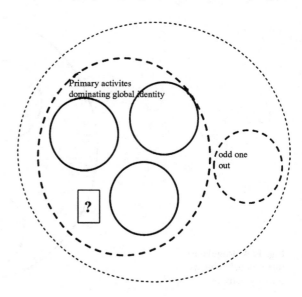

Fig. 12.5 Organization's
identity dominated by some
of its primary activities

primary activity is likely to be underdeveloped, simply because formally no one is recognising it; this fact may affect its performance. It can be argued that the total organization collapses into the virtual organization; senior management is focused on the most significant cluster of primary activities, leaving the others unattended. Managers of these others feel that no one is interested in what they do. It is difficult to recognise where the synergy between primary activities is. The identity of the organization is related to the dominant synergistic cluster.

It can also be the case that the global level fails to work out synergistic relationships among its primary activities failing to recognise a global transformation different to the individual transformations of its constitutive chunks. This is the case of global managers who do not have a business *of their own* and are likely to be more concerned with the activities of subsumed primary activities than with their own business. These are organizations ready to be split up. From a black box perspective the global organization does not have an identity; from an operational perspective the policy-making relationship (3) in Fig. 12.3 is failing to be creative and to *add value* to the enterprise. This is the *negative synergy archetype* (Fig. 12.6).

An identity archetype emerging at the operational level is observable when people in a *primary activity work for inconsistent purposes*. Often people in an

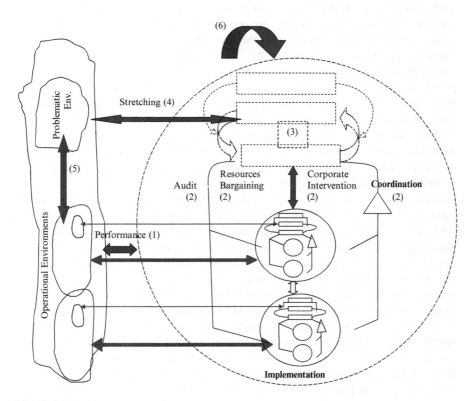

Fig. 12.6 Negative synergy archetype

Examples can be found in multiple dot.com companies, which have failed to adjust to the evolving requirements of their markets. The speed of change in these markets was too much for them. They have failed to recognise primary activities with potential for viability let alone necessary organizational processes in order to maintain stability. As reported by a 2003 paper: 'And this relentless redesign of the organization was occurring simultaneously with the construction, emergence, consolidation, dissipation and reconfiguration of the industry itself. "What is New Media?" This was the question we encountered numerous times scribbled on whiteboards in brainstorming sessions during or just prior to our meetings in various interactive companies. Or, as one of our informants posed the question: People are always trying to come up with a metaphor for a website. Is it a magazine, a newspaper, a TV commercial, a commu- nity? Is it a store? You know, it's none of these... and it's all of these and others, in many variations and combinations. So, there's endless debate'. (Girard and Stark 2003) Many of these organizations have not clarified what business they are in; their boundaries are unclear to them and to their customers.

The above archetypes show black box identity problems intertwined with oper- ational relationship problems. In particular, the pressure of customers affects the achievement relationships (1) in Fig. 12.3, which in turn makes it necessary for the organization to adapt and change its transformation. These are the foci of the archetypes related to the cohesion, policy-making, stretching and citizenship relationships; (2), (3) and (4) and (6) in Fig. 12.3.

Hierarchical relationships between cohesion resources and primary activities are at the core of the *weak primary activities archetype*. People responsible for produc- ing chunks of the organization's transformation that should operate as primary activities are reluctant or do not know how to become entrepreneurial. They are unwilling to create new policies and to some degree to make their own decisions. Their identity is defined for them rather than worked out by them. Rather than taking ownership of their tasks managers are henchmen doing what they are told. In this case primary activities do not take responsibility for their autonomy and behave as if they were in a hierarchy. The relationship is one of dependency rather than one of autonomy and alignment of interests. This relationship is archetypical in hierar- chical organizations and often has cultural underpinnings.

In the wider sense of the stretching relationship (3) the *outside and then* is left to the attention of mainly global resources, who hopefully but not necessarily, develop a vision of the organization's future. The variety amplification entailed in a distributed adaptation is lost since the embedded primary activities operate without the *local long term framework*. The idea of middle level or local primary activities inventing their own futures is not considered. Thus the links of local and middle level primary activities with their *problematic environments* are weak and mostly reactive (Fig. 12.8).

The hierarchical archetype is common in the divisions of large corporations, triggering the *middle level manager archetype*. This archetype is the result of divisional (intermediate level) managers being seen either as amplifiers of senior management vis-à-vis local primary activities, and/or filters of local activities vis-à-vis senior management, rather than as parts of a managerial level in its own right. The

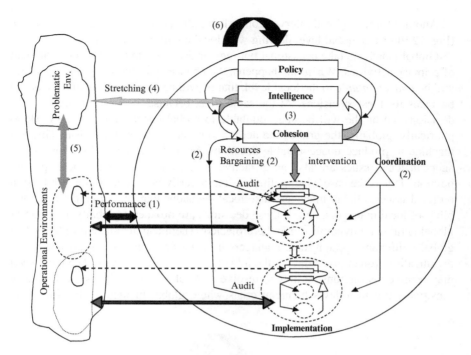

Fig. 12.8 Weak primary activities archetype

division is often no more than a high status manager and his or her own staff, which operate as a communication channel rather than a primary activity with its own autonomy. These managers do not develop policies of their own; they are gate keepers, co-ordinators and distributors of information. Often middle managers are seen as ritualistic channels in charge of producing 'integrated reports' for which they don't have requisite variety.

The hierarchical archetype also has implications for business units in large corporations, as they wait for corporate management to decide their investment programmes and strategic goals. This lack of entrepreneurship is reflected in the *lack of competitiveness archetype* common to strategic business units (SBUs) vis-à-vis smaller independent organizations working in the same business. But this problem is not only characteristic of large corporations; it is the same for any organization whenever the units producing their products and services (i.e., its primary activities) do not develop an identity of their own and/or lack in local problem solving capacity, only that smaller enterprises do not have the survival umbrella of a powerful business.

In many corporations it is easy to see that people's commitment decreases with distance from the corporate level. It is not possible to talk about *viable* local primary activities. They only exercise operationally discretion, but show little sign of autonomy.

Another form of global intervention in local affairs is the *politicians' archetype* (Fig. 12.9) or the global level dealing with local environmental issues.

Global managers take occasional but regular decisions in the local environment of primary activities. When this happens, the chances are that the global manager will be *unaccountable* to the local level, that is, will be outside the local checks and balances for these decisions. At the same time, because the local nature of these decisions, he or she will be unaccountable to global checks and balances. Metaphorically, globally, the grid of the net is too broad to catch 'local' fish. This is a machine to produce unaccountable decisions. Sporadic decisions by global managers in local issues are also an attractive strategy to manipulate local (public) opinion. This is the case when politicians temporarily but regularly focus attention on local issues. Global managers take local decisions that should be the responsibility of local managers, and, if these decisions are broadcast globally a mirage of global action and dynamism may be projected. There can also be a problem when global politicians appoint local managers in quasi-autonomous non-governmental organizations (quangos) reducing the influence of local democracy. The local level may receive instructions on how to resolve particular issues. This is a particularly sensitive point in today's financial crisis where global financial authorities may

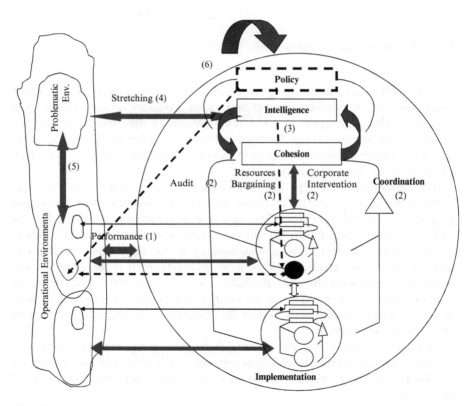

Fig. 12.9 Politicians' archetype

instruct managers of nationalised banks to give credits by-passing requirements for local scrutiny. However this archetype should not be confused with Beer's algedonic signals (Beer 1981), when the local level, whether people in the environment or the primary activity, asks for global intervention in situations that go beyond their control.

As it was illustrated by the bank's example in Chap. 8 often large corporations adopt functional structures that fragment their performance. In these structures, units such as loans, customer services and risk management are kept apart and people find it difficult to align their efforts. However, in one form or another, often at a high cost and endless meetings, units develop operational relationships which support their day to day activities. These informal structures are embryonic, unrecognised virtual primary activities, which illustrate the *unsupported self-organization archetype*.

Another example of this archetype in large corporations is the difficulty of supporting simultaneously the viability of several market segments and production plants. Sales people have to secure production capacity for their clients and production people have to develop and make good use of their assets. In other words, marketing people have to optimise customer support and manufacturing production capacity. These, often conflicting, requirements imply endless communications and co-ordination meetings, which could be avoided if sales, production and technology were integrated operationally in a virtual organization rather than just using middle level managers (see Chap. 5 in Espejo et al. 1996).

But perhaps the most common archetype reflecting a poor management of complexity, and more significantly poor interpersonal relations, is the *control dilemma archetype* described graphically in Fig. 12.10 (Espejo 1989b).

As illustrated above, today, managers of primary activities, at all levels, are dealing with increasingly complex environments. Under pressure these managers often find the need to respond locally to changes, without involving their supervisors. This may lead to a sense of unease in the latter; there are more and more things happening locally of which they are not aware. Senior management feel the need to take firmer control. They issue *more commands* and demand *more reports*, eating far into primary activities management time. This leads to situations where more of the primary activities resources are spent dealing with control requests and less with environmental complexity. This happens precisely when more time is needed to deal with an ever increasing environmental complexity. Local managers feel they are over controlled while senior managers feel they are under controlling. The latter feel that local people are doing whatever they like, taking no notice of them. Local managers are lacking in motivation; in their eyes whenever they take the initiative they trigger further control. This is a common experience for managers at all levels, and, in fact, for people in all walks of life. For instance a divisional manager tightening the budgetary procedures for travelling in reaction to a business unit decision to make more customer visits. What the divisional manager may be unaware of is that the business unit requires an increasing understanding of customers' local environments to become more competitive. For more illustrations see (Espejo 2008).

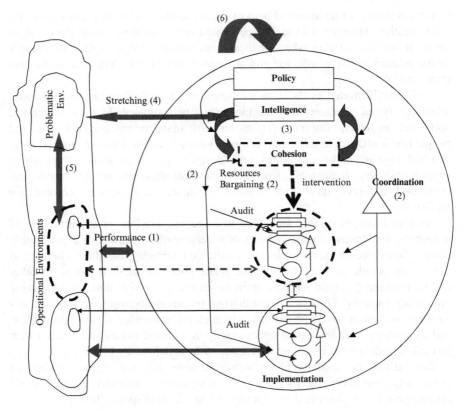

Fig. 12.10 Control dilemma archetype

Often managers feel more comfortable dealing with issues relevant to subsumed primary activities rather than those appropriate to their structural level. This behaviour may be the outcome of previous *local* experience, making it easier for them to handle local issues rather than the as yet unlearned global issues. In any event the result is a variation of the *control dilemma* and managers dealing with far more complexity than they should, thus affecting theirs, and the organization's global performance. In this situation local managers feel restricted in dealing with their tasks; intermediate or global managers are too close for their comfort. There are unmanaged intermediate or global issues and overworked and under pressure senior managers. They are dealing with far more issues than they can reasonably cope with. They may be experiencing an *information overload syndrome*.

The control dilemma can be compounded when the global or intermediate levels do not monitor their immediate embedded primary activities. This is the *no-monitoring archetype*. This is a common archetype throughout the organization that may affect some functions more than others. If local primary activities business functions are not monitored by those responsible for their over viewing, the quality of their communications will suffer. Without knowledge of local operational activities intermediate managers cannot make sense of the information they receive from local managers, to the extreme that reporting is transformed in a ritual rather than in a serious attempt to integrate efforts and steer processes (see cohesion mechanism in Chaps. 6, 9 and 10). From the perspective of the local managers, lack of monitoring is tacitly or explicitly constructed as lack of interest in their activities. The outcome is an environment of mistrust; the two sides are aware that they do not understand each other. Communications are mainly based on formal reports and not on involving local people in conversations, occasional audits and so forth. Relations are perceived as hierarchical and not as participative. Global and intermediate managers confess that they do not know what is going on at the intermediate and local levels respectively, and often experience surprises in their expectations about performance. Therefore contrary to the view that monitoring is an infringement on someone's autonomy, monitoring primary activities is crucial to the development of responsible trust in an organization (Espejo 2001).

A variation of the no monitoring archetype is the *micromanagement archetype* (see Fig. 12.11) or intervening and monitoring at the wrong level.

Global intervention and monitoring of primary activities removed two or more levels below are poor complexity management and possibly a recipe for conflicts. On the one hand global managers get involved in too much detail, thus hindering

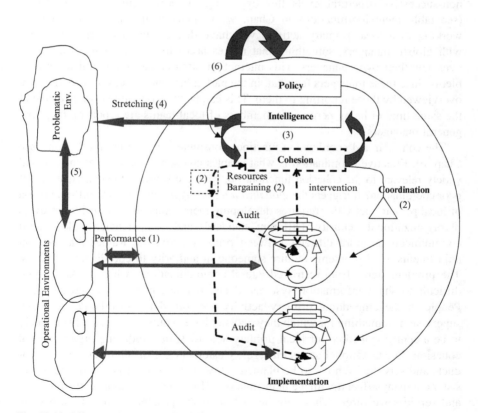

Fig. 12.11 Micromanagement archetype

their performance; on the other, intermediate management feels global management is intruding in their territory, and weakening their position vis-à-vis local primary activities. Altogether intervening and monitoring at the wrong level confuse lines of accountability and increase conflicts in the organization; global management may use its local knowledge *to surprise* intermediate managers with local knowledge that they don't have. This is likely to create resentment and conflicts between them. This is compounded when intermediate managers do not monitor local primary activities. This archetype often happens at a personal level when a local person develops a special relationship with a global manager (two or more levels above), who, this way, learns a good deal about local problems, knowledge he might use to control the intermediate manager (who should be responsible for 'this monitoring'). This behaviour creates mistrust and conflicts (see example in Espejo 1989b).

At a more formal level, for good operational reasons sometimes, people in charge of a global function interact with and monitor local people by-passing the intermediate structural level, possibly creating the impression that local people are accountable to global and not intermediate managers, and possibly creating the structural conditions for an *archetype where local people overview intermediate managers*. This is often the case when capacity for a function is available at several, non-successive structural levels, thus bypassing one or more of the existing levels (see table recursion/functions in Chap. 9). In practice this means that people working in a local primary activity will have direct functional reporting lines with global managers, something that makes accessible to them information to overview their own managers. This interaction often creates communication problems since these managers feel that, in the particular function of concern, they are overviewed by those reporting to them. This can be the case with specialists that at the same time of being permanent members of local teams are reporting to global general managers.

The cohesion and coordination functions constitute the cohesion mechanism (see Chap. 6). Effective coordination is what enables autonomy and reduces the residual variety relevant to the cohesion function. So, what are some of the consequences of poor coordination? It triggers the *globalization archetype*. Enabling the self-regulation of local primary activities requires developing their competencies to similar levels of organizational maturity. Different standards and competencies make lateral communications more difficult between primary activities. Rather than mutual adjustments local problems require someone in authority to coordinate activities. The problem stems from restricted lateral communications, which make it more difficult to share information systems, decision rules, procedures and so forth. People in the embedding primary activity are forced to co-ordinate by direct supervision, something for which they may not have requisite variety. This is likely to be a centrifugal force for local primary activities, thus reducing organizational cohesion. Organizational stress emerges. Customers get different quality of products and services. Who is to be blamed? How does the poor performance of my sister company affect my image in the market? How can we harmonise the products and services we offer? These are but a few of the problems likely to stress the organization's mechanism of cohesion. In a globalised world, where enterprises are likely to operate in different countries and cultures, we are more likely to find these sources of imbalances, triggering the *globalization archetype*.

Several archetypes relate to the distribution of resources and discretion in the organizational system. Problems emerge from highly interrelated functions that are parts of the same value chain but operate at different recursion levels (see Chap. 10). A solution could be *centralizing the local function or decentralizing the global function* to operate them at the same structural level. This is the *broken business process archetype*.

This archetype takes multiple forms. Often two or more activities, which operationally are highly interconnected operate at different structural recursions and are connected by a low capacity communication channel (e.g., a local boss). Since this channel is regulating the connectivity between the operational activities its low capacity becomes a source of frustrations. Frustrations because of delays as the related activities wait for the local boss's decisions in situations where these 'authorities' have little or nothing to add to the process. Delays in projects, contracts, tasks happen because relevant documents and reports are waiting for the attention of 'busy' managers. People often by-pass these managers as they realise that they can get results without their intervention. Often in these cases conflicts ensue (see Espejo 1989a).

Sometimes organizational resources are necessarily centralized even if this centralization might be undesirable, (see criteria for centralization and decentralization in Chap. 9). Of course some other times centralization may be desirable. For functions that offer an overview of the organization like finance it makes sense to centralize related resources. Naturally while it is functionally desirable to distribute resources if these are focused on particular tasks, when resources are scarce or highly specialised it makes sense to keep them centralized. This seems reasonable, but in this case people and global resources are dealing with local issues, that is, with problems specific to local primary activities. This becomes a problem if *resource centralization* is not accompanied by *functional decentralization*. In the past functional decentralization was more problematic than it is today. ICTs permit virtual decentralization (see example of bank in Chap. 8). But if this decentralization does not happen or the virtually decentralized resource is not effectively integrated with other local resources fragmentation ensues. This is the *resource and functional centralization archetype*.

The dual archetype is *resource decentralization and functional centralization*, which we relate to the *leading primary activity archetype*. Resources are functionally centralized in one local primary activity, which uses them for its own purposes but also to service all other sister primary activities. Since it is a scarce resource, otherwise it would have been made available to all of them, the tendency for the leading primary activity is to serve its interests first at the expense of the others. Sister primary activities perceive they are not receiving a good service or that the distribution of the resource is not even. This fact is used to justify performance problems. Conflicts emerge between the owner of the resource and the others. Much energy is spent in dealing with this internal problem.

while those at the intermediate level with local knowledge through monitoring are aware that their knowledge is of no use in decision making.

An alternative form for this archetype is resources bargaining between the intermediate and local levels but monitoring from the global level. This archetype gives some lights about the case of 'Baby P' in the UK (*The Economist* 2008). Baby P died in the hands of his mother and two others. In the last 6 months of his life the child had been seen not less than 60 times by doctors and social workers. Not long after his death the UK Social Services regulator issued a report, which recommended that the national regulator carried out yearly *visits* to every social service department in the country. The regulators were off the mark; social service departments are part of local authorities and not directly of a National Social Services, thus in terms of structural recursion it should be expected that the monitoring of their activities is done by their respective local authorities and not by a national body. The reason for this is simple, one must assume that corporate managers in local authorities negotiate with social service departments (as with all other service departments) the allocation of resources for their programmes and therefore that they should be the ones assessing their capabilities and monitoring their performance. In the end, it should be the responsibility of each local authority that the services' performance is adequate.

The stretching relationship (4) in our reference VSM model (Fig. 12.3) triggers adaptation archetypes. In particular the w*eak stretching archetype* is common in situations where strong environmental challenges are necessary to improve policy processes (Fig. 12.14). Stakeholders in the problematic environment should put pressure on the organizational system to get the best out of them in their own interest, however, over time they can become closely related to organizational actors, losing independence and therefore offering a weak stretching. Vociferous opponents become tame stakeholders, thus reducing the organization's accountability to its silent stakeholders (5 in Fig. 12.3). For sensitive policy issues, such as nuclear waste management, on the name of dialogue NGO representatives are slowly but surely integrated in the group of experts and policy-makers reducing the strength of their challenge (Espejo and Bowling 2002).

Figure 12.3 also makes us aware of the relationship for organizational citizenship (6). An archetype emerges from the organization's management of its *belonging* relations with embedding meta-systems or enabling organizations. For instance a local authority is a meta-system for a manufacturing plant operating within its geographic boundaries. An industrial association is a meta-system for industries in their sector. In such cases belonging is sometimes weak and there are doubts about *organizational citizenship*. Citizenship cannot be assumed. When this belonging is taken for granted, and not enough effort is put to work for it, otherwise cohesive and high performance organizational systems may find, to their chagrin, that they are hit by an unfriendly and possibly indifferent embedding meta-system. This is the *organizational citizenship archetype* (see Fig. 12.15). The meta-system may have different expectations and views about them. This break may happen even with a great sense of local comfort and autonomy.

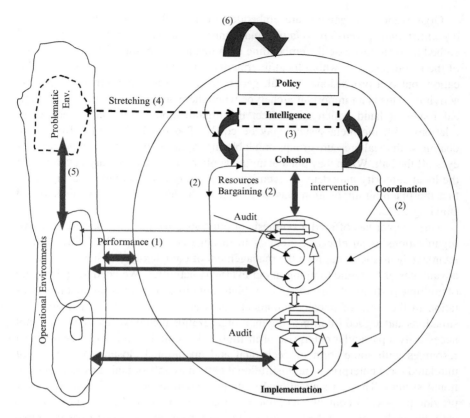

Fig. 12.14 Weak stretching archetype

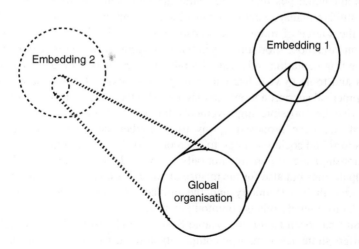

Fig. 12.15 Organizational citizenship archetype

Organizations in general are embedded in more than one meta-system. The *organizational citizenship archetype* may emerge with any of these relevant global embeddings. In this case the embedding organization is not the all-powerful owner of the resources, with whom local/intermediate management negotiates their allocation, but is a professional, social, geographic, environmental embedding of its activities. This is an important archetype when there are environmental or ecological issues at hand which may affect the organization's legitimacy. Indifferent relations with the meta-system may be costly. Too much time and effort spent dealing with local pressure groups and lobbying groups may take the organization's eyes off the ball. When they put a planning application for a necessary development the local authority may deny it, even if a rational argument would have suggested that the planning application was beneficial to the local community (Espejo and Bowling 2002).

This chapter has offered a synthesis of our book. We have advocated recursive organizations as an effective strategy to manage complexity. The VSM offers a recursive heuristic to improve the management of complexity. We have argued the advantages of systemic thinking in our everyday activities. We need the joining up of multiple participants in particular problem situations. We are aware that fragmentation in the form of poor communications is at the root of many performative situations and argued for improving their organizational context. This context is not necessarily a particular enterprise or institution but could be the self-organizing of resources with some form of decisional and operational closure. A network of unrelated local enterprises and institutional parts may self-organize as an organizational system. These organizational systems, underpinned by political will, may provide purposeful contexts that, not only make meaningful the situations of concern, but make apparent the resources and relations necessary to produce desirable changes. Particularly for situations emerging in contexts with unclear organizational frameworks we have identified identity and structural weaknesses that may need attention to counter possible future challenges and enable desirable ones.

The intuitive management of organizational complexity is what we all do but it may be the source of more or less costly mistakes. By increasing our ability to observe and diagnose shortcomings in this management we improve our chances to overcome fragmentation and create desirable futures. This book provides concepts, methods and tools to visualise and manage complexity. In this chapter we have offered practical support not only to diagnose shortcomings in this management but also to visualise possible improvements for a better future. This last aspect is important; we have proposed a way to strengthen complexity management in organizations and society at large to overcome costly historic practices. Hierarchical relationships are responsible not only for wasted talents and reduced organizational capabilities but also for the misuse of natural resources as we fail to *visualise and manage* their systemicity and the implacable consequences of using them blindly. Unfortunately this is common practice.

Our aim has been to use the Viable System Model to think systemically. This model offers strategies to manage complexity at the least cost to people and organization and can be used to observe how organizations manage their complexity.

Everything we have said about managing complexity suggests that in the end constructing a systemic world is a *learning process* where the transformations we want to produce are adjusted and modified as we hit walls that make apparent that the cost and consequences of pursuing them are unacceptable. The Law of Requisite Variety asserts itself in all situations but systemic thinking can help us anticipate these walls or regulatory failures to avoid unnecessary pains. Behaving as if these walls did not exist is inviting backslashes of one kind or another.

References

Argyris C, Schön D (1978) Organizational learning: a theory of action perspective. Addison-Wesley, Reading, MA

Argyris C, Schön D (1996) Organizational learning II. Addison-Wesley, Reading, MA

Bauman Z (2000) Liquid modernity. Polity Press, Cambridge

Beer S (1981) Brain of the firm, 2nd edition. Wiley, Chichester

Eisenhardt KM, Martin JA (2000) Dynamic capabilities: what are they? Strateg Manage J 21 (21):1105–1122

Espejo R (1989a) P.M. Manufacturers: the VSM as a diagnostic tool. In: Espejo R, Harnden R (eds) The viable system model: interpretations and applications of Stafford Beer's VSM. Wiley, Chichester, pp 103–120

Espejo R (1989b) The VSM revisited. In: Espejo R, Harnden R (eds) The viable system model: interpretations and applications of Stafford Beer's VSM. Wiley, Chichester, pp 77–100

Espejo R (1997) Structural archetypes; Internal document for the Contraloria General de la Republica de Colombia. Syncho, Ltd., Birmingham, UK

Espejo R (2001) Auditing as a trust creation process. Syst Pract Action Res 14(2):215–236

Espejo R (2008) Observing organizations: the use of identity and structural archetypes. Int J Appl Syst Stud 2(1/2):6–24

Espejo R, Bowling D (2002) Structure for transparency in nuclear waste management: report on the system of waste management in the UK. Syncho, Ltd., Lincoln

Espejo R, Bula G, Zarama R (2001) Auditing as the dissolution of corruption. Syst Pract Action Res 14(2):1, 39–56

Espejo R, Schuhmann W, Schwaninger M, Bilello U (1996) Organizational transformation and learning. Wiley, Chichester

Girard M, Stark D (2003) Heterarchies of value in manhattan-based New Media Firms. Theory Cult Soc 20(3):77–105

Nachira F, Nicolai A, Dini P, Louarn ML, Leon LR (2007) Digital business ecosystems. European Commission Information Society and Media, Brussels

Reyes A (2001) Second-order auditing practices. Syst Pract Action Res 14(2):157–180

Sennett R (2005) The culture of the new capitalism. BBC Publishing, London

Tapscott D (2009) Grown up digital. McGraw-Hill, New York

Teece JD (2008) Technological know-how, organizational capabilities, and strategic management: business strategy and enterprise development in competitive environments. World Scientific Publishing, London

The Economist (Nov 20, 2008) Harm done: the tortured life of baby P. *The Economist*, London

Index

A

Achievement relationship, 235, 242
Actors, 120
Additional methodological support for variety
    engineering, 199
Algedonic signals, 103, 245
Aligning business, organizational and
    information processes, 208
Aligning informational and operational
    domains, calculus for
    self-reference, 82
Aligning organizational processes with
    business process, 207
Allopoietic systems, 15
Amplification, 52
    creating new variety, 58
    increasing the resolution of the source
        variety, 58
    maintaining source variety over
        time, 59
    strengthening the source variety, 58
Amplifier of complexity, 55
Amplifiers and attenuators, designing, 55
Analyzing centralized functions, 179
Archetypes
    identity and structural, 234
    observing relationships, 234
Arturo Rosenblueth, 23
Ascribed purpose and purpose-in-use, 125
Ascribe purpose, 49
Ascribing different purposes, 119
Ashby, 36
Ashby's Law of Requisite Variety, 28, 40
Assessing consequences of actions, 211
Assessment of relationships, 214
Ataxia, 23
Attenuation, 52

making situational variety time
    dependent, 60
reducing the resolution of the situational
    variety, 59
selecting situational variety, 59
weakening sources variety, 59
Attenuator of complexity, 54
Attenuators and amplifiers
    balance of, 55
    complexity drivers, 56
Authenticity, 224, 228
Autonomous components, 93
Autonomous systems, 12
Autonomous units
    design and self-organization, 96
    requirements for, 97
Autonomy, self governing and self producing, 97
Autopoietic systems, 14
Avoiding fragmenting service delivery, 188

B

Balance between centralization and
    decentralization, 188
Balance of complexity, 52
Bauman's liquid modernity, 240
Beer, 58, 213
    identity, 115
Beer's First Regulatory Aphorism, 10
Beer's homeostatic loop, 70
Beer's Syntegration, 195
Biological Computer Laboratory, 25
Black box, 26
    complexity of a, 37
    description, 237
    identity, 115
    system description, 10
    systems, 13

R. Espejo and A. Reyes, *Organizational Systems*,
DOI 10.1007/978-3-642-19109-1, © Springer-Verlag Berlin Heidelberg 2011

CPI Antony Rowe
Chippenham, UK
2017-04-25 22:14